ALL THE WAY
JOSE

ALL THE WAY
JOSE

THE INSIDE STORY OF
CHELSEA'S GREATEST YEAR EVER

HARRY
HARRIS

JOHN BLAKE

Published by John Blake Publishing Ltd,
3, Bramber Court, 2 Bramber Road,
London W14 9PB, England

www.blake.co.uk

First published in paperback in 2006

ISBN 1 84454 213 0

British Library Cataloguing-in-Publication Data:

A catalogue record for this book is available from the British Library.

Design by www.envydesign.co.uk

Printed in Great Britain by Bookmarque

1 3 5 7 9 10 8 6 4 2

Pictures reproduced by kind permission of Action Images, Cleva, Empics,
the Daily Express and Getty Images.

Papers used by John Blake Publishing are natural, recyclable products made from wood
grown in sustainable forests. The manufacturing processes conform to the
environmental regulations of the country of origin.

Every attempt has been made to contact the relevant copyright-holders, but some were
unobtainable. We would be grateful if the appropriate people could contact us.

What a first season and what a partnership! It's difficult to imagine Chelsea without Jose or Jose without Chelsea. The Carling Cup was a classic and their performance in the Premiership has given us a real season to remember – the Double's not bad for starters. Cheers!

Contents

To my father in law Ken, who was there in '55 and has never stopped dreaming of the day The Blues would do it again. Enjoy your dream come true!

Acknowledgements

To my publisher John Blake, who had faith in my pre-season prediction that Chelsea would be crowned champions.

To Charlotte, who acted beyond the call of duty to complete the final rush to ensure the book was out in record time.

To Andy Sutherden and Steve Bradley at Hill & Knowlton.

To Jose Mourinho, captain John Terry, the PFA Player of the Year, Sports Writers Footballer of the Year, Frank Lampard, and the rest of the Chelsea squad for providing so much pleasure and exciting football throughout an historic season.

Introduction

So, it came to pass, the greatest season in Chelsea's history. The perfect symmetry, the first title in 50 years in the club's Centenary season.

Their championship win smashed records set by Manchester United for the most points earned in the Premiership and also, the highest number of league wins. Ironically, these records were broken in the penultimate match – at Old Trafford against Manchester United. Mourinho was proud of this latest Chelsea success, 'We needed two points to beat the record and played with very fresh minds. We showed a fantastic quality of football. It was the perfect way to beat the record in such an amazing stadium and against a team like Manchester United who, in Sir Alex, have such an example of success. This season we've been fantastic with only one defeat, a record of points, goals, victories and clean sheets. Everything the team did was fantastic and this would be the perfect-end.' Indeed the perfect end it was!'

Yet, for all the glory of a Double, the championship and the Carling Cup, and a double individual year for John Terry, the PFA Player of the

Year and Frank Lampard, the Football Writers Footballer of the Year, there was a lingering undercurrent of disappointment that Jose Mourinho, having arrived as the winner of the Champions League with Porto, had not taken the team to Istanbul for the Final against AC Milan. Mourinho looked on at the near hysteria at the Bridge when the first Premiership trophy was presented to the team, finally in blue hands. But his thoughts were of the future – of strengthening the side and aiming to win the Premiership, Champions League, FA Cup, Carling Cup and even the Community Shield. It is a measure of how far Chelsea have emerged as a dominant European power in such a short time when Mourinho said, 'The only thing that would make me happy would be to win everything. If you ask me if I am happy, I say yes I am happy. But not 100 per cent. I am like this and I don't change. This is the motivation. When you have a job in football it is for three reasons. One reason is because you love it. Another reason is because you want a good financial situation for the future of your family. And the next reason is to win titles. So you cannot lose the ambition of winning titles, or the passion you have for the game. The day you lose it or you feel it is going a little bit down is the right moment to leave. The day I feel I don't have the same passion and motivation, I will quit.'

Terry earned the nomination from his fellow players for being an inspirational leader in an unforgettable campaign, and like his boss he too was smarting from failing to reach the Champions League Final. Terry said: 'We've got to do better in Europe next season. We were a better team than Liverpool over two legs but they beat us, so good luck to them. I hope they now win it.'

Although the future was very much on everyone's minds, the celebrations of their achievements so far are set to continue for some time yet. Chelsea's championship party got into full swing after Claude Makelele's last-minute winner saw off Charlton. It was the Frenchman's first goal for THREE years as he scrambled the ball in after his penalty was pushed out by Stephan Andersen.

Players from the 1955 championship-winning side were at the ground to witness the trophy being lifted. Terry said: 'This is unbelievable. It's been a long time coming and I've been here so long and at last it's ours. Now I've got my hands on the trophy it's so special.'

Mourinho added: 'I'll let the players enjoy it and feel the sensation of the moment. But this is only one season. I'm proud but we have to try to repeat it as it's a fantastic feeling.'

This extraordinary season was filled with behind the scenes controversy and meticulous organisation on the pitch. Yet also, a special camaraderie developed by the new coach, which was best demonstrated by the way the players celebrated on the pitch. The trophy celebrations were extended to all – partners and children joined in, Robert Huth commandeered a truck, and Mourinho insisted that virtually everyone involved behind the scenes was recognised for the team's achievements. Chelsea pensioners formed a guard of honour and backroom staff were fêted along with the players.

Mourinho's wife Tami and daughter Matilde, nine, and son Jose, five, posed with the trophy, then the kids were off to bed so that dad and mum could hit the town with the team.

Mourinho's desire was to end his first season in England defending his Champions League title in Istanbul, instead he led the team to a post-season friendly against the Suwon Bluewings in South Korea. Mourinho had always intended to keep the players back until 25 May and having failed to reach the Champions League final, the club arranged a promotional tour to mark their new shirt sponsorship deal with Samsung, who own the Bluewings. Chelsea's season finally ended on 22 May with an open-top bus parade and civic reception at Hammersmith and Fulham Town Hall to celebrate their first championship in 50 years.

Mourinho said: 'Now we have to repeat it. I told my staff a couple of days ago "we have won the Premiership but we are not 100 per cent happy because we lost the semi final of the European Cup". This is the nature of my staff. I have chosen them for their mentality, what I have created in them and what they have by themselves. That's why we are together for the third consecutive season. And it is the same for the players. Next pre-season I have to see that from the players, but I know them from working with them for a year and I know which ones are the people with ambition and desire to win it and win it and win it.'

And so it seems, there is far more yet to come from Jose Mourinho and his Chelsea team!

Jose Mourinho

'THERE'S A BIT OF THE YOUNG CLOUGH ABOUT HIM. FOR A START, HE'S GOOD LOOKING AND, LIKE ME, HE DOESN'T BELIEVE IN THE STAR SYSTEM.'

Brian Clough on Jose Mourinho.

Designer stubble, expensive grey overcoat and scarf, brooding, explosive, animated, flashy, arrogant, young and glamorous. But Jose Mourinho has proved to be more substance than style.

Mourinho was voted the best club coach in the world in 2004 by the International Football Federation of History and Statistics, finishing well ahead of Arsene Wenger and Didier Deschamps of Monaco, and the nomination came just as he was on the verge of engineering a shift in power within English football away from Highbury and Old Trafford.

It's incredible to realise that Mourinho has performed a meteoric rise – six years ago he was a glorified interpreter at Sporting Lisbon, Porto and Barcelona.

Some say Mourinho's defining moment was when his Porto team won the Portuguese League Cup for the second year running, and then overwhelmed Monaco for the European Champions title last May. Perhaps, though, his seminal moment had come in Lisbon four years earlier when, after just nine matches, he walked out on the famous Benfica club. 'It wasn't right,' says Mourinho. 'I could have stayed around, but I knew my work could not prosper there. My ideas could not develop.'

When Roman Abramovich interviewed Mourinho on his yacht moored in Monte Carlo, the Chelsea owner had had 24 hours to read a document sent to him by his prospective coach. It was a stunning appraisal of the situation of the club that had become the richest in the game.

English football writers put to Mourinho some theories about the course of this season, which has been so dominated by Chelsea. They spoke of a renaissance at Arsenal and a rally by Manchester United. Mourinho frowned. 'Do not tell me about your movie. I am in a movie of my own.'

The choice of metaphor is not accidental. Mourinho loves films. On away trips he carries his Sony Vaio laptop with him – the night before last season's Champions League final he planned to watch a DVD of *The Punisher,* starring John Travolta – and when he describes meeting Abramovich it's like a scene from a James Bond flick: the French Riviera, the speedboat, the monumental yacht. And the pressure Mourinho is under? That brings another screen reference. 'Worthy of Don Corleone,' he says.

Mourinho is star-struck. 'I don't have many invitations to social events in London,' says the workaholic, not previously known for his liking for parties. When he arrived in June he moved into a flat in Eaton Square, Belgravia. In Eaton Square, with its Doric columns across terraced facades, his neighbours include Abramovich and the former 007, Roger Moore. 'English actors know me,' he says proudly. 'But the Americans don't. We can meet on the street, because we all live near. It is usual to be walking down the street and cross paths with Sean Connery. One of my deputies, Brito, lives in the same building as Monica Bellucci. Jeremy Irons lives near me also.'

If Mourinho's life is a movie, then its pre-production has been extensive. 'He's an overnight sensation who is twenty years in the making,' says Andy Roxburgh, UEFA's technical director. Roxburgh has been acquainted with Mourinho all that time. It was through

Roxburgh that Mourinho acquired his first coaching badge, when he attended a Scottish Football Association course in Largs, Ayrshire. 'We used small-sided games on that course and it had a profound effect upon him. I know that players appreciate his training methods and attention to detail. He is also very personable and has good communication skills.'

For Roxburgh, Mourinho was a willing, enthusiastic and, above all, interested student. His public image – ice-cool, dispassionate, detached – is misleading, though even his wife, Tami, has said she had to learn to 'decodify him'. Indeed, he has quickly forged a strong bond with Abramovich who likes his style – from the speeches to the stubble. Abramovich finds Mourinho good and convincing company. Travelling on the team bus and sitting in the dug-out for training sessions are things Abramovich would not have considered last season.

Roxburgh says that far from the public perception, Mourinho does not 'need the limelight'. 'With big-name players you sometimes see that they do,' Roxburgh adds, 'but because of his background that's not the case.'

Mourinho enjoys the good life, but sees it as merely a reflection of success. 'I have a good car, but only one at a time. I like good holidays with my family, I like us to live in a nice place [Eaton Square], but as a football man the most important thing is to be working with the right people and with the right approach to things,' he says.

There is a little secret to his success. He calls it his 'methodology.' Mourinho calls it his ability to 'smell' what to do. 'There is an impression that he is a purely analytical robot,' Roxburgh says. 'The enigma is that he is all that but is also very passionate and emotional.' Mourinho himself appears to concur, 'I have a new way of thinking the game, the players and the practice,' he says. 'I defend the globalisation of the work, the non-separation of the physical, technical, tactical and psychological. The psychological is fundamental.'

Mourinho's ideas are stored on his laptop. He used the machine to make his famous 'Power point' presentation to Abramovich in which he analysed Chelsea's strengths and weaknesses with forensic detail. Also, on the computer is Mourinho's 'bible': an extraordinary document that contains his theories about teamwork (its first line is 'The team is more important than the player'), his philosophies, beliefs and even his definition of what the role of club chairman should be. He never shows it to anyone. It's his secret – as are the notebooks he keeps hidden in his coat and his private diary.

There is a locked cupboard at Chelsea's training ground full of dossiers and DVDs, many of them compiled by Andre Villas, a reformed addict of the Championship Manager computer game, who heads what Mourinho calls his 'Opponent Observation Department.' Villas takes four days at a time to compile detailed reports on forthcoming opponents. Mourinho used to do the same for his father. Sometimes each player receives a document running to ten pages, sometimes it is simply a DVD showing which way a player turns or shoots. Villas is just twenty six and is known as 'Mini Mourinho', and, like all of Mourinho's staff has known his boss for several years. 'With my staff things are clear in one respect – they grew up with me,' says Mourinho.

It is the same with some of the players. He signed four from his homeland, but resisted the urge to acquire more. 'The core had to be English. I wanted to show my players that I could build a team without the need to bring in all my "children".'

Whatever the player's nationality, Mourinho can be brutal. There were initial fears that Damien Duff was injured too much and might not fit in. When he went to see the winger play for the Republic of Ireland in Dublin, he did not even speak to him. That was calculated. But Duff responded and is now a vital part of his team. It shows that Mourinho can also be won round.

The Premiership has changed him. Mourinho claims he is calmer and, so far, there have been few of the histrionics that have studded his career. He says the football is 'more honest', likes London and wants to remain here. He has spoken of the need for his children not to change schools constantly.

What strikes all who encounter him is his remarkable belief in himself – a belief that allows him, unusually among managers, to sleep easily. 'I think it's normal that a coach – the night before a match – doesn't sleep well,' he says. 'Some sleep badly because they are afraid but, since I do not sleep badly, I don't consider it to be normal.'

But his wife Tami is really in charge. When she ran out of cigarettes, there was no argument over who nipped out to their local in Belgravia in the cold and wet, still wearing his slippers. Mourinho says, 'It's a fantastic life in England but it's difficult. I have been to a pub only once, the one near where I live. My wife sent me out to buy a packet of cigarettes. I didn't have a drink. I just used my coins to buy cigarettes from the machine.

'I am enjoying life in England but it has been difficult to distinguish the main differences between English life and Portuguese life because I do not have much contact with the reality of the daily thing as work and family take up almost the entire time I have. In Portugal, I am what is known as the three F's. Fatima – Portugal's best known shrine – Family and Football. First and foremost, I'm a family man, but I am religious and Catholic and I'm from football, no doubts about that. I can be a good Catholic but I have not been to Fatima for six months.

'I'm not stuck to the symbolic thing. There are times I go to church and others not so much. At Porto I was going to Fatima once a month; at Leiria, my previous club, every week. I have full days. I wake at 7.15am and I leave home not long after that. I usually arrive at Chelsea training ground around 8.30am and have breakfast with the players and my assistants. I meet my assistants after that to organise work and then I meet the medical staff. Around 12.15pm, I end the training session and, if I don't have to go to a Press conference, I have lunch. If I don't have an afternoon session I leave at about 5pm to be with my wife and kids. Sometimes we go out together or we stay at home. Other times I just go out with my wife, to the movies or for dinner. I never go to bed until around midnight.

'It will be very difficult to go back to Portugal. Yesterday I was in my house looking at a Portuguese Cup quarter-final. In the Benfica stadium, which holds 87,000, there was just 12,000. I prefer it here, with the enthusiasm, the atmosphere. Every stadium is full; every team can fight for a result. Every country is different and the professionals have to adapt to the country, not the other way around. I have to respect what is important for the people who rule football here. In the future, I know if I do things on the touch line I will be punished. So I will not do them again.'

Mourinho's favourite hobby is quad-biking, and he enjoys skiing and snowboarding. He admits, 'I love quad-bikes but the guys from the insurance company which covers Chelsea told me "no way", otherwise I would be breaking the contract. I have a lot of hobbies but I don't have the time to practise them. I love snow, but I only had the chance to do snow sports when I left Benfica. I also love the summer and everything related to water, like swimming, but there is never any time for me to enjoy these things. Any spare time left over from my professional life is spent with my wife and kids.'

Mourinho also indulges in more genteel pastimes such as reading and going to the theatre. 'I like to go out for dinner, to go to a show or read a book. My wife suggests books for me to read because she is an insatiable reader. My latest is the autobiography of Colombian Nobel Prize winner Gabriel Garcia Marques. Reading allows me to distract my mind from the rest of my worries.'

In an interview with UEFA's technical director, Andy Roxburgh, the former Scotland manager, the Chelsea coach reveals his international ambitions and also laughs off suggestions that he is arrogant. Mourinho points to the way he was encouraged to develop when assistant manager at Barcelona, first to Bobby Robson and then Louis van Gaal as a key period in his career.

'Louis gave me the responsibility of taking the team in some friendlies or cup games and he monitored the way I handled things,' he says. 'I was prepared to take charge of a team; I had developed my know-how and confidence. Confident? Yes. Arrogant? No. My friends laugh when they read articles which label me as arrogant – they know it is not true. When I say I think we will win, I am only saying what most coaches think before a match.'

After his time at Barcelona, Mourinho returned to Portugal, ready to become a coach in his own right, and he admits it was not all plain sailing at Porto, with whom he would go on to win the UEFA Cup and Champions League. 'The first six months were difficult because the club and the team were in a very bad situation. I changed players and reorganised the team – it was a crucial period of rebuilding. The next season was fantastic because we won the UEFA Cup and the treble in Portugal. It was a great process, but it did not happen by chance. I have been influenced by some people, although I have never been the type to just accept the truth of others.'

Mourinho is an assiduous note-taker, but only during the first half of games. 'During the half-time team talk I try to control my emotions and be what the team needs me to be – this means I can be cool or I can be emotional because the team needs a certain response. There is always something to tell them at half-time, but after the match not one word, because the players are not ready to be analytical at that moment.' Instead, he analyses the second half at home.

'I am very demanding during training. We go for quality and high intensity during short periods. Players want to work, as long as the training is well organised and serious, and they know the purpose of the exercise.'

Mourinho took a gamble by recruiting Didier Drogba for £24m, but believed he had similar attributes to Thierry Henry – power and speed. Drogba reveals that Mourinho banned running during training, unless the players have a ball at their feet. 'I haven't jogged a single step since I got here,' says Drogba. 'We never run, except with the ball.' Talking about his first day of preseason training, he adds, 'I turned up with jogging trainers on. Mourinho looked at me with surprise and said, "You can put them back at the bottom of your bag. With me you'll never be needing them."'

Mourinho took more pleasure from winning the UEFA Cup – when

Porto beat Celtic – than he did from the club's triumph in the Champions League. 'The emotion was much greater when winning the UEFA Cup than beating Monaco in the Champions League final because of the game of football. The match against Celtic was dramatic until the last moment. But after the dust has settled, the Champions League title is the greatest prize. The night we won it was difficult because I was full of conflicting emotions, knowing that I would be leaving the team.'

He possesses a meticulous attention to detail when discussing what he looks for in a player. 'I have produced profiles for each position in terms of personality, athletic qualities, technical skills, etc. If a player lacks speed he has no chance at the top level.' Mourinho gets frustrated by some aspects of the English game. In particular, he believes it is unfair that Chelsea counter-attacks are often stopped by 'technical fouls', with most referees failing to issue yellow cards, and he joins the chorus of managers demanding that action be taken on the offside rule. 'The interpretation of the offside law is very confusing and it must be very difficult for officials to make decisions.'

His new-found fame has come at a price, but he has few complaints. 'My life has changed. It is part of the job to deal with the demands. However, a principle for me is that I never miss a training session due to other claims on my time. Professional duties always come before external business requests. Football is my job but also my passion.' He is ambitious and desperately wants to repeat the success he achieved at Porto with Chelsea. And then? 'One day I would like to be the head coach of Portugal, but not now. I would not like to retire without having been the Portuguese manager.'

Spirit, motivation, togetherness. It used to be the prerogative of 'The Invincibles,' as Arsene Wenger's players indulged in on-the-pitch pre-kick off huddles. For Jose Mourinho the bonding takes places in the privacy and sanctuary of the dressing room. Just before the players go out, they take it in turns to deliver a brief motivational speech.

Frank Lampard explains, 'It's about bonding and it's a way of bringing out people's character. We stand in the dressing room, put our arms around each other and one of us says a few words and finishes by asking, 'Who are we?' Everyone shouts, 'We are Chelsea.' There are a few lads who are a bit quiet, Damien Duff for instance, and it's a way of bringing them out of themselves as well as getting everyone motivated.

'John Terry swears an awful lot when he does it. There was a pre-season game against Celtic and he was effing and blinding and I was thinking, "Hang on, John, it's only a run-out!" Scott Parker did the best one at Newcastle in the Carling Cup. It was the most aggressive speech I've ever heard, about being ready for battle. We already had a good spirit but the manger has taken it a step further.'

In his pre-Premiership existence he was 'sent off' and subsequently suspended for preventing an opposition player (Lazio's Lucas Castroman) taking a throw-in at a crucial moment during a UEFA Cup semi-final game. He explains, 'I did it by instinct. It wasn't that I was waiting for a chance to interfere with the game and stop the opponents' throw-in.'

That suspension meant that Mourinho was not allowed to communicate with his players after arriving at Lazio's stadium in Rome for the second leg of that tie. For the coach it was more than an inconvenience. 'What it came down to was that I wasn't going "into battle" with them,' he recalls in a new book, written with a Portuguese journalist friend, Luis Lourenco. 'I cried because I couldn't be in the war with my men.' To overcome such an adversity, he watched the game from the stands, aided by a 'small, sophisticated communications device' to enable him to keep in touch with his coaching staff.

There is no room for jokes, raised voice or any other gimmick in Mourinho's team talks. 'He is simply meticulous,' says Lampard. 'Everything is explained in such detail that the minute he does make a change, we can adjust. We're able to do it because he leaves absolutely nothing to chance; he even tells us how to play if we go a goal up or down. He knows every opponent inside out. Even their subs. He talks to us as a team but also individually. No player likes to be blanked by the manager because even if you're playing well, you still wonder what he's thinking.'

Dressing room fun and games sum up the camaraderie in Mourinho's squad. Terry and Lampard are gunning for pranksters Kezman and Robben after they keep on being left exposed. Kezman and the Dutch winger were nicknamed Batman and Robben during their days at PSV Eindhoven. But the pair have combined to play the Joker with Terry and Lampard, in a series of stunts that have the rest of the Chelsea squad in stitches – and left Terry and Lampard without a stitch to wear.

Terry confesses, 'There are plenty of wind-ups at the training ground. Kezza and Robbie keep cutting up mine and Lamps' pants. But when it happens four days on the spin, you're like, "Lads, leave it out". Actually, we still owe 'em for that.'

Terry adds, 'The team spirit we have here is great. There are PlayStation competitions, we go go-karting and paintballing together. Going into the games we all want to fight and die for each other. We also have the pre-match talks now, when everyone has their turn to say something. I had to do it in the first game under Jose, against Celtic. Mine was all effing and blinding but other lads will read out a quote. It always gets us pumped up. Jose's so thorough. He always wants to win. Even in training he doesn't like players conceding goals. We know what the opposition are about before we go into the game. And we always know what the boss wants you to do.'

Lampard expresses how much the atmosphere has changed due to Mourinho's regime, and how much Chelsea have raised their expectancy levels and status, 'Fans and other players are always asking the same thing: "What's it like at Chelsea? What is the manager like? What's Roman Abramovich like?" Even on England duty, people like David Beckham, Gary Neville, and Wayne Rooney all ask about it. They want to talk about Arjen Robben, Damien Duff and John Terry. It just shows the level that we have reached now at Chelsea, and it is terrific. There's an amazing buzz about the place. The buzz of a club that's going places, where something big is happening, and we have become such perfectionists about everything we don't feel it strange to look down and see Manchester United and Arsenal below us. Right now I think Chelsea is the most exciting club in the world. In the past you'd look at clubs like United, Real Madrid or AC Milan and wonder what it would be like to be there. Now, people look at Chelsea, and so much of that is down to Mourinho.'

The atmosphere has changed, as Lampard added, 'The build-up is much more relaxed. We used to have no music, no TV, no nothing. Now before a game we have it all. The night before a game is more relaxed, the pre-match meals are more relaxed.' Tiago reveals 'one of the secrets' of Mourinho's astonishing success. 'He's like a friend to us,' Tiago says with a smile, and a shrug. 'He's one of us.'

That was evident in the rich warmth Mourinho, a youthful forty two, displayed as he embraced his players following the Carling Cup semi-final victory over Manchester United at Old Trafford. Much has been made of the lack of dissent within Chelsea's squad from those players who have been 'rotated.' Largely that has to do, as Mourinho himself offers, with their hunger for success. They want trophies. Tiago is one of those players fighting for a place. But he doesn't regard the competition – from Joe Cole and Alexei Smertin – as a struggle, because, he says, 'They fight the same way as me. We are all friends. We all know if I play well it's good for me but for them also, because we are top of the league and if we stay there all of us will be champions. So, yes, it's a fight but a different kind of fight.'

Tiago was Mourinho's fourth purchase in the flurry of comings and goings following the manager's appointment 'In Portugal everyone admired Mourinho,' Tiago says, 'because he won everything. In Portugal and in Europe. He's a coach who, I think, every player wants to work with.'

But why is he so effective? 'I don't know,' Tiago says. After a pause he adds, 'I think he's very clever. He works fantastically hard, not just him but all his staff. They are fantastic people – and the players know exactly what they have to do.'

Abramovich made up his mind he wanted Mourinho when he inspected the AC Milan trophy room and was taken aback by all the silverware. He came to the conclusion that Mourinho had won so much in just two years, compared to Claudio Ranieri's record over his entire career, let alone his four trophy-less years at the Bridge. Abramovich and Mourinho talked on the Russian billionaire's yacht, 'Le Grand Bleu', moored at St Tropez.

Mourinho immediately stamped his personality on Chelsea, as he was not interested spending fortunes on stars such as Ronaldinho, Roberto Carlos or David Beckham.

Whereas Ranieri recommended only three new players, Mourinho wanted four or five. Ranieri put forward a short list of new players: a striker, a central midfield player and centre half. Ranieri suggested Gerrard for the midfield berth; Fernando Morientes of Real Madrid, Didier Drogba from Marseille or Samuel Eto'o from Majorca as the new striker; and after his first choice, Walter Samuel signed for Real, a number of alternatives were suggested for central defence.

Mourinho wanted three of his Porto stars – Paulo Ferreira, midfielder Costinha and playmaker Deco – Tiago, and wouldn't have said no to Gerrard if he could be prised from Liverpool. Ranieri did not want to be too hasty in offloading players such as Jesper Gronkjaer, while Mourinho kicked out a dozen of the Italian's squad. Mourinho shared Peter Kenyon's conviction that Chelsea were vastly over-staffed. Melchiot, Petit, Stanic and Bogarde came to the end of their contracts and they were free to go; Hasselbaink and Desailly with a year left could also go on free transfers, and if they could not fix themselves up with clubs there was no place for them in the first team. Gronkjaer attracted a host of clubs including Birmingham and was sold off at a reasonable price. Others on loan such as Zenden at Boro and Carlton Cole at Charlton were also available. Zenden's move would become permanent, while Cole switched loans to Villa.

Chelsea were looking to recoup some of the fees paid out for Argentina internationals Crespo and Veron.

But Mourinho would have to revise his targets with Deco signing for Barcelona. Porto midfielder Costinha also expressed a desire to follow Mourinho. 'I still have two years left on my contract at Porto but of course I'd love to go with Mourinho,' he said. 'I know if I go I will have more success.'

Mourinho arrived with his family at Heathrow on 1 June. Mourinho's contract was worth 6m euros (£4.1m) a year plus 1.5m euros (£1m) in bonuses triggered if he repeats the success he enjoyed at Porto in winning the championship and the Champions League. Kenyon negotiated a compensation package for Mourinho and his back room team of 2.5m euros (£1.75m). Chelsea poured money into Porto's academy to help them spot and coach players and, in return, will get preferential treatment if they want to bring Portuguese youngsters to Stamford Bridge.

The most important of Mourinho's back room team is his assistant Baltemar Brito. The 53-year-old Brazilian has known Mourinho since the Portuguese was a teenager. Having left his homeland to play in Europe towards the end of his career, Brito played under Mourinho's father Felix at the small northern Portuguese club Rio Ave. A centre-half who acted as the on-pitch lieutenant of Mourinho senior, Brito helped Rio Ave to the final of the 1984 Portuguese Cup and became a close family friend. But it is to Jose Mourinho's wife, Tami, that Brito owes the progression from friend to Champions League-winning coach. Brito is aware of his debt to Mrs Mourinho, referring to her as his 'madrinha', or godmother, in recognition of her influence on his career.

After leaving Benfica in October 2000, Mourinho headed for the more modest side Uniao Leiria. Tami reminded her husband of the commanding personality of Brito, and Mourinho appointed him as his right-hand man.

Porto's 28–year–old fitness trainer, Rui Faria, is another key part of Team Mourinho. Born in the central Portuguese town of Barcelos,

Faria was, like Mourinho, a graduate in physical education who had never played football of any distinction. He met Mourinho at a seminar day at Barcelona's Nou Camp, where Mourinho was working at the time as Louis van Gaal's assistant. Mourinho was impressed and stayed in touch, and when he took the job at Uniao Leiria in April 2001 he appointed Faria fitness coach and video analyst. Uniao Leiria struggled to attract 2,000 fans to its home games. But three years later Mourinho was in charge of a Champions League-winning team. No modern-day coach had achieved it at such a young age, or on Porto's meagre budget.

In his two full seasons in charge of Porto, the team won all but one of the six serious competitions they entered – two Portuguese titles, one UEFA Cup, one European Cup, one Portuguese Cup – and lost only two matches of consequence: the Portuguese Cup final and the one-off European Super Cup against Milan. Yet, in each of his close seasons he sold their most valuable player – centre-half Jorge Andrade to Deportivo La Coruna in 2002, and striker Helder Postiga to Tottenham Hotspur in 2003. The final ninety minutes with Porto reflected well on Mourinho, who made two contentious selections: Brazilian teenager Carlos Alberto started ahead of Benni McCarthy, Porto's leading scorer and conqueror of United. Alberto scored the first goal. And Pedro Mendes was picked ahead of Dmitri Alenitchev, who came on to set up the second goal and to score the third.

Mourinho picked his team for the final weeks beforehand. 'I decided the line-up a month ago,' he revealed. 'I first had the idea when Porto played Coruna [in the semi-final] and I saw Monaco in Chelsea. I was very clear about it. I was also clear that if we were not winning at half-time, I would put on McCarthy instead of Pedro Mendes, pushing Carlos Alberto back. But we scored and then had the chance to play in the style we prefer. I told Alenitchev to be the most attacking part of my midfield diamond and we mustn't lose the diamond shape. If you play in a perfect diamond, you control the match.'

Mourinho enjoys role reversal games, swapping places with his players and sometimes carrying out their orders while they act as manager. That's what happened to former Manchester United star Karel Poborsky when he told Mourinho – then in charge of Benfica – what position he wanted to play. Mourinho, who saw Poborsky as a winger, called him in and said, 'Right, you're the boss, why do you want to be playmaker?' He listened, let Poborsky pick his own place in the next match and took him off after half an hour. Poborsky says, 'Mourinho then told me, "Right, I'm the manager again. I gave you the chance to prove you were right and you proved nothing. You will play where I tell you from now on, and if you do not want to, you'll play in the reserves."' Porto scout Gil Rui Barros says, 'I have never known a manager prepare his training sessions so thoroughly. Like Zidane with a ball at his feet, Mourinho has this thing that cannot be taught. He is the Zidane of managers.'

Mourinho's special attributes attracted the attention of English clubs even before FC Porto's European Cup victory. He was wooed by Liverpool in the spring but demurred. Five years ago Sir Bobby Robson asked him to join the staff at Newcastle United with a pledge that within two years he would be head coach. Mourinho declined. Spurs had made inquiries through intermediaries regarding their then vacant manager's job. 'It was in December or January,' said Mourinho. 'There was a contact but not direct. I was not interested at that time, I do not like to leave clubs in the middle of the season, so I thought, at that time, no chance.'

Mourinho, a deeply religious man, was struck by tragedy when his sister died in a diabetic coma during his spell with Barcelona. The experience reinforced his strong bonds with wife Tami, his seven-year-old daughter, Mathilde, and his son Jose, four. It was to see them that he left the scene of Porto's triumph so hurriedly – on the way to Chelsea.

Mourinho's uncle Mario Ledo owned a sardine cannery and grew rich under dictator Antonio de Oliveira Salazar's regime. Ledo died in

1972 and Salazar was later ousted leaving Mourinho's family on the wrong side of the political divide.

The canning factories were confiscated and Jose and his sister Teresa moved with Felix and mum Maria to a more modest home. He never talks of Ledo, whose death badly affected him as a nine-year-old.

Teresa died in 1997, aged 37. The official explanation was her diabetes. But others believe the drugs she began using after her marriage broke up caused the infection that killed her. Mourinho refuses to discuss it.

Before every kick-off, he kisses a photograph of his two children, and a crucifix.

The Premiership

'LET'S HAVE SOME FUN.'

Jose Mourinho in his first programme notes.

JOSE MOURINHO DELIVERS a message of intent at his unveiling at Stamford Bridge. 'We have top players at Chelsea,' he says. 'And, I'm sorry if I sound arrogant, we have a top manager as well. I don't want to be compared with coaches from the past, nor do I want to be viewed as the face of young managers in the game. I have won the Champions League. I'm not one who comes straight out of the bottle. I'm a special one. I am a winner because I'm good at what I do and because I am surrounded by people who think the same.'

The club's chief executive Peter Kenyon admits, 'I don't think we'll need to work on his confidence! He has been charged with being arrogant, but I don't think he is. He's very confident and self-assured and thoughtful about what he does. He's deliberate and has a gameplan.'

Mourinho adds, 'I want to win. Over the last two years I've had the taste. As a manager you want to feel the biggest success you can achieve. I want to keep this taste. I don't want to lose it. I don't want to get to 2010 or 2012 with just the same titles I have now. I want more. The people here have the same ambitions and mentality. We shouldn't be afraid to say, 'I want to win.'

'I accept that if I don't win this year it will be a failure. If I am sacked, I can always find another job. But I have not come here to give myself nightmares. I have come here to sleep well.'

Mourinho also responds to sniping from the outgoing coach Claudio Ranieri. 'I didn't like what he said about the Portuguese league being an easy one to win. I prefer to use my head and not react to other people's opinions. But what I suggest is that if someone is Mr Ranieri's friend, or has contact with him, you should explain to him that if a team is to win the UEFA Cup or the Champions League, it has to play clubs from other countries. I didn't win the UEFA Cup and the Champions League playing 20 Portuguese teams. I played and beat players and clubs from his country Italy, from England and Spain. Porto beat everyone in Europe. What has Ranieri won in 20 years? The Spanish Cup. I could say things like Ranieri has been in football for 20 years and the only thing he has won is the Spanish Cup. I could say that. I don't like to, but I could.'

Then Mourinho turns his attention to Sir Alex Ferguson, Arsene Wenger and Sven-Goran Eriksson.

After Porto had beaten Manchester United in the Champions League in Portugal, Ferguson said the opposition were divers. 'Ferguson had a reaction – something out of nothing,' says Mourinho. 'But I felt my players were big enough to cope with that type of pressure. I had to show them I was not afraid of him and that their boss was ready for a fight. After the second game at Old Trafford he came to the dressing room and congratulated me. And I have respect for such important people. I have not come here specifically to fight. I have come here to win. But at the right moment, if I feel my players, my group and my club are in a situation where they need my help, it's like family. And they will get it.'

Arsenal? 'Their manager is one of the best in the world. As for any weaknesses in his side, how can you identify weakness in an historic team? I need to learn about him and his side. In Portugal I could smell the changes managers would make at half-time. So I now need to look at Wenger and his players and discover their philosophy and playing style. That is why my scouts will watch his stars at Euro 2004 and then again in pre-season friendlies. When you go to war you have to know the opposition's strengths and weaknesses.'

As for Eriksson, Chelsea's first choice to replace Ranieri, Mourinho shrugs his shoulders. 'It is only natural they went for him. Mr Eriksson is a manager with a lot of prestige in the world. He also had a close relationship with Chelsea and, because of that, he was their number one choice. I don't mind ... because now I'm the man.'

Finally, Mourinho speaks of Roman Abramovich and the suspicion he will be difficult to control. 'I don't have to control Roman Abramovich – he has to control me! But, as in any business, you have to communicate with the top man. I spent two days with him on his yacht and he never once mentioned what he expected from me. Instead I gave him a four-page document about how I work and what I am. He is the owner and the first person in the club. But what I need to do I have already done. I have established clearly what my position is and my functions in the club.'

Claudio Ranieri was loved at Stamford Bridge and there was anger at his treatment. But he had won nothing of real consequence in nearly two decades in management; Mourinho has won the UEFA Cup, Portugal's league and cup double and the European Cup in two coruscating seasons at Porto. But Mourinho's mentor Sir Bobby Robson is concerned about his move to English football. 'The fact is Jose is coming into an area he doesn't know. He won't find the Premiership anything like the Portuguese league. He is joining the big boys and the big teams, where every game is a potential blip. In Portugal, if you can defeat Benfica and Sporting home and away, you are likely to win the title. What he has done on five or six occasions in European competition over the last two seasons is beat the big teams. He has to do that 38 times in the league.' Sir Bobby adds, 'I never thought of him as being a coach. I always felt his vocation would be in education because he had been a PE teacher.'

Mourinho responds diplomatically, showing his deep affection for Robson, 'I still see Sir Bobby as a father to me. My early times with Bobby were really important, and the way he put faith in me gave me confidence and taught me to be strong in believing myself. Tactically and dealing with players I could not ask for a better teacher, and I could not have learned from anyone better. It was an experience that was invaluable and I still telephone and talk to him now. He is a leader to me and I will go on respecting him as a great manager. He is always close to the players and that is something as a manager you must always be. They are your blood and the most important thing of all. They have to respect you and that is something that I learned form Bobby in the way they respect him and will always play for him. A little something from everything I achieve will always be dedicated to him.'

Mourinho prepared for his new job by sending a code of conduct to each of his stars. Porto's players were handed the same document and they responded. Gone are the days of late-night partying, weekend trips abroad and snubbing the press. Under the new regime all players must stick strictly to the rules or faces heavy fines or even suspension.

Split into seven sections, the rulebook states how players should behave with each other and the public – and the punishments they face if they break those rules. Players will be fined £250 for being 15 minutes late, with a further £500 penalty for the second quarter of an hour. Any later arrivals will mean a fine decided personally by Mourinho as he attempts to organise the training system right down to the smallest detail. Celestine Babayaro, notorious for his poor punctuality, arrives early for pre-season work!

At a time when the image of footballers off the field is under scrutiny, Mourinho has devised a clause to cover behaviour away from the club. 'Players must know that they're role models for children and adults, and they must always have an ethical and correct social behaviour. Players are not allowed to be away from their residence after 0.00pm. On the night before a resting day/free day, players are allowed to be away from their residence till 2.00am.'

The rulebook says, 'Player misconduct towards technical staff, medical staff, kit staff and press staff will not be tolerated. Players' misconduct towards each other, be it in training sessions, match days, travelling or in the club's installation, will not be tolerated and will be considered a serious offence. All misconducts will be analysed by an executive director and the manager resulting, if appropriate, in a financial penalty and/or suspension by the club. Players who miss the appointments made by the medical department are subject to penalty fees and a disciplinary process. Direct red cards will be judged by the manager and the team captain. Disciplinary action will be taken if appropriate.'

Snacking before matches and ordering food and drink on room service during away trips is out. The code of conduct continues, 'Smoking and alcohol drinking is not allowed in the rooms. The medical department is responsible for choosing the meal menu. The players are allowed to choose or ask for a different pre-match meal according to their culture and their habits. Players have an absolute duty to maintain a lifestyle that protects their capacity to play to the best of their ability. This requires that they follow a healthy diet, drink alcohol in moderation, avoid drugs and ensure that they have enough sleep. Injured players, foreign or not, may only leave the city or the country if permitted by the medical department and the manager.'

Mourinho calls for players not involved in Euro 2004 to attend Stamford Bridge on the first Monday of pre-season training at 8.15am. Hernan Crespo is the one player who does not show up. When Crespo arrives on Wednesday he is told decisively what his options are. Mourinho says publicly, 'We spoke in a very open way about whether he can find the motivation or the happiness for himself and his family to stay. For me, the player's desire is crucial. I told Hernan about the style, the quality of players I want, and the motivation. I was upset that he was not at our breakfast. You have always to be there – if the plane is full from Argentina, you come by bus. You can call. There is always a solution. He gave me excuses – some I could accept.'

Mourinho says he finds empathy from day one in Adrian Mutu, and that Eidur Gudjohnsen is a better player and a more willing enthusiast than he expected. He speaks at length about Mateja

Kezman, who lives the family life Mourinho admires, and who on the pitch represents his belief that 'modern' football demands that you defend from the front. And he speaks longingly about Didier Drogba, the Ivory Coast striker, who Olympique Marseille insist is not for sale, even at Chelsea prices.

Outcome: Mutu stays, but ends up being kicked out after a failed drugs test; Crespo is let go on loan to AC Milan; Seba Veron is similarly released on loan back to Italy; and Chelsea successfully pursue Drogba for a record transfer of £24m.

Marcel Desailly also leaves, Jimmy Floyd Hasselbaink departs to Middlesbrough, Mario Melchiot to Birmingham City, and Mario Stanic retires with a knee injury, all in the first week. Boudewijn Zenden, Jesper Gronkjaer, Emmanuel Petit and Winston Bogarde also depart.

Scott Parker talks positively about battling for his place in central midfield. 'I came to Chelsea to improve myself. I know it's a big task to get into the side in my best position in central midfield because Frank is a good player and Claude is as well. I want to kick on and establish myself as a Chelsea player, and fortunately Chelsea squashed the rumours that I would be one of those moving on pretty early in the summer. Every day there are rumours around this place, but that's the way it is going to be with such a big club.'

From Carlo Cudicini, the goalkeeper facing competition from the young Czech, Petr Cech, there is the acknowledgement that 'the challenge will be on the pitch, not in the contract' and the early indication is that goalkeepers are to be more involved in the whole group, not trained apart.

From Gudjohnsen there is the comment – enjoyed by Mourinho – that every movement, every moment, of the training sessions is controlled and organised. 'I read that Eidur said my training lasted exactly 90 minutes, and that the work and the rest were timed to the last stretch on the last stroke of 90 minutes,' muses the coach.

Frank Lampard's first meeting with the new boss is etched on his mind. Mourinho stared into his eyes and asked him, 'Are you a winner?' Lampard recalls, 'It was a strange scene, but it felt right and walking out we all thought, 'We're going to win something this season.' In a way he asks us that question every day. There is never a moment when you are allowed to relax. He'll have a joke, but you know with him the only thing that matters is winning and that has rubbed off on everyone.'

So does Mourinho genuinely believe Chelsea can win the Premiership in his first season in charge? 'Yes, I do,' he replies prior to the new season's opening game with Manchester United. 'One hundred per cent. I have no doubts that we can.'

As Mourinho prepares for the first match of the season, the issue that Sir Alex Ferguson refused to shake hands when Porto beat United in last year's Champions League is put to him. Not so, according to Mourinho! It suited the media to suggest bad blood, but he stresses, 'I have no problems with him. He complained about certain things in Porto, but he shook my hand after the match, and at Old Trafford he came to the dressing room to do it. I have respect for every manager when they have respect for me.'

The opening Premiership encounter will be 'entirely different' to the last time the two managers met in the Champions League, Mourinho insists. 'There is no comparison between a league match and a knockout competition. Also, my players at Chelsea are completely different – with the exception of Ferreira and Carvalho – from the ones I had at Porto, and the way we play here at the moment is different. Manchester United will also be different. When we played them last season it was at a time when they weren't feeling good. They weren't playing well. This season we have them in the opening game, and at the start everybody feels good and ready.'

Peter Kenyon, who was chief executive at Old Trafford before being lured to Stamford Bridge, has worked with both Ferguson and Mourinho, and he believes Chelsea's new manager can build dynastic success in the same single-minded way as the Scot has done at Manchester United. Mourinho responds in typical fashion, 'I don't want to be compared with other people. I am what I am, I've done what I've done, and I will try to do well again in the future. But I know that one day, instead of being a champion at the end of the season, I'll get the sack. These things happen in football. I don't think I'm the best in the world when I win, and I don't think I'm the worst when I lose. I'm just me.' And the showdown with Manchester United? 'If we win, we are not champions, and if we lose, we are not out of the fight. It is just one match, no more important than any other.'

The mind games are under way from the start. 'When Jose Mourinho goes to bed at night,' remarks an onlooker from Manchester United, 'his tongue gives a round of applause.' Ferguson says, 'Mourinho won the European Cup last season and the UEFA Cup the year before that, which is a great feat. You can't dismiss that sort of record. I'm sure we'll have a glass of wine together after the game.'

The United manager is invited to comment on how Mourinho has been talking himself up. 'Ach,' shrugs Ferguson. 'We'll just have to see how that develops. The personal aspect doesn't come into my thoughts. I'm more interested about new players coming into other clubs than new managers. Over the years we've had a great record at Stamford Bridge and we've probably been favourites most times, but Chelsea were second in the league last year and they've bought eight new players this year – big, international players – so it's not going to be easy.'

Normally, Ferguson would relish starting a campaign with such a big game. 'Not this season,' he says. 'Not with the injuries we've got. I'd rather have played someone else. You don't want to be three points behind one of your main rivals on the first day of the season.'

SATURDAY, 15 AUGUST

MANCHESTER UNITED 0, CHELSEA 1

Jose Mourinho offers Sir Alex Ferguson a glass of Chelsea's cheapest plonk after sending the Manchester United boss to his first opening-weekend defeat in eight years. Gudjohnsen's first-half strike seals the points. Mourinho and Fergie shake hands and then share a bottle of Argentinean Shiraz in the manager's office.

But even as he admits his side are fortunate to start their campaign with a win, Mourinho is happy with the way his team are coming together. Mourinho says, 'Silvestre said we didn't have enough time to create a big team spirit – and he was wrong. I could have told him that my players have been fantastic from the first day and that mentally we are a team. When you consider we've only been together for a month it is great that we showed we have created this spirit and want to fight together.

'I don't think United deserved to lose. They controlled the game and made us change the way we played from what we wanted. But everybody gave one hundred per cent and showed the character we need and didn't allow them many chances at all.'

Fergie moans about Gudjohnsen's 'sloppy' winner and vows to step up his search for a striker after his injury-depleted side fail to test Cech. The United boss says, 'I didn't need him [Mourinho] to tell me we were unlucky. In a game like that you've got to make one of your chances count.'

The single goal comes with barely a quarter of an hour gone; yet Chelsea are already aiming to play on the break by then. 'Sometimes you have to play a little different to how you would like,' says Mourinho. 'We did not play better quality football because of our opponents. Sometimes football is beautiful because of competitiveness and organisation. Defensively we played fantastically with unbelievable team spirit. United pushed us back and I had to control the game.'

Ferguson is unsurprised by Chelsea's approach. 'I expected them to defend because of the way Porto played when they went 1–0 up against us,' he says. The goal comes when Geremi beats a sluggish Quinton Fortune to the ball, and Didier Drogba rises high to redirect a diagonal pass into the space behind United's defence. Howard's reaction lacks conviction, allowing Gudjohnsen to flick the ball goalwards. Not even Roy Keane's despairing sliding intervention can stop the ball crossing the line.

Eager to protect Gudjohnsen's early goal, Chelsea and their coach are consumed with caution. Petr Cech resorts to time wasting as

United's siege intensifies. One of Euro 2004's most impressive stoppers Ricardo Carvalho is introduced into midfield to kill off the match. Chelsea's leading contributors are two defensive midfielders: the outstanding Claude Makelele and the debut-making Russian Alexei Smertin. This pair give Chelsea the midfield steel that United, for all their pressure, cannot overcome.

As well as a full complement of points, Chelsea fans will also take heart from Cech's assured display. Tall and mobile, the Czech Republic international looks comfortable whether collecting crosses or dealing with shots. Ferreira endures one or two problems with Giggs but still exudes promise. Drogba plays an important part in Gudjohnsen's goal, confirming his aerial strength, but clearly requires time to pick up the pace and physical demands of the Premiership.

Team

Cech, Ferreira, Gallas, Terry, Bridge, Geremi (Carvalho), Makelele, Lampard, Smertin, Drogba (Kezman), Gudjohnsen (Parker).

So early in the campaign Arsenal's 4–1 rout of Everton bears overtones of the sweeping verve that carried the double to Highbury in 1998 and 2002. Arsenal's impressive win at Everton is without question the result of the opening weekend of the Premiership season. Alan Hansen writes in his *Telegraph* column: 'The victory was a clear message that said "Move over Manchester United" and also showed Chelsea that, whatever they spend on new players, Arsenal will continue to pulverise their opponents. Arsenal have yet to take United's mantle as the dominant force in English football, however, despite going through an entire league season without defeat last year. United's success over the last five years entitles them to that distinction and Arsenal have to overcome the obstacles faced by Sir Alex Ferguson's team if they want to become the undisputed top team.

'Four or five years ago, United's midfield of Paul Scholes, Ryan Giggs, David Beckham and Roy Keane would frighten anybody.

Nowadays, opponents will look at United's team sheet and fancy their chances. That is why I believe United will struggle to regain the title this year. Arsenal are beating them on the pitch and Chelsea are beating them off it, in the transfer market. I can only see the title being contested by Arsenal and Chelsea, with United probably having to be content with third place.

SATURDAY, 21 AUGUST 2004
BIRMINGHAM CITY 0, CHELSEA 1

Mourinho hails the team spirit that he feels can propel Chelsea to the title. 'It was amazing; I have never known anything like it before. The players who weren't involved were all calling into the dressing room on their mobile phones encouraging and cheering on the players who started the game. Perhaps that is normal for you in England but it is unheard of where I come from and it's a sign that we have a fantastic spirit and determination here.'

This is Joe Cole's day from the moment he is called on just after the hour mark and he delivers with style. Cole's entrance comes after Steve Bruce's five-man midfield has strangled the life out of Chelsea. The best chances fall to Julian Gray, but he cannons his first shot off Cech's right-hand post. Mourinho has no option but to make changes at the break, dragging off Smertin and Gudjohnsen and replacing them with Tiago and Kezman.

Cole then emerges and is told to play behind Drogba and Kezman. He flits out to the left, takes a pass from the otherwise unimpressive Lampard and makes tracks towards Maik Taylor's goal. His shooting from range isn't normally enough to trouble any keeper, but this time he finds the target with a deflection off Taylor's leg.

Mourinho blasts Robbie Savage for an elbow attack on Kezman that floors the striker ten minutes from the end. 'If an elbow situation happens in my country, or in Spain or Italy, then we accept it as part of our culture. But when I see it over here in England I am shocked and surprised as well as angry. England and the English people are the kings of fair play and that's why so many people love your game.

So when I saw that blond player elbow Kezman, sure, I was upset, but also shocked. I hope that you see it on film and that a disciplinary panel will deal with it.'

Bruce is gutted. 'We've been kicked in the teeth. But if you don't take four or five glorious opportunities that fall to you, you know you are going to get punished. We matched Chelsea in virtually every department, but we've wasted our chances... and they've taken the one that fell their way. Chelsea are a hard-working side, but if you look at Mourinho's team – and at his Porto team last season – they don't look remotely interested in entertaining. But what will he care? He's got six points out of six and we are left to lick our wounds.'

> **Team**
> Cech, Ferreira, Terry, Carvalho, Bridge, Geremi (Cole), Makelele, Lampard, Smertin (Tiago), Drogba, Gudjohnsen (Kezman).

Chelsea sit joint top of the Premiership with Arsenal after winning the first two games. But, while the reigning champions have scored nine times in two games, Chelsea have eked out two 1–0 wins based on defensive solidity and organisation. It is a comparison Mourinho believes is unfair. He wants his team to play 'beautiful' football, but first he wants to win – and he reckons teams from this country, including Arsenal and the national side, have not enjoyed international success in recent years simply because they do not defend well enough. 'Football people in England should stop and ask yourselves for what reason English football has not been successful abroad. Spanish, Italian and Portuguese clubs have all won UEFA competitions, but England can't do it. You have to think about the reason the English national team has a top manager and top players and goes to the European Championship and World Cup and can't win. England has wonderful football but when you go outside this country they cannot do it. Manchester United was the last one when they won the Champions League in 1999. Why is that? You have to think about it because it is not normal. My philosophy is the philosophy which gave me six titles at Porto in two years. To win.'

Mourinho says his side should not be compared with the team Wenger has been nurturing since 1996. 'When I have a boy of seven years of age and when I have a young human being of seven weeks, the boy of seven years can run, jump, speak, communicate: you can see what he is. After seven weeks, when I had my daughter and boy, you just take care of them and try to create conditions for the little baby to grow. So you want to compare a team of seven years with the same manager, with the same spine year after year, with a team with 50 per cent new players, a new manager, new everything? You should compare the first two months of Mr Wenger in English football with my first two months. At the moment there are two teams – one is from the moon and one is from hell, but both have six points.'

TUESDAY, 24 AUGUST 2004

CRYSTAL PALACE 0, CHELSEA 2

Didier Drogba's first Premiership strike and a thumping clincher from Tiago make it three wins and three clean sheets out of three for Mourinho. In front of Sven-Goran Eriksson at Selhurst Park, Cole mounts a persuasive case for playing a major part in the World Cup campaign. He is the catalyst for a display that suggests the new-look Blues are beginning to take shape. He is a non-stop menace, liberated by a coach who wants to test out his impish skills.

Mourinho takes a leaf out of the Tinkerman's book with five changes, including full debuts for Tiago and Kezman. Danny Granville is the only survivor of the last Premiership clash between the sides, a 6–2 Chelsea win at Stamford Bridge six years ago, except then he was playing for the Blues. And he does his old side a favour when unmarked he heads wide of the gaping target from ten yards. It is a brief interruption as Chelsea take up the reins again and Cole draws a fine diving save from Julian Speroni after an instinctive give-and-go with Kezman.

But Chelsea are in front after 27 minutes. Kezman threads through for Babayaro, replacing the injured Bridge, to deliver a cross that begs for the powerful downward finish from the Drogba. Seventeen minutes from the end Tiago puts the seal on his personal display as he collects from Drogba and drills a fine shot into the corner.

> **Team**
> Cech, Ferreira, Gallas, Terry, Babayaro, Makelele, Lampard, Tiago, Cole (Geremi), Drogba (Gudjohnsen), Kezman (Mutu).

Mourinho says he plans to turn Lampard into the best midfielder in Europe. He missed UEFA's gala awards ceremony in Monaco to work with Lampard and his team-mates ahead of the home clash against Southampton. At those awards, Porto midfielder Deco was handed the Champions League Player of the Year award. Mourinho arranges for his own award for winning the Champions League to be given to him at Chelsea's home European clash against his old club. He targets the next Player of the Year award for Lampard. 'I want to change Frank Lampard as a player. I want to make him a better one. I want him to win the same trophy that Deco won on Thursday night. How can I achieve this? By winning, because Deco is the same player that he was two years ago. The only reason he won on Thursday was because he is a European Champion. Frank will be the same player but he will be adapted to a different philosophy.

'At the moment we do not have Arjen Robben or Damien Duff in the team wide on the left, but when they are in the team that will make it easier for him. Frank was involved in four of the six passing channels against Crystal Palace on Tuesday night. He was the player most in the opponent's final third coming from behind. And, with Tiago, he ran the most – 11 kilometres. In the last 15 minutes of the game when everybody's level was going down, he ran more than he did before.'

SUNDAY, 29 AUGUST 2004

CHELSEA 2, SOUTHAMPTON 1

They may not quite have the look of champions in waiting, but Chelsea beat Southampton more convincingly than the score-line suggests to make their best start to a season in the top flight. 'You can't do better than take 12 points from your first four games,' says assistant coach Steve Clarke. Chelsea should be three or four ahead by half-time, despite falling a goal behind to a wonderful strike from James Beattie within 12 seconds of kick-off. After equalising through a Beattie own-goal and then taking the lead with a Lampard penalty, Chelsea fail to kill off a Saints side who rarely threaten.

Wayward finishing, outstanding goalkeeping and goal-line clearances keep Chelsea down to a one-goal winning margin for the third weekend running. 'Missing chances is not a concern while we are winning games – it might be if we were losing,' adds Clarke.

Yet an unlikely upset looks briefly possible when Chelsea kick off and Cole's wayward pass sits up invitingly for Beattie to hit a beautiful volley that dips over the arching body of Cech from 25 yards. Gudjohnsen heads wide from close range, Drogba has a shot blocked by Antti Niemi and Lampard thumps a drive over the bar, all inside the opening ten minutes. Then Lampard swings in a corner, Gudjohnsen flicks the ball with a heel and it flies off Beattie's hip on to the crossbar and down over the line despite Anders Svensson's efforts to clear.

Svensson is in action again, clearing a header from the impressive Tiago off the line, but Chelsea soon have the decisive goal. Lampard swings in another corner and Claus Lundekvam handles under pressure from Drogba. Southampton argue for a push and are still unhappy after Lampard scores the resulting penalty, claiming he touches the ball twice.

The second half is less one-sided, although Niemi is still the busier keeper. 'That was probably our best performance so far this season,' says Lampard. 'We really played in the manner we want. We had a cutting edge in the box and, with better finishing, could have won by four or five. We've had a tough start to the season and won them all. We know Arsenal have been very good but we'll do our utmost to challenge them all the way.'

> **Team**
>
> Cech, Ferreira, Carvalho, Terry, Bridge, Makelele (Geremi), Tiago, Lampard, Cole (Duff), Gudjohnsen (Kezman), Drogba.

Mourinho says that what happens to him in football is second to his relationship with God. 'I'm scared of God. I'm a religious man, although I don't practise religion by going to church every day. I believe what I believe. There are certain things in this life that we cannot control. The first thing in my life is to have the people I love healthy and happy. I have no fear of losing, no fear of the critics. It is important to do your best, wake up every day with good ambition and go home to sleep well knowing you have done everything.'

The Premiership season takes a break with Chelsea losing 19 players to international duty, leaving Mourinho to work with only three first-team squad players and the injured Carlo Cudicini. 'It's more than frustrating,' he says after running through a series of videos and discussing tactics with his re-assembled squad. 'You can do nothing to improve your team. He adds, 'I told them the only chance we have at Aston Villa is to forget the internationals and next Tuesday's Champions League. Aston Villa are too difficult to be thinking of other things.'

SUNDAY, 12 SEPTEMBER 2004
ASTON VILLA 0, CHELSEA 0

Merely ending Chelsea's 100 per cent record is an achievement for Villa. Huth, Duff, Parker, Bridge, Johnson and Geremi are not even required on the bench to emphasise the strength of Chelsea's squad compared to Villa. David O'Leary changes his team, aping Chelsea's formation and thus curbing his wide players, Nolberto Solano and Gareth Barry. O'Leary says the changes are made with victory in mind but they seem primarily designed to stymie Chelsea.

The score-line suggests it works, but O'Leary is helped by Mourinho's refusal to involve Duff. Yet even without the width he offers, Chelsea have chances enough to win. In the opening half flowing moves create opportunities for Cole, who miskicks, and Drogba, who hits the bar.

Chelsea dominate after half-time, but Mourinho withdraws Cole and the link between midfield and attack is lost. Darius Vassell wastes a chance to put Villa ahead before Chelsea revive and Drogba is robbed of a penalty when felled by Ulises de la Cruz and is ludicrously cautioned for 'diving' by Rob Styles. An incandescent Mourinho justifiably criticises refereeing standards before claiming, 'It would have been two penalties in some countries. It was ridiculous.' Four wins and a draw is an excellent start to the season, but it still leaves Chelsea behind Arsenal who record their fifth straight victory.

Team

Cech, Ferreira, Carvalho, Terry, Babayaro, Makelele, Tiago (Smertin), Lampard, Cole (Mutu), Kezman (Gudjohnsen), Drogba.

Later Styles rescinds the yellow card shown to Drogba after watching video replays of the incident. Makelele announces his retirement from international football to concentrate on his club career. 'I think that a player like me cannot afford to answer international calls if he is not going to play. I shall be 33 in 2006. My future is with Chelsea.'

MONDAY, 20 SEPTEMBER 2004
CHELSEA 0, TOTTENHAM HOTSPUR 0

Mourinho feels cheated by an opposition who come solely to achieve a stalemate. Ledley King is the game's pivotal figure and he never looks like being caught as he marshals his side's defences. So Chelsea fail to capitalise on Arsenal's draw against Bolton the day before, and the gap at the top remains two points.

Mourinho is furious. Not with his players, who, for the second successive Premiership match, do not score, but with Jacques Santini, his team and their alleged time wasting. 'I think it is frustrating for me, the players, for every Chelsea supporter and for every football supporter. Because people are not paying money to see one team play and for another to keep falling down, kicking balls away, sending for the medical department and spending five minutes to change players. My team played fantastic football. They may as well have put the team bus in front of the goal.' Mourinho ends the match with four strikers – something he says he would never normally do. Santini is unrepentant. 'They have big international players, and that obliged my young team to defend.'

Chelsea extend their unbeaten run against Spurs to 29 league games, but that matters little in the context of this Premiership season. They need the three points. It is almost none. Cech pulls off the save of the match in pushing away Robbie Keane's header in the second half, although Gudjohnsen also strikes the base of the post, and Paul Robinson reacts smartly to dig out Lampard's fierce free-kick.

It is Lampard's 114th consecutive Premiership match – a new record – but he figures little. Chelsea only really start to fire in the final 20 minutes once Duff comes on and offers width. There are five minutes of added time at the end. 'There should have been 15,' says Mourinho.

Team

Cech, Ferreira, Carvalho, Terry, Bridge (Smertin), Makelele, Tiago (Kezman), Lampard, Cole (Duff), Drogba, Gudjohnsen.

SUNDAY, 26 SEPTEMBER 2004

MIDDLESBROUGH 0, CHELSEA 1

Before kick-off a minute's silence is immaculately observed in memory of local legend Brian Clough, born just a mile from Boro's former home, Ayresome Park. Clough scored a phenomenal 204 goals in 222 league and cup games for the club.

Mourinho's pre-match media conference is dominated by his view that he and his side have superseded Sir Alex Ferguson and

Manchester United as the ones most in football love to hate. Chelsea, however, might just win a few friends if they can replicate more performances like this and add a few goals for good measure. Chelsea only have Drogba's 81st-minute goal to show for their overwhelming superiority.

Mourinho concedes the paucity of goals is a cause for concern: just seven in as many Premiership matches. He complains that 'the knives always go in Chelsea's direction and the flowers in the other direction'. But he adds, 'One day a team will be unlucky: we will score from every situation and win 4–0 or 5–0. We had a lot of chances to score and the only surprise was that we scored so late.'

The goal comes when Lampard pulls a free-kick into the middle for Drogba to crack a right-footed effort from 15 yards that Mark Schwarzer can only help into the net.

The home side are not helped by the loss of Jimmy-Floyd Hasselbaink for ten minutes after sustaining a bloody head wound resulting from a dangerously high boot from Terry. While Hasselbaink receives stitches, Drogba and Duff, making his first start, both threaten and Smertin smacks a shot that Schwarzer parries. Moments later Boro are dealt another blow when Ray Parlour is carried off with a gashed knee after a jarring duel with Gallas. When Hasselbaink emerges for the second half, he is ordered to change his blood-caked shirt. With no ready-made replacement to hand, he sports injured defender Ugo Ehiogu's shirt. Steve McClaren admits, 'We lost Chris Riggott and Szilard Nemeth before the game. We lost Ray and Jimmy for a while. We didn't have another number 18 shirt for Jimmy. We didn't have enough of anything.'

Team

Cech, Ferreira, Carvalho, Terry, Gallas, Smertin (Tiago), Makelele, Lampard, Duff (Huth), Gudjohnsen (Kezman), Drogba.

Mourinho's side is taking shape. Lampard, Terry, Makelele and new signings Cech, Ferreira and Drogba have started every game. Gudjohnsen has started seven and come on as a substitute in the other two. Gudjohnsen has failed to recapture the form of the 2001-02 season when he scored 23 goals, but Mourinho has taken to him from the outset. The 26-year-old is an intelligent footballer whose excellent movement and touch creates space for his colleagues – rare attributes that were rewarded in the summer with a new £55,000-a-week contract.

With the strikers and back five largely picking themselves, the fiercest competition has been in midfield, with Cole, Duff, Tiago and Smertin sharing the remaining two places alongside Makelele and Lampard.

Cole has impressed at the head of the diamond until Duff's return from a shoulder injury reduced his workload, while Tiago and Smertin have started four games each on the right of a deeper midfield three. Smertin's emergence is surprising, though fully justified, but more of a shock is the disappearance of Scott Parker, who this time a year ago was among the most impressive performers in the Premiership.

The reigning PFA Young Player of the Year has played just eight minutes and only made the substitutes' bench on one other occasion. Parker's career appears to be going nowhere. The only experienced players further from the first-team than Parker are Glen Johnson and Carlo Cudicini. But 20-year-old Johnson has time on his side, while Cudicini, who returned to the bench for the Champions League victory over Porto, has been out for much of the season with an elbow injury and would walk into any other Premiership team.

Gallas reveals that Mourinho began his Chelsea tenure by telling his players their standards were not good enough. 'I think the atmosphere is very good, like it was last season. But Mourinho said at the start, "There are a lot of good players at this club, a lot of international players, but you haven't won anything. With this team we must do it." And that is true. This season is our season and everybody feels the same. We know it will be difficult because we know Arsenal are very strong and there's Manchester United, but we want to win all the games. Everybody is fighting on the pitch together and that's important. We play with our hearts.'

Lampard says the studious attention to detail that characterises the new regime means the team expect to win every game they play. That is the biggest change under Mourinho. Lampard says, 'The most important change is that the mental attitude now is: win, win, win. At times it wasn't like that last season. Now the accent is on winning every game we play – and every competition we're in.'

Lampard adds, 'In training, virtually everything we do is intended to replicate a match situation. That has helped the players technically and made us more tactically aware. The work we do with a ball, day in, day out, is the foundation of the team's strength. We're not conceding goals and look strong and solid because we hammer away at getting it right every day in training. The organisation is becoming ingrained. It's not that we've just got the one way of playing, but if we do change we really do know what we're doing because it has been mapped out beforehand. In the build-up to the game the manager will have prepared us for every possibility. He'll say, "If this happens, we might change to this." It's never off-the-cuff, as it was under Ranieri, it's always something that has been pre-planned.'

Is Mourinho happy winning 1–0? 'Of course he is. We all are,' says Lampard. 'The manager does like to play good football; he's not one of those who wants to defend, content to play unattractive football and nick a result. He'd be happier, obviously, winning 3–0, but 1–0 will do as well.'

Last season was easily Lampard's best. This time his football has improved again. 'The manager is great at giving individuals confidence. In my case, I'm taking free-kicks and corners, which I was never entrusted with before. He has given me that responsibility; it's something I've added to my game and it has made me believe in myself even more. He is bringing the best out of me. What I haven't got is as many goals, and that's something that bothers me because I think like a striker – if I haven't scored I'm not happy, however well I've played. I do need to get among the goals again. I've got one for Chelsea and one for England, which isn't enough.'

Chelsea's next opponents are Liverpool. 'We're ahead of them in the league, but they are making progress under their new manager,' says Lampard. 'It's usually a tight game, and last season they beat us 1–0 at our place. We can't allow that to happen again. The way Arsenal set the pace these days, you can't afford to lose many, and we need to keep winning.'

SUNDAY, 3 OCTOBER 2004

CHELSEA 1, LIVERPOOL 0

Joe Cole scores the winning goal and leaves with a bottle of champagne from Sky as their man of the match, but also with a stinging reproach from his boss. Mourinho accuses Cole of neglecting his defensive duties after the goal and hints that the England international finishes the game playing to the gallery, which includes Sven-Goran Eriksson, rather than for the team.

But Cole catches the eye with the neat finish he applies to Lampard's free-kick and the invention he brings as an auxiliary striker after coming on in the first half for Drogba. Mourinho, though, says Cole's display is 'not good enough' from the moment he finds Liverpool's net. 'Joe Cole scored a goal; that's very important. He gave us good dynamic and played really well in terms of that attacking dynamic. When he scored the goal the game finished for him. After that I need 11 players for my defensive organisation and I had just ten.'

Cole responds by saying, 'The boss has no axe to grind against me. He just wants to make me a better player. I will sit down with him and talk to him and listen to whatever he has to say. He's a fantastic manager.'

Mourinho also hits back at critics who have lambasted his team's four 1–0 wins. 'It is not fair. I think they should criticise the teams playing against us. Against Tottenham we created the chances and they did not have a shot. Liverpool came here with just Cisse up front and I think had one shot and Middlesbrough had one up front. But it is fair to say we should score more goals. Today we played for an hour with just Eidur as a pure striker. He is a good target. Duff is playing fantastic. The midfield is working very well and defensively we are playing great. So Arsenal are playing beautifully and we are playing not so good and not scoring many goals and we are just two points behind them – so in one weekend it can all change.'

With Drogba forced off through injury after 38 minutes and Kezman not on the bench, Cole is brought onto the right flank. He makes an immediate impact, setting Ferreira free down the line to cut inside and produce a pinpoint cross only for Lampard to send his diving header well wide.

Cole then hits the side netting before striking a half-volley from the edge of the area that Chris Kirkland manages to take the pace off before Harry Kewell heads off the line. But in what appears an expertly planned routine Lampard plays a delightful low free-kick for Cole to burst ahead of his marker and clip the ball first time past Kirkland.

Cech has to make an important late save from Steve Finnan, while Gudjohnsen and Cole also come close in the final stages. But once again it is 'one-nil to the Chelsea'.

> **Team**
> Cech, Ferreira, Terry, Carvalho, Gallas, Makelele, Smertin (Tiago), Lampard, Duff (Geremi), Drogba (Cole), Gudjohnsen.

Just eight goals in as many league games does not seem to compare favourably with Arsenal's 26. But Opta Index statisticians reveal Chelsea have had more shots than the Gunners and Manchester United. Chelsea have had 111 shots in the league compared to United's 102 and Arsenal's 101. Chelsea's goalscoring chances are hit by the news that Drogba needs minor surgery on the groin injury that forced him to limp off against Liverpool. And Adrian Mutu reveals a dispute with the coach. Mourinho claims Mutu has been injured and cannot play for Romania. But Mutu insists he is fit and flies out to face the Czech Republic. Mutu storms, 'I am in an open conflict with Mourinho who forbade me to go to my national team and said I was injured. It is not true – I have been in good condition for five days and he knew that. I don't care about being fined. I want everyone to know that the national team is the most important thing for me. Mourinho has promised me that I would play in the first team for some games. Then I wasn't even in the squad and I don't understand why. Probably the only solution, even if I don't want it, is to find another team.'

SATURDAY, 16 OCTOBER 2004
MANCHESTER CITY 1, CHELSEA 0

Mourinho's unbeaten record ends in a flurry of frustrated continental-style arm waving at the City of Manchester Stadium. After guiding his men through eight Premiership games without losing, he finally looks hot under the collar as a first-half Nicolas Anelka penalty brings the curtain down on the impressive start.

On a day when Arsenal are the only winners in the title race, Mourinho has to swallow defeat against a revved-up City side who deserve their win for a collective effort that leaves Chelsea for once unable to conjure a spark of magic.

The game is just ten minutes old when controversy strikes – leaving Chelsea a goal down and lucky to survive with 11 men. An easy-looking take for Gallas close to the halfway line suddenly turns into a nightmare as the defender slips on the greasy surface, presenting the ball straight to Paul Bosvelt. The Dutchman launches a long ball forward triggering a chase between Anelka and Ferreira, who grapples the Frenchman to the ground as they both surge into the area. Referee Howard Webb instantly awards a penalty but enrages Kevin Keegan by producing only a yellow card to punish Ferreira when, as last man, he should be sent off. A furious Keegan remonstrates with the fourth official before and after Anelka coolly sends Cech the wrong way with his penalty.

With Mourinho becoming more agitated at perceived each mistake, City fans have fun at his expense by mimicking his gestures as he waves his arms in exasperation. Having replaced Gallas with Bridge at the break, Mourinho then gambles by sending on Cole for Tiago with just over an hour gone. Despite Chelsea's escalating threat, City remain unruffled on the pitch even if Keegan's nerves are fraying.

This first defeat for Mourinho's side sees them drop five points behind Arsene Wenger's spectacular team. John Terry says, 'We want to win the title this season. But Arsenal are five points ahead of us now. A gap has started to form already and we simply cannot afford to let that gap get any bigger. We have had some great performances so far this season. But they go out the window when you suffer a defeat like this.'

On a day when Jimmy-Floyd Hasselbaink smashes in a hat-trick, the wisdom of selling the Dutchman has to come into question. Terry adds, 'We are getting chances but also getting caught offside too many times for my liking. We need to be more clinical, like Arsenal. When they get a chance they take it.'

Mourinho blames the international break. 'After the last two international breaks we have drawn with Aston Villa and now lost against Manchester City. Players go away for their internationals and managers have different ways of treating them. They come back in different conditions. Some play two games; some do not play at all. It is not an excuse but an important fact.'

Team

Cech, Ferreira, Terry, Carvalho (Geremi), Gallas (Bridge), Tiago (Cole), Lampard, Makelele, Duff, Kezman, Gudjohnsen.

Adrian Mutu's situation at the club becomes even more tenuous with the news that he has failed a drugs test. Mutu says he was tempted into taking drugs by the belief it would improve his sex life. The 25-year-old striker insists, 'I am not hooked on drugs. I categorically deny this. The only reason I took what I took was because I wanted to improve my sexual performance. It may be funny but it is true. I did not take cocaine. I took something to make me feel good.'

The Romanian, who joined Chelsea from Parma in August 2003, has had little impact on the team since falling out of favour with Claudio Ranieri in the second half of last season. Mutu has managed only two brief substitute appearances under Mourinho and claims that even before his failed drugs test he had come close to physically assaulting his new coach during a row. 'I have to admit that in the heat of our confrontation I did actually threaten Mourinho about what would happen if he ever went to Romania. In a moment of total madness I almost hit him too. But now I am calmer and I must say I have nothing against the coach.'

Chelsea refuse to comment but Gordon Taylor, the chief executive of the PFA, says, 'I have been in contact with the player but it would be wrong to say what he thinks. It's a matter of some concern because any action will apply internationally as well.'

Andrea Pretti, one of Mutu's representatives, adds, 'We are awaiting the counter-analysis. We don't think it will take long for things to happen, possibly a couple of days. You can imagine how the player feels. He already had technical problems at Chelsea and now this has just made it even worse. Until this situation is cleared up his future will is secondary.'

Mutu has four advisers, all apparently representing him. All are quoted in the press and all adapt different strategies in representing their client. The most famous, former Tottenham and Romania defender Gheorghe Popescu, arrives at Heathrow airport with another of Mutu's agents, Victor Becali. Before attending a meeting with Chelsea chief executive Peter Kenyon, Popescu confirms that Mutu will not be requesting the all-important B sample. 'I told him not to ask for the second sample so as not to prolong his agony.'

Mutu's fourth agent, Victor's brother Ion Becali, disowns his client in an extraordinary outburst live on Romanian television. Becali says, 'I found out about the drugs test last Tuesday. Jose Mourinho was a gentleman and called me up to tell me. I was very unhappy with Mutu when I told him about the test. I cannot protect him any more. Twice in the past I have wanted to break our contract because I was fed up with his attitude. He told me he had been given an illegal drug at a party. I know he has attended many, many parties like this. I think he wanted to copy David Beckham. But he was a very bad copy. Beckham is very professional.'

It emerges that Mutu was deliberately targeted by the doping authorities at the request of his manager. Gordon Taylor announces, 'Mutu's accepted that he did test positive for cocaine, and so we've got to deal with it under the social drugs procedure that we have in line with the FA. If the player accepts he is guilty and is prepared to undertake rehabilitation, to be checked regularly, to be clean, there is great sympathy towards the player.'

Mark Bosnich, also drug-tested at the request of the club, was sacked in 2003. If Chelsea sack Mutu, it would mean writing off the £15.8m they paid for him a year ago. 'Bearing in mind that investment, they've as much interest in getting the player back on track as the player has himself,' Taylor suggests.

Mourinho admits that it was a mistake for Chelsea to have bought Mutu and says he would have burrowed deeper into a player's lifestyle before signing him. 'When you spend big money with a player, you can't bet; you must be sure what you are buying,' Mourinho says. 'But sometimes you make mistakes. The best way is to analyse them in training because you cannot follow 16 hours a day outside. When you see a player committed, concentrated, strong, ready to do complex exercises, for sure his life outside football is good. When you see a player is tired, finds it difficult to concentrate, one day is very happy, another day is lonely and quiet, then you put the question mark and think, perhaps ...'

Chelsea decide to sack Mutu but reserve the right to claim compensation if he is not banned by the FA and is given a second chance in the Premiership or at a top club in Europe. 'We want to make clear that Chelsea has a zero-tolerance policy towards drugs,' a club statement says. 'This applies to both performance-enhancing drugs and so-called recreational drugs. They have no place at our club or in sport. In coming to a decision on this case, Chelsea believed the club's social responsibility to its fans, players, employees and other stakeholders in football regarding drugs was more important than the major financial considerations to the company.'

Mutu is charged and suspended by the FA. Kenyon defends the club's decision to 'target-test' Mutu and then sack him on grounds of gross misconduct. Gordon Taylor accuses the club of target-testing Mutu 'with a view to getting rid of him'.

Mourinho reveals he confronted Mutu over suspicions the player was using cocaine just days after joining Chelsea. 'When I met him on his first day in the pre-season in July and he was with his two agents Mr Becali and Mr Popescu I told all three, "I have information that you are on cocaine." All three were laughing, denying, saying this was a lot of lies about Adrian. After that I did not speak with them again because they denied the situation. For a long period we saw now and again strange behaviour. Arriving late a few times, not coming in to train other times. A doctor visiting his house and the apparent reason was just headaches. Injured when nobody knows how it happened – for example he was on the bench and did not play against Paris, yet the next day he was injured. We spoke about it. Is he pushing us to let him go in December? Is he doing this to get into a conflict with me [so I] say I don't want this player here? Or is he involved in other things? We began to question and the club doctor, because he has some experience that we do not have, was analysing with different eyes and he arrived at the decision that, maybe, yes. I would never sign him again. Not just because of the drug, but because he called me a liar.'

It is the first verbal attack from Chelsea as the battle lines are drawn ahead of a costly legal process. The club engages Jonathan Taylor, head of Hammonds' sports law group, with the FA appointing as prosecuting counsel Mark Gay, a board member of the British Association for Sport and Law. As well as representation from the PFA, Mutu's advisers are in advanced negotiations with Nick Bitel to act as defence counsel. The Culture, Media and Sport select committee called Bitel as an expert witness in its formulation of a drugs in sport report, and his testimony supports the FA's allowance in its rules for a divergence in the considerations of recreational and performance-enhancing drugs. This, along with Mutu's willingness to undergo a programme of rehabilitation forms the basis of Mutu's defence.

It is not, however, a discrepancy Mourinho appreciates. 'Recreational drugs are private life but football players, especially the pros of the big teams, they have a very, very big responsibility. The club bought [Mutu] to be ready to play football and in this moment he will be out of competition for a long period. The first one to break the relation was the player so he cannot complain.'

Mutu responds, 'Chelsea have destroyed me – I don't know what I am going to do. I am shocked and surprised by their decision. I didn't expect them to pay me while I was suspended but I never thought they would sack me either. Why didn't they wait to do this? Now my career is in ruins. I might as well walk away from football. What is there left for me?'

Peter Kenyon claims the player ignored their efforts to help him with his drug problem. Kenyon says, 'Players are given ample support these days and we fully support the PFA. But the same support was there for Adrian Mutu. He chose to ignore it, to lie, and as a consequence of that the rules are quite simple. To suggest there was no support and that we hung him out to dry because we wanted to get rid of him is absolute rubbish. We could have come to the decision in the summer, to move Mutu out and get a transfer fee for him. But we embraced him and wanted him to be very much part of our squad.'

Kenyon adds that Chelsea would dish out the same treatment to any player who fails a drug test. He claims both Mutu's contract and the FA's guidelines give Chelsea the right to sack their player, even before he has been through the FA disciplinary procedure.

SATURDAY, 23 OCTOBER 2004
CHELSEA 4, BLACKBURN ROVERS 0

Eidur Gudjohnsen produces a sublime hat-trick to hand Abramovich an early 38th birthday present. Chelsea's league goal tally increases by 50 per cent! This is the response to those who say Chelsea do not possess the attacking power to keep pace with champions Arsenal. Gudjohnsen says, 'I think we've been threatening to score a few goals in a match. We've been playing well, creating a lot of chances and it is just a matter of putting those chances away. Today we did that, plus the fact that we got another clean sheet, which is also fantastic. I've scored two goals for Chelsea on quite a few occasions but never a hat-trick. It's very pleasing and something I'll treasure.' Duff completes the rout with the fourth goal against his old team.

Mourinho gives Scott Parker and Glen Johnson their first starts under his reign. But with Parker sitting in front of the back four and Gudjohnsen as the only recognised striker, this does not look like a day for spectacular, free-flowing football. However, when Chelsea break, Duff and Smertin produce enough width to cause Rovers major problems.

After a Paul Dickov penalty appeal is waved away by referee Graham Poll, Chelsea seize their chance with two strikes in a minute. Cole's fantastic touch supplies the first in the 37th minute when he picks up a short Parker ball 35 yards out and chips a pass into Gudjohnsen's run a few yards from goal. With more shin than boot Gudjohnsen angles the ball past Brad Friedel. Seconds later another long ball – this time from Lampard – has the same timing and precision to give Gudjohnsen the chance to volley in.

Gudjohnsen's commitment pays off in the 50th minute when a surging run tempts Craig Short to bring him down just inside the box for a clear penalty. Gudjohnsen gleefully slots away his hat-trick.

At times Parker's desire gets the better of him – he picks up a needless booking for a rant at Poll – and much of his work is over-ambitious. But his presence at the base of midfield releases Lampard. Arjen Robben comes off the bench for a devastating 26 minutes, eight months after Chelsea agreed a deal with PSV Eindhoven. Mourinho says, 'I think our fans can now see what a blow it has been to have him out all this time. He is really important for us and we have been counting down the days until he was finally ready to play because he's one of the best in the world. He has super speed but he's not the type of player who has pace but lacks vision or the final ball. When he gets into position he chooses well when to pass, when to cross or when to shoot. He created a lot of chances for our strikers during his time on the pitch and I don't see why he couldn't play at the same time as Damien Duff.'

It is Duff who completes the scoring in the 74th minute. Mourinho adds, 'It was a good day for us after a difficult week. It was important for Eidur's confidence that he got the hat-trick. Now I can watch the Manchester United – Arsenal game with a smile. If United win we close the gap and if Arsenal win we distance ourselves from United. I still hope it's a draw, though.'

> **Team**
> Cech, Johnson, Carvalho, Terry, Bridge, Parker, Lampard, Smertin (Tiago), Duff, Cole (Robben), Gudjohnsen (Kezman).

Arsenal go down to a contentious and significant 2–0 defeat to Manchester United that reduces their lead to just two points. Everton, who visit Chelsea in two weeks, and who were many experts' tips for potential relegation, are surprisingly just a point further behind.

After his impressive display against Blackburn, Robben reveals he could well have ended up at Chelsea's big rivals Manchester United. United moved for the winger first, only for Chelsea to act decisively when Old Trafford negotiations stalled. Robben says he has no regrets. 'There was some interest from Manchester United. I went there but the second step is that the clubs have to come to a deal. They didn't. Chelsea were very quick and gave me the feeling that they wanted to get me. It wasn't a difficult decision because that gave me a lot of confidence. I had a meeting with four people, including Peter Kenyon and Claudio Ranieri. It was a good meeting.'

The subsequent managerial upheaval did not worry Robben. 'That wasn't a problem as I had that before at Eindhoven. When I was signed there, it wasn't long before Guus Hiddink came to the club. At Chelsea I knew Mr Mourinho was a good coach. I have a lot of confidence in him as a trainer. I can learn a lot from him. The only thing you have to do as a player is show what your qualities are, then it doesn't matter which manager is there.'

Good judges in Dutch football, such as the outstanding former Holland midfielder Wim van Hanegem, believe that ultimately

Robben's best position will be as a classic 'number 10', playing behind and around the main striker. As a child and in some of his teenage years he played that role before moving to the left wing when he became a professional. At PSV Hiddink pointed out to Robben a negative aspect to his game, one that has continued to dog him since Euro 2004 – a reputation as a player who goes to ground far too easily. But Robben feels that his style of play makes it inevitable that he will fall regularly. 'That's always the case when you are a fast player and you go past people. If they just touch you a little, sometimes you are out of balance. I know I'm not a diver. For me it's not a problem, but I know people call me that and I have to be aware.'

Adrian Mutu is suspended from football for seven months and fined £20,000 following the FA's disciplinary hearing. Mutu's ban is conditional on him successfully completing a period of rehabilitation and is backdated to start on 25 October. That means the suspension concludes on 18 May.

Peter Kenyon criticises the seven-month ban claiming the FA have been too lenient. In a statement Kenyon says, 'Chelsea are extremely disappointed with today's verdict. We believe it is far too lenient and sends out the wrong message about drugs in football. It is also indicative of a lack of direction within the FA at this time. As a club we can only take the action that we believe is right for Chelsea. However, the FA have a much wider responsibility to look after the interests of the game as a whole and, in this case, we believe it has shown itself to be weak over the issue of drugs.'

Gordon Taylor reveals the striker's thoughts after the hearing. 'Adrian admitted the charge from the beginning and accepted his responsibility,' declares Taylor, with Mutu standing just behind him. 'He is sorry for the problems that have been caused and he very soon wants to restore his good name in the international football world and particularly in his homeland of Romania. He is now looking forward to getting his career back on track in top-class football after next May.'

Mutu apologises to Chelsea's fans, blaming injury problems and loneliness for his 'mistakes' – but he insists he never tried to cheat. 'I am still disappointed with myself but now, because I know what I'm going to do and know what the ban is, I can breathe easier. I needed help and expected Chelsea to help me and I think he [Kenyon] wasn't so fair. They terminated my contract before the FA made a decision. In Tony Adams and Paul Merson's cases they were being helped by the club and that means a lot for a player.

'I first took the drug in February. I didn't want to cheat on football. I had been injured in that time and because I was very sad that night I got drunk. I don't drink usually so it's easy for me to get drunk. I made a mistake and I know that now and I am very sorry about this. I know I have disappointed them [the fans]. I wish them all the best, and I wish to see Chelsea at a good level and come back to Stamford Bridge and play against Chelsea. I've made a mistake and I am sorry. Who doesn't make mistakes in this life?'

Mutu fires his agents and signs a new deal with an Italian management company led by Alessandro Moggi, son of Juventus managing director Luciano Moggi. And he fires a parting shot at Mourinho. 'I am sure Mourinho didn't notice that I had a busy private life because he simply didn't care about me. My problem with him was to do with the national team. I will always have a problem with a coach who doesn't let me play for my national team. As a coach Mourinho is very good, but as a person I have a big question mark about him.'

SATURDAY, 30 OCTOBER 2004
WEST BROMWICH ALBION 1, CHELSEA 4

Mourinho repeats his claim that Chelsea are statistically the best team in England after their second successive four-goal Premiership win sends them level on points with Arsenal, who are surprisingly held to a draw by Southampton. 'Our first-half display was our worst performance this season,' says Mourinho. But it got much better in the second half and the substitutions worked. With the other results it was a fantastic day for Chelsea. That is the beauty of the game in

England – if I was five or six points ahead in Portugal, the title would be over. Over 14 matches in all competitions we have a better statistical record than Arsenal because we have won 12 and drawn two, while they have won 10 and four draws – now that gap has widened. I would say they have just been better than us in the Premiership.'

Chelsea break the deadlock late in the first half when Terry dives to guide a looping Lampard delivery across the face of goal. Albion freeze and Gallas volleys home a rare strike. Mourinho is still not happy and hauls off Cole and Bridge. Robben spices up the attack and, within two minutes, sees a shot drift wide. Gudjohnsen makes it 2–0, heading home Duff's 51st-minute cross. Albion give themselves hope when Zoltan Gera lashes the ball into the net. But their hopes are short-lived as Lampard runs 70 yards and releases Duff, who clips his shot over Russell Hoult and inside the far post. Lampard then makes it four in the 81st minute with a stunning strike.

With eight goals in two Premiership games and a five-point deficit on the Gunners wiped out, the table has a different complexion. Yet Lampard, the driving force behind this impressive victory, admits he feared the worst at Arsenal's record-breaking start to the season. 'It's nice to see Arsenal are human after all,' says Lampard. 'They have been unbelievable this season and they almost didn't seem human when they were winning every week. Arsenal have been phenomenal and everyone has been talking about how well they have played, but points are all that matters. We have come back at them and that is how a football season works. They have conceded a few points and now we need to make sure we keep our own results going. We have been accused of being boring but, in the second half, we were strutting about.'

Robben catches the eye with his ability to switch wings, track back and run at people. Mourinho says, 'He brings something different to the team. He was fantastic and always dangerous every time he had the ball.'

Team

Cech, Ferreira, Terry, Gallas, Bridge (Carvalho), Smertin, Makelele, Lampard (Tiago), Cole (Robben), Gudjohnsen, Duff.

Following an impressive 1–0 win in Moscow to romp through to the knock-out stages of the Champions League with two games to spare, Chelsea now have the advantage of concentrating on the title, with Arsenal wobbling and United uncharacteristically inconsistent in Europe. Mourinho says, 'We've put pressure on ourselves as we've not asked for time. We said from the beginning that we want to win every game and to be one of the best teams in Europe. Of course next season my team will be better and in two seasons even better, but at the moment we're fighting for results and coping well with the pressure. We can achieve something big this season.'

Arsenal's blip raises expectations of the title coming to Stamford Bridge for the first time in 50 years, but Mourinho tells his players to concentrate on themselves. He says, 'We can't think about Arsenal. We have to win our own matches and see what they do. They cannot win every match but will not lose points every weekend. Maybe tomorrow they will lose points or they will return with a victory at Crystal Palace, but we must make sure we win our game and stay on top of the league. We've lost one game to Manchester City, but after that won five consecutive games, which is very important. You have to show you're strong enough for the fight.'

SATURDAY, 6 NOVEMBER 2004

CHELSEA 1, EVERTON 0

Robben tells his team-mates in a pep-talk before the game to play so well that Arsenal will 'shit in their pants'. Mourinho likes a player to address the team in the dressing room prior to kick-off and it works. Robben declares, 'I kept it simple and said, "Let's continue what we have been doing. Arsenal are playing after us today so let's pressure them, make it hard for them."' Robben's gloriously spectacular second-half strike on his first Premiership start ends the only unbeaten away record in the Premiership, and Arsenal are later held to a 1–1 draw at Crystal Palace.

Chelsea rotate their team with Johnson, Gallas and Parker giving way to Ferreira, Babayaro and Tiago. Makelele and Tiago spend the first half trying in vain to wriggle out of Everton's midfield straitjacket. Kezman replaces Tiago, but his settling-in period is proving long and laboured, and it is not until 20 minutes from time that Nigel Martyn is exposed, only for Gudjohnsen to waste a Terry knockdown.

Kezman's appearance at least galvanises Gudjohnsen and it is his superb turn and floated pass that leads to the breakthrough. Robben dashes clear and not even David Weir's desperate tug can prevent the tricky winger from lifting a delicate lob over Martyn. Tim Cahill's unchallenged header late on is a notch short of the power needed to beat Cech, who is proving the shrewdest of all Chelsea's purchases.

Robben acquires a new nickname, 'The Catalyst', because of his ability to turn games around after coming off the bench. There is an expectant buzz from the crowd whenever he is in possession and he comes desperately close to scoring a magnificent goal midway through the first half when he chips the ball cleverly over Weir's head, then lets fly from the edge of the D. But Martyn brings off a top-class save.

Mourinho acknowledges Everton's performance. 'They have players who are strong, experienced and were good defensively. But we kept the faith, and when Arjen scored we were able to change our organisation and come away with the points. I told the players at half-time if we want to be champions, we have to play like champions – we have to play risky. The alternative was to stay comfortable and enjoy life but, if we play that way, there will be no trophies for us at the end of the season. At the end it felt like a cup final in the dressing room. That is how it must be for the rest of the season.'

Robben, on the mark at CSKA Moscow in midweek, adds, 'It was nice for me to score again but it's been a great week for the team. I can tell you now that we aren't going to win all the games until the end of the season. We will lose and that's all part of the game. But you have to try to win all the prizes. That's how it should be. The Premiership is much tougher than the Dutch league, with big games every week, but I am ready for the physical challenge. I came here to win championships and believe I can do that with Chelsea.'

Everton boss David Moyes says, 'I thought we could hold out but Robben proved the difference. If I had £12m, I would buy a player like that. But the fact is if you can't shop at Armani, you have to shop at Marks and Spencer.'

Team

Cech, Ferreira, Carvalho, Terry, Babayaro, Tiago (Kezman), Makelele, Lampard, Duff (Huth), Gudjohnsen (Geremi), Robben.

Mourinho dismisses speculation linking him with a January move for Real Betis winger Joaquin and Tottenham's Jermain Defoe. He is adamant that his 23-man squad is strong enough to cope with the dual demands of the Premiership and Champions League and has no plans to replace Adrian Mutu. Mourinho says, 'I don't need any more strikers or any other players in January. Duff and Robben are playing well and linking together. We don't have a pure outside-right player, but have two left-footed players who can play together. Eidur Gudjohnsen did a very good job at the start of the season. If everybody is fit I have a lot of options.'

But while he is happy with the team, Mourinho calls on Chelsea fans to be more vocal. He tells Chelsea TV, 'When I can hear 2,000 Everton fans behind me and 35,000 Chelsea fans not being too enthusiastic, I feel we need more.' He also says he wants his long-term future to be at Stamford Bridge. 'I'm so happy with English football, my players and the people that surround me at the club that I want to be here at Chelsea for many, many years.'

John Terry also shows his commitment to the club by signing a new five-year contract just 18 months after putting pen to paper on his last deal. 'I want to be here for the rest of my career,' he says. 'The manager is a key figure. He's made me club captain and I want to stay here and play for him.'

Mourinho looks for an English solution when it comes to strengthening his squad. He believes it is crucial for the development of the team to keep the core of his side as English as possible, and only 'crazy' fees will stop him from scouring the country for new talent in the future. Mourinho says, 'John signing a new deal for us was crucial. It was very important to keep the core of the team English, with players of a strong mentality. We must only go abroad to buy what we don't have here. If you don't have a special player for a special position in the English market you have to look abroad. But the most important thing is to try and look for English players first. But sometimes the fees are crazy amounts, so we have to look elsewhere.'

Next up for Mourinho's table-toppers are local rivals Fulham at Craven Cottage, while Arsenal face a high noon showdown at Tottenham. Mourinho taunts Arsenal by insisting Chelsea are so far ahead of the rest that they will win the Premiership two weeks before the end of the season. Mourinho has only been top for seven days but is determined to stay there for the long haul. He says, 'Just ten minutes ago I was driving down the King's Road with one of my assistants and he said that on 14 May it will be crazy because that's the final day of the season. But I said maybe we should do it two weeks earlier and celebrate then.'

SATURDAY, 13 NOVEMBER 2004

FULHAM 1, CHELSEA 4

Arsenal win 5–4 at the Lane in the midday kick-off, but Chelsea respond in style to restore their two-point lead with another Robben-inspired performance. Mourinho chooses a Chelsea side almost unrecognisable from the team that beat Newcastle in the Carling Cup in the week, making seven changes.

Chelsea take a deserved lead through a fantastic Lampard free-kick into the right corner from almost 30 yards. Fulham simply cannot get a foothold in the match and, after Papa Bouba Diop has made a great last-ditch clearance following Terry's header across goal, the home side are lucky not to concede a penalty. Robben feeds Lampard on the edge of the box after 36 minutes, and the England midfielder's shot hits Zeshan Rehman's raised arm, but referee Uriah Rennie waves play on. Lampard is again unfortunate in first-half stoppage time. Although he appears to be tripped in the area by Moritz Volz, he is booked for diving.

Fulham produce a stunning equaliser on 57 minutes – and it has to be to beat Cech. Terry's headed clearance drops to Diop 30 yards out, and the Senegalese midfielder's vicious volley shoots into Cech's right-hand corner for a memorable first club goal.

But Chelsea regain the lead two minutes later as Robben shows wonderful footwork to elude Zat Knight, Rehman and Mark Pembridge before firing in with his left foot from 15 yards. That proves the catalyst as Gallas seizes on a Diop miskick and heads in from three yards at the far post. Chelsea then seal it with a delightful fourth goal nine minutes from time. Tiago feeds Robben down the left, and the winger's marvellous back-heel gives the Portuguese player time and space to arrow a 16-yard shot into the right corner.

Once again Robben is the difference, with arguably his best performance so far. He takes the match to Fulham, sets up the fourth goal and tops his display with one of the goals of the season. So was it Ranieri, or was it Kenyon who snatched Robben away from Manchester United? 'If it was Mr Ranieri, then congratulations, thank you very much,' muses Mourinho. 'If it was Peter Kenyon or Mr Abramovich, then I say perhaps they should both become managers, because they know a lot about players.'

Chelsea's goal difference is closing in on Arsenal's, and Mourinho taunts Arsenal's defence for conceding four times at Spurs. 'I didn't see Arsenal's game, but 5–4 is a joke result. It is not a real football result; it was like a hockey match. For a team to give away four or five goals, the defenders must be a disgrace. I often play three versus three in training and if the score gets to 5–4 then I send the players to the dressing room and stop the game! They are obviously not doing their job properly and it is no point going on with it – and that's just in a three-a-side game. In a true game I cannot believe the defenders are doing their job properly at all and as a manager this would be a nightmare. Some people may go away thinking it was the best game they had ever seen but as a manager how could you be happy?' While the Gunners have conceded four goals in one game, Chelsea have conceded just four Premiership goals all season.

Mourinho adds, 'I do not think I am vain or arrogant but I believe that now we are top of the table Chelsea can go on to win the championship. I don't say this just for the sake of it – I say it because I truly believe we are good enough to win the title. This was a big test for us and we had the answer. We showed we could handle the pressure. I still remain convinced that we can become the champions.'

Once again preparation is meticulous. Robben says, 'Before every single match you are given a full dossier on your direct opponent – not the team but the precise man you will be playing against. For example, my direct opponent against Fulham was around two metres tall and the coach wanted me to know that in advance and prepare for it.' Terry reveals that the derby status of the game was explained in no uncertain terms to all the new players. 'Before the game we made sure that everyone in that dressing room knew exactly what games between Chelsea and Fulham mean. The rivalry between the clubs and the history of the fixture is very important to our supporters and to get the result against our neighbours that puts us back on top of the league is even better.'

> **Team**
>
> Cech, Ferreira, Terry, Carvalho, Gallas, Lampard, Makelele, Smertin (Tiago), Duff (Kezman), Robben, Gudjohnsen.

The search to replace Mutu takes Roman Abramovich, accompanied by Kenyon, to the Ajax Amsterdam Arena at the weekend to watch Feyenoord starlet Salomon Kalou. The Ivory Coast-born striker has hit an impressive nine goals in 12 games in the Eredivisie – flourishing under the tutelage of Ruud Gullit. The 19-year-old has a quiet game in the 1–1 draw with Ajax but is earmarked for great things at the De Kuip Stadion.

Valeri Bojinov has caught the eye of Mourinho with eight Serie A goals for Lecce. The 18-year-old is just one goal behind Andriy Shevchenko, Inter's Brazilian ace Adriano and Roma hitman Vincenzo

Montella. Mourinho sends assistant Steve Clarke to watch the Bulgarian international in action against Juventus and Siena. Arsenal, Barcelona, Marseille and Borussia Dortmund are also chasing Bojinov.

Mourinho says he is delighted with how quickly the team have gelled. 'It was the big question mark. I'll never forget a word I had with Mario Stanic. He left the club but he was with me on the first day and said something like, "A lot of people have arrived in England and they adapt to the English reality of football. But I know that your methods and your philosophy and your way of thinking are very special. Don't ever change, even if it takes time, don't change." I'll never forget what he said. So it was a question for me whether the players could adapt. I followed an Italian manager, and it cannot be easy when you follow a manager who thinks very differently.

'At the moment I feel we are a very strong team defensively. I don't say we are a defensive team. I say we are a strong team in defensive terms, but at the same time lacking sufficient fluidity in attack, because that will take time to come. But we play very good football at times. The only thing I would like is to have more control of the game in terms of possession. In five years I have never had a match where my team has had less possession than the opponents. Never, never. We could play Real Madrid, we could play Deportivo La Coruna, even Manchester United; we always had a bigger percentage. Again, that takes time, but the team is going in the right direction.

'We must think more about our football and not play by instinct. When you play another team with the same qualities as you, normally the better one wins. But when you play against other teams who can stop during the game and think collectively, it becomes much more difficult. You see how Spanish, Italians, Portuguese play football? I don't say that they are perfect. English football has a few things to learn from them in the same way they have a lot of things to learn from English football. I have a lot to learn from English football and am completely open to good influences. But I also have things to give. The lines of communication between me and my players are wide open and the intention is to improve the whole team by each one of us giving our best. I believe it can make us a strong team. I cannot say we will win the Champions League or the Premiership, but I know that we can do it. Real Madrid have a group of stars and they have a group of young boys who are not ready to cope with that pressure and that quality. What is missing is what I call low-profile players. For example, in my team I love to have Geremi on the bench because he's a low-profile player who is ready to help, to fight for the team, to do the job I want him to do. If I need him to play right-back, he can play right-back. If I need him to play right-winger, he can play right-winger. If I need him to pick up a man and mark him out of the game, he does it.'

SATURDAY, 20 NOVEMBER 2004

CHELSEA 2, BOLTON WANDERERS 2

Never before in his managerial career can Mourinho recall losing a two-goal lead. 'No, no, no, never. Never, never, never,' he insists. A club record ninth successive victory in all competitions is snatched away by the set-piece specialists who earn a draw from two free-kicks, the second three minutes from the end.

The noisiest roar of the afternoon greets the news that Arsenal have mysteriously failed to see off West Bromwich Albion at Highbury, but that is eventually followed by 40,000 groans at Bolton's equaliser. The surprise bulletin on Arsenal's latest lapse arrives well before the finish at Stamford Bridge, where traffic and transport chaos delay the kick-off by 30 minutes.

Duff makes a blistering start after all the delays, scoring after 36 seconds. Robben feeds Lampard for a shrewd through-pass to Duff, just about onside. His first touch seems to have taken the ball too wide, but he uses the wet surface to slide forward and knock the ball into the empty net from an angle. A goal right at the start of the second half by Tiago seems to have extended Chelsea's advantage at the head of the table to four points, but Kevin Davies and then Rahdi Jaidi do Arsenal a huge favour.

A measure of Bolton's effectiveness is that they have met last season's top five Premiership teams and remained unbeaten. Sam Allardyce rightly praises the 'resilience, belief and team spirit' that keeps them in contention, while admitting, 'We've nicked a point.'

Mourinho is dignified in his disappointment. 'I don't think many people like the way Bolton play, but they're effective and dangerous. It was a bad result because we want to win every game. Yet we have to be fair. It is very difficult to play against them. Bolton can beat everybody because they create danger from nothing. It is a style I don't like – but we have to give them credit. I'm happy we only have to play them once more.'

Mourinho describes how Bolton attack as 'ugly', but confesses his team had no answer to the aerial bombardment. That is despite spending 20 minutes before kick-off going through a video of Bolton's set-pieces with his players.

But for a long time the only scare for the home side is self-inflicted, Carvalho almost turning the ball into his own net as it bounces awkwardly at him from a free-kick by Bruno N'Gotty. Bolton hold out until the interval, only to be undone again two minutes after it. In the home side's first attack of the second half, Duff controls Robben's corner from the right and lays it back to him for a cross that Tiago meets with a vicious low volley.

But Bolton's self-belief has been boosted by their unexpectedly good results and a set-piece soon revives them and their supporters, who have been complaining about the £40 admission price. Speed swings in a free-kick that evades Cech, and Davies heads it past him off the shoulder of Jaidi. It is only the second Premiership goal Mourinho's team have conceded on the ground all season and the first in almost three months.

Chelsea have chances to extend their lead, but Jussi Jaaskelainen beats away Lampard's fierce drive, Gallas's shot from the rebound painfully strikes a defender, and Gudjohnsen's effort from a corner is held by the keeper on the line at the second attempt. Gudjohnsen then strikes the crossbar, and the sucker punch comes three minutes from time when N'Gotty pumps another free-kick forward and Jaidi latches on to Davies' knockdown to shoot past Cech. Having scored at Highbury in another 2–2 draw earlier this season, the Tunisian has been as even-handed in the championship race as the rest of his side.

Despite Cech flapping for the first goal, Mourinho insists, 'I have no criticism of my players. We're top of the league. My confidence doesn't change; my happiness with the players doesn't change. I never speak about my players when they make big mistakes. I never consider one player individually guilty for a defeat; if anyone is guilty, it's the manager. Petr will face Charlton with my confidence.'

Team

Cech, Ferreira, Carvalho, Terry, Gallas, Tiago, Lampard, Makelele, Duff (Kezman), Gudjohnsen (Johnson), Robben.

Charlton call an end to their simmering feud with Chelsea ahead of their match at The Valley. First there was the row over the Stamford Bridge 'beach' a couple of years ago when the Premier League fined Chelsea £5,000 for failing to inform Charlton about the state of the surface. The Addicks felt less bruised about the outcome of the Scott Parker stand-off a year later, their first confrontation with the Abramovich regime. While unhappy that their star player had pushed too hard for a move and suspicious about the advice Parker was getting, the basic £10m fee Charlton eventually agreed was good business.

Part of the midfielder's deal included provision for striker Carlton Cole to stay for a second season on loan with Charlton. When he chose not to stay in the summer another row blew up. Chelsea loaned Cole to Villa instead, and when the Stamford Bridge club could not offer Charlton an acceptable alternative, Valley lawyers combed the small print of their contracts. The Premier League again were called in but the clubs managed to settle things on their own and Chelsea paid an undisclosed but significant compensation fee.

Prompted by back page headlines in three national papers, Mourinho rules out a move for Tottenham's Jermain Defoe in the

January transfer window. Mourinho says, 'It is completely untrue. Not because I don't like the player – I like him. He is a very good young player but we are not interested.'

Arsene Wenger says he believes Chelsea will make a fresh move for Steven Gerrard at some point. Gerrard was close to a £25m switch in the summer but made a massive U-turn and pledged his future to the Merseysiders. Wenger says, 'Chelsea get who they want sooner or later, so it might be only a temporary decision. But I am not jealous of their money. I find it exciting to fight a team with much bigger potential, financially.'

The Gunners' loss of form has coincided with an injury to Sol Campbell, but Mourinho says, 'Arsenal, Chelsea and Manchester United all have big squads, which offer solutions to all the problems that come up. So there should be no excuses. Ourselves, Arsenal and United have all had injury problems, but ones we can cope with.'

SATURDAY, 27 NOVEMBER 2004

CHARLTON ATHLETIC 0, CHELSEA 4

John Terry and Frank Lampard are once again the driving force behind another Chelsea victory. Terry's second-half goals, separated by just three minutes, are a testament to his determination to get forward, as well as marshal the meanest defence in the top flight. While Lampard gives a performance that is a fitting tribute to his grandfather who passed away the day before.

Another lightning start sees Duff on the scoresheet after 229 seconds. Gudjohnsen gets the ball deep and flicks it hard and low into Duff's path. The Irishman sweeps past Paul Konchesky and arrogantly pokes the ball into the far corner of Dean Kiely's goal.

The only blemish in a near-perfect first half comes when Carvalho plants a diving header on to his own post. But Mourinho is far from happy with just a one-goal interval lead and lets his team know it.

Charlton's hopes go into decline within five minutes of the restart as Terry stages his scoring spree. First he bustles in with a header from Duff's looping corner, which bounces just in front of Kiely giving him little chance. Then he taps in after another Duff corner is headed back across goal and Radostin Kishishev can only clear the ball to the Chelsea captain.

Just before being replaced by Drogba, Gudjohnsen holds himself onside just long enough to score the fourth after a stunning low pass from Lampard leaves him the simple task of tapping past Kiely.

A year ago Alan Curbishley's side gave Ranieri's title pretenders a harsh lesson as they beat the Blues 4–2 on Boxing Day. But Mourinho's Chelsea are a different class and the efficiency of their victory echoes around the dressing rooms of Highbury and Old Trafford.

Team

Cech, Ferreira, Carvalho, Terry, Gallas, Tiago, Makelele, Lampard, Duff (Geremi), Robben (Babayaro), Gudjohnsen (Drogba).

Arsenal lose 2–1 at Anfield, leaving them five points behind Chelsea in a remarkable turnaround at the top of the table. Their hopes of retaining the title are dealt a further blow when Vieira is ruled out of the crucial showdown with Chelsea at Highbury after receiving his fifth caution of the season. Vieira says, 'When we are going through a difficult time like this, I have a big part to play and I will try my best. As a team we have to improve. It is up to us. If we really want it, we are going to do it. The quality and the hunger to keep the title is there. We know what we have to do.' With Brazilians Gilberto Silva and Edu injured, Wenger has no option but to field an inexperienced central midfield duo of Mathieu Flamini and Francesc Fabregas against the league leaders. After just one win and four draws in the last six Premiership games, Arsenal desperately need the win against Chelsea to revive their title challenge. Vieira adds, 'We know we played better at the start of the season. We need maybe a bit of togetherness to help us win the games. Three or four years ago maybe we would have won the game at Liverpool. We are disappointed because we wanted to start winning again.'

But first up for Chelsea are Newcastle under new manager Graeme Souness. The Scot believes fans will look back in future years and acclaim Mourinho's Chelsea for their starring role in a golden era in the game's history. As a player Souness was a hugely influential figure during Liverpool's golden era. 'People often talk to me about the good old days, but in 20 years' time what we are doing today will be considered the good old days. In my opinion these are the glory days and as a manager it's a privilege to be involved. In years to come I think they'll be saying, "D'you remember the great Chelsea and Arsenal teams at the start of the century?"

'It's easy to be dismissive of Chelsea's success and say they've achieved this and that simply because of the money they have,' adds Souness. 'But the manager still has to do the job. He has to sign the right players, pick the right team and get them to win consistently. He's done all that in my opinion with some style. You also have to say that he has an outstanding pedigree. You don't win the Champions League and the UEFA Cup without talent and without making the right decisions. But what I've learned is that no manager gets everything right. Yes, you enjoy the highs, but there are lots of lows too. That's the price on the ticket. There's a great sense of responsibility when you're the manager.'

SATURDAY, 4 DECEMBER 2004
CHELSEA 4, NEWCASTLE UNITED 0

Chelsea consolidate their position at the top with four second-half goals. Drogba stands in front of the adoring Chelsea faithful bellowing 'I'm back!' in celebration of his superb strike. The curse that normally comes with both the Player and Manager of the Month awards is lifted as both Mourinho and Robben receive their accolades before kick-off and again make their own special contributions. The deepest joy, though, is reserved for Mateja Kezman's first league goal: an absolutely delightful chip from the spot.

Lampard breaks Newcastle's resistance with the opener in the 63rd minute, and substitute Drogba adds the vital second five minutes later before Robben and Kezman wrap up the points with two goals in the final minutes. Unchanged from the team that thumped Charlton, Chelsea have a Terry header correctly ruled out for offside early on. In a lively opening Cech brilliantly pushes aside a Laurent Robert free-kick from 25 yards, while Craig Bellamy should put the visitors in front when Dyer carves open the Chelsea defence with a perfect through-ball. Once again Cech thwarts his man and Chelsea escape again when the ball runs loose to Robert from the keeper but the Newcastle winger sends his effort wide.

Gudjohnsen is then left in the clear with just Shay Given to beat after a defensive mix-up, but the Icelandic striker shoots wide with the goal at his mercy. Mourinho replaces him with Drogba at the interval. Robert brings another excellent save from Cech from a free-kick before Lampard makes no mistake from six yards after latching on to a Drogba knockdown.

Five minutes later roles are reversed as Drogba runs on to Lampard's crafted long ball and beats Given with a clever left-footed shot inside the right-hand post. Chelsea are now irresistible and, after Kezman hits the post, Robben wraps up the points after weaving his way into the area. And there is still time for Kezman to break his Premiership duck from the penalty-spot in stoppage time after Given brings down Duff.

'For the last three or four months I've been unlucky,' insists Kezman. 'I hit the post again today but all the players have helped me with my confidence. I know all the lads were behind me, so you can try anything. I worked hard every day to get to this moment. I've played more than 1,000 minutes this season and had only scored one goal in the Carling Cup, so it has been very difficult. Goals are my life. That's me. Without goals I have a difficult life. When you have scored 20 or 30 goals every year for the past seven or eight years and then go three months with just one, it is very hard. You could see our spirit after I scored. Every single player came to me. That was fantastic and that is our strength this season. That is how we can be champions.'

It is the fifth time in seven Premiership games that Chelsea have scored four times. Newcastle, like Blackburn, West Brom, Fulham and Charlton before them, are simply blown apart. Chelsea are now

33–1 for a clean sweep of the Premiership, the FA Cup, the Carling Cup and the Champions League.

Team
Cech, Ferreira, Terry, Carvalho, Gallas (Bridge), Tiago (Kezman), Makelele, Lampard, Robben, Gudjohnsen (Drogba), Duff.

Both Arsenal and Manchester United win 3–0 at home later in the afternoon and Sir Alex Ferguson says he expects Chelsea to slip up in the title race. 'Chelsea will have a blip. They will lose games. It's then a case of how their players react which will be important. Arsenal and ourselves have got that experience. We have seen title challenges be over by March. Chelsea don't have the experience of winning when it really matters.'

Contractors move in to relay the pitch at Stamford Bridge, which should be ready for their next home game against Norwich in 12 days' time. The surface has deteriorated severely and the win against Newcastle was played in particularly difficult conditions.

Chelsea warm up for the title showdown at Arsenal with a Champions League defeat at Porto. 'Every defeat hurts and we're used to winning,' says Terry. 'It doesn't change the group but we wanted to win the game. We don't like losing games and picked a strong team to win it. We're all angry after defeats, including the manager, but we can see the bigger picture. We've got a more important game on Sunday.'

Claudio Ranieri will be in the stands to watch his old side for the first time since being sacked. 'Italian television have asked me to be the commentator for this match and I plan to go to the game,' he says. 'I won't see anyone at Chelsea but plan to go straight to the stadium. I've had no contact since I left the club and am a very reserved man. If they don't want to see me that's fine and I'm happy with the way things have turned out. I don't want to disturb anybody and will just watch the match and see some old friends.'

Having led Chelsea to second place in the Premiership and the Champions League semi-finals last season, Ranieri is convinced they can go one better this time around. 'Chelsea must be one of the favourites for the Champions League because Mourinho has won it before and my players had a good experience last year. It's possible for them to win the Champions League and the Premiership. Why not? Chelsea are very strong. We did a very good job last year putting the foundations in place and they're continuing to progress.'

Chelsea's dramatic victory in last season's Champions League quarter-final may have been the high water mark of Ranieri's reign but that should not detract from its significance after 17 games without a win over their London rivals. Ranieri adds, 'I was very happy Chelsea got Drogba because in my last meeting with Abramovich in Milan I said he should sign him. He wanted to know my ideas for new players, and I said Drogba, another central defender and Steven Gerrard. It was my idea to sign Robben and I met him in Eindhoven. I'd watched a lot of videos of him and was very impressed. I'm not surprised by his success and when I met him I was sure straight away. I told him he could play on the left, on the right and he could swap with Damien Duff. I knew very well they could play together.'

Robben reveals he feared he had testicular cancer at the beginning of the year. He needed an operation to remove a lump – and then faced an agonising wait while tests were done. 'I was very scared – it was a very difficult time. I found a little lump and went to the doctor. He told me I needed an operation. I then had to wait for the results and I didn't know if it was going to be good or bad news. The waiting was terrible for a few days. I didn't know what was going to happen to me. It was a horrible wait. Then I heard the news was good and it was a massive relief. At that time football was no longer important – the most important thing is to be healthy and for your family to be healthy. It's good to talk about it and put it out in the public domain. Why would you be embarrassed about it? It can happen to any man at any time and can lead to terrible consequences.'

Arsene Wenger sends his stars to the bowling alley to ease the pressure ahead of the game. While Mourinho was pushing his stars through a gruelling training session, Arsenal's first-team squad enjoyed skittles for three hours. The Arsenal manager insists his side are back to top form after crucial wins over Birmingham and Rosenborg – and will prove it with a victory at Highbury, even without the suspended Vieira. 'We just want to win,' says Wenger. 'I don't think their fans will laugh when they lose the game. We are ready. We have won two games since last week. We have the talent and the spirit and we believe we will do it. We're looking forward to the game.'

But Mourinho sees things differently. 'At the end of the game Chelsea will be top of the league. So it's not a question of whether this game can decide a change of positions. It's not a case that because of this game Arsenal could go top and Chelsea go second. The only question left is: two points difference, five points difference or eight points difference? And I tell you eight points difference is a lot. If we win, it is significant. If we draw, it's five points; if we lose, it's two points. But our next two matches are at home against Norwich and Aston Villa. So it's significant if we win.'

Wenger is sure the neutrals are behind Arsenal because Chelsea are backed by Abramovich. He says, 'I am surprised that more people are not behind us because we have less money than Manchester United and Chelsea, with whom we are direct competition. We have 30-times less investment capacity.'

But Mourinho ridicules that notion, 'When Thierry Henry signed for Arsenal was that for free? Did Juventus give him to Arsenal? When Vieira came here was that on loan? Did they rent him for £100,000? Was Reyes free from Sevilla? That surprises me, the fact that Sevilla made Reyes a Christmas gift. Ha! How much have I spent at Chelsea? Sometimes you confuse things by saying how much Chelsea have spent. We don't spend too much – maybe Man United spend more than me.'

Mourinho has splashed £70m of Abramovich's money on five players in his short time in charge, and, even though Wenger has laid out £95m, his net expenditure is just £9m in eight years. Wenger hits back, 'Of course we've spent. I didn't say we hadn't. I don't feel we're poor. But if I ask who has the biggest financial potential, Chelsea or Arsenal, what would you say? Arsenal? I don't think so. We bought

Thierry Henry with the money we generated from Nicolas Anelka – less than half of it. We bought Patrick Vieira for £3.5m at that time so you cannot say that was a big investment. It forces you to be a little bit more creative.'

Mourinho says that Vieira's suspension will be a big blow to Arsenal, but he points to the fact that Arsenal's magnificent, free-scoring run at the start of the season came without the Frenchman, who was recovering from injury. He says, 'They will miss him. The same way that I would miss John Terry if he was not involved in the game. And, to be fair the best period of the season they have had was at the beginning when they beat everybody scoring four and five. And Patrick was not there. It looks a contradiction because Patrick is a fantastic player. But it's reality. They didn't miss him in that period. I think they have a lot of potential. Their young players are good. Flamini is good, Fabregas is good, Robert Pires can play in the middle as he is top quality and has a lot of experience. So I think they have an answer and I think they have a great side.'

Mourinho adds that he has used Kezman in training as a double for Thierry Henry. The coach explains, 'Henry is one of the best strikers in the world; there's no doubt about it. What he has done in English football in recent years speaks for itself. He's a threat; he can score. You have to try to control his movement, but not just his movement but what the team tries to create for him. We've studied the movements he makes on the pitch and for the last two days we have tried on the training ground to practise our defensive movements in relation to Thierry's attacking movements. Kezman took on the role of Henry, and now I think we are ready to fight him.'

Mourinho also points out that he has not lost a big game in his entire career. In two and a half seasons with Porto Mourinho was unbeaten in games against major rivals Benfica and Sporting Lisbon. So far this season Chelsea have already beaten Liverpool and Manchester United. 'In 12 or 13 big games with Porto, classics as we call them in Portugal, we never lost. I've got a very good record in important matches and have every confidence in my team.'

SUNDAY, 12 DECEMBER 2004

ARSENAL 2, CHELSEA 2

A global television audience of 600 million watches events underline the growing interest in Chelsea's attempt to oust their London rivals as Premiership champions. The players demonstrate how a tense, competitive fixture can be spectacularly entertaining and still promote its finer virtues.

One of only four Englishmen in the starting line-ups, Terry's leadership is as important as the contributions from more glamorous names. But Mourinho is angry Thierry Henry's quickly taken 29th-minute free-kick is allowed to stand, even though referee Graham Poll has not blown his whistle and Cech is still busy lining up his defensive wall. Mourinho is grateful for a late let-off as Henry misses a glorious 77th-minute chance to wrap up victory for the Gunners, who are still left trailing leaders Chelsea by five points.

Mourinho says, 'I don't want to talk too much about it otherwise I will have to go before the FA, spend time in the stands and it might cost me money I would rather spend on Christmas presents. But I am more than unhappy. Unhappy is a nice word and I cannot say the word which is in my heart and soul. Because I cannot forget Arsenal's second goal I don't think it was a fair result. But my players gave a big performance and the result keeps the distance between us and the other teams. The game had a dark moment and it's difficult to forget that. The way both teams fought and performed made the result fair but Chelsea scored two goals and Arsenal only scored one.'

Henry responds, 'The referee asked me, "Do you want to wait for the whistle and for the players to go back ten yards?" He said, "You can have a go," and I was just waiting for Eidur Gudjohnsen to move out of the way.' Poll adds, 'The whistle doesn't need to be blown. I asked Henry, "Do you want a wall?" He said, "Can I take it, please?" He was very polite, and I said, "Yes". I gave the signal for him to take it and he did.'

Mourinho claims that a leading referee – it was, by coincidence,

Poll – visited the Chelsea training ground in the close season to clarify some of the rules. 'One of the things he explained to us was free-kicks – walls, distance, whistle – everything was clear,' says the Chelsea manager. Henry scored in similar circumstances against Aston Villa last season and Ian Harte once did the same to net for Leeds against Arsenal.

Terry is furious with his team-mates for the lapse in concentration, and gives Cech a serious dressing down. 'We have worked on that. I wasn't trying to dig him out. We made someone face Petr so he can direct the wall, and the others the play, so they can see what is going on. We didn't do that so it was disappointing.'

Later Cech tells a Czech newspaper, 'Maybe he's [Poll] an Arsenal fan or it was just a failure. We were able to win the game but the referee scored a goal for Arsenal and that was earth-shattering. It's not acceptable. Referee Poll has cheated us. He clearly showed he will give a whistle. We prepare ourselves for these situations. We had seen this in our preparation. Henry is very quick thinking and he tries it. He tried it recently in the Champions League. That's why Eidur Gudjohnsen was directly stood in front of the ball. Eidur asked the referee three times whether he gives a whistle first. Graham Poll ordered him to get away from the ball. Eidur asked him if would give a whistle and he said he would, but there was nothing.'

Gudjohnsen claims Poll helped Henry so much that it was like watching a training ground routine. He says, 'We asked the referee to blow the whistle and he told one of our players what he was going to do. I saw in Henry's reaction that he didn't want the whistle and in the end it looked like a set-piece from the training ground, where one player stands in front of the ball and just jumps out of the way. Sometimes they go for you and sometimes they go against, but luckily Arsenal didn't gain any points on us because of something like that.'

Henry sets the tone for a pulsating contest when he scores within 75 seconds. Cesc Fabregas picks out Henry with a great ball forward, and his nod-off allows Jose Antonio Reyes time to find the striker once again with Chelsea unaccountably standing off. Henry controls with his right foot before spinning to arrow home with his left.

Manuel Almunia, given the nod ahead of Jens Lehmann once more, and who looks far more confident throughout, shows his quality with a flying leap to turn aside Lampard's rocket. Yet when Robben swings in the resulting corner, Sol Campbell is inadvertently blocked by Henry to allow Terry a free header.

On the half-hour Robert Pires earns a free-kick after tangling with Terry and Makelele. Poll stands over the ball with Henry and Gudjohnsen refuses to retreat. But Poll gives the nod and Henry beats the unprepared Cech with a deflection off Tiago's shoulder. Chelsea are furious but the goal is legitimate.

Mourinho's interval switch, with Drogba and Bridge coming on, leaves Arsenal trying to work out their marking duties. Within 35 seconds of the restart, Lampard delivers a free-kick from the left, Gallas outjumps Ashley Cole and nods down into the six-yard box for Gudjohnsen to loop the ball in with a stooping header.

Chelsea take control, and for a while they seem set to score with every free-kick or corner they launch into the box. Lampard is disgusted with himself for failing to hit the target from six yards. Then Almunia does just enough to divert Robben's shot wide after a wonderful dribble past three defenders.

But it is Arsenal who squander the best chance, with Henry the guilty party. Mathieu Flamini's energy and Fabregas's vision put Pires into space on the right, he pulls back but Henry's outstretched left foot can only fire into the North Bank.

The hugs between Terry and Henry at the end are proof of mutual respect. Henry, though, has shown why Abramovich waved a £50m cheque in front of Arsenal vice-chairman David Dein for his services a year earlier. Even without Henry, Chelsea remain favourites to lift the league crown. With him, it would be no contest. Arsenal are left in third place behind Everton, but the Merseysiders are punching well above their weight.

To twice come from behind against the champions at Highbury says something about Chelsea's character. 'I thought my players were fantastic after Arsenal's second goal,' says Mourinho. 'They kept cool, remained in control and gave proof of their strong mental state. When a strange thing has happened, players can lose control. But after Arsenal's second goal – if you can call it a goal – my players were fantastic. We cannot promise anything yet as we don't know. Maybe we'll finish second or third, but maybe we will finish first.'

For Terry, nothing less than first will do. 'We have been too close too often and I am fed up with it now. I want to win something this year. The Premiership would be fantastic, and we showed in the Carling Cup that we are in every competition to go and to win everything we are in. You could see that by the determination of all the lads. We have great experience in the side and we want to go that extra length and go and win the Premiership. We have an edge over them now – and we showed that when we were 2–1 down against a side who have been so great for so many years.'

> **Team**
> Cech, Ferreira, Carvalho (Drogba), Terry, Gallas, Duff, Tiago (Bridge), Makelele, Lampard, Robben, Gudjohnsen (Parker).

During the match yobs singled out Vieira, who was watching from the stands, for sickening racial abuse. Anti-racism group 'Kick It Out' demand action. Spokesman Leon Mann says, 'Their chants were racially offensive, but I am sure there are Chelsea supporters who were disgusted. The problem is a minority can become vocal and give the club a bad name. I'd urge supporters to come forward and ensure these morons get what they deserve. I'll be in contact with the clubs to ensure these people are punished. We have a good relationship with both clubs who've done a lot of anti-racism work. And I will ask Arsenal to see if they can highlight the incident on CCTV cameras and see if Sky Sports footage picked it up.' An FA spokesman says, 'We have not had any complaints regarding any racist chanting. But we would be prepared to investigate if there were any complaints.'

Cech continues to talk about his anger over the Henry goal suggesting Poll must be suffering 'an uneasy conscience'. But former Premier League referees' chief Philip Don says, 'The referee does not have to blow the whistle to restart the game – it can be the voice, the hand, the arm or the nod of the head.'

Jermain Defoe urges Tottenham to sign Joe Cole, who is now a peripheral figure in Mourinho's squad. 'Joe would fit in well down here,' says Defoe. 'He can play on the left, on the right or behind the front two. He is such a good player. Hopefully he will come to Tottenham.' But Cole is determined to stick it out until the end of the season even though he has not started a Premiership game since the win at West Brom in October and has even failed to make the substitutes' bench in recent weeks. Mourinho insists, 'He is ready to fight for a place here and, in fact, that's the same feeling that I have. We have had a conversation and I said, "No chance of leaving. Don't think about it because I need everybody." It's just a question of getting a chance. I've told him he's a good player, he works well and has a lot of ambition but at this moment the team is winning, playing very well and I'd be stupid to change it too much.'

Sir Alex Ferguson switches his psychological attack to Chelsea. He says, 'Chelsea? They will find it difficult coming north to get points. Without doubt, Chelsea are the new force. Yet their form is not much different from last season. If you look at the last few seasons, Chelsea have always been up there at this time. It is when they come up north you will see. They have got to go to Liverpool and Everton. It's different after New Year – different pressures, you see. I always think the league starts on New Year's Day.'

Mateja Kezman says he considered walking out on Chelsea shortly after joining the club, depressed at failing to hold down a regular place in the side. Only a heart-to-heart with Mourinho prevented his premature departure. Kezman says, 'On more than one occasion I just wanted to drive to the airport and jump on the first plane home. My wife and I were struggling desperately with the situation. I even remember saying to myself, "If this doesn't change by January, I will have to find myself a new club." I had to tell him how I was feeling. It is not in my nature to keep quiet. I knew if I was burdened by unhappiness it would eventually go terribly wrong for me on the pitch. I wasn't frightened to approach Mourinho. We talk a lot anyway, so I didn't find it too difficult to have showdown talks with him. I'm pleased to say he immediately calmed me down and said, "Don't worry, it will work out. I have immense confidence in your ability as a striker." I assured Mourinho that I had not come to Chelsea for the money. I know other players love the money and big contracts, but for me the football is far more important.'

Kezman adds he feared he would go broke in the opening weeks. He says, 'We initially hired an apartment in Kensington which is extremely close to Harrods. I thought I would go bankrupt. My wife seemed to think there was only one shop in London so she went shopping at Harrods all the time. Fortunately we have now bought our own place: a house which needed a few things doing to it. Nevertheless we feel at home there.'

He adds, 'There are a lot of similarities between me and the manager. Mourinho is a very emotional man. He is passionate about everything he does. He has what I call a proper Portuguese mentality, one that is very similar to a Serbian. Mourinho is arrogant, but in a way you respect. And if we want to be the best and win big trophies, it's vital the manager comes across as a winner. Mourinho makes sure he does. All the time he is telling us we are going to win all the big trophies this season. He emphasises the point so often that the players now believe they are born winners. Honestly, we actually believe we are going to win the league and the Champions League. I think Mourinho has brainwashed all of us. I rate him among the best coaches in the world. He is unbelievable when it comes to analysing games and putting players in the right frame of mind to maximise their effectiveness. No matter who we play, Mourinho always knows every minor detail about that team. Believe me, he is as sharp as a knife. Nothing eludes him.'

Kezman reveals the human side of Abramovich, who hangs around the dressing room cracking terrible jokes. 'I have been so surprised by the incredible atmosphere among the squad players. A lot of that is down to Mr Abramovich. He comes down to the dressing room after every game. He talks to us individually and he shows his warm character. Believe it or not he is actually a very funny man. He cracks jokes every time he comes in. He makes us laugh because most of them are lousy. I think people see him as the big untouchable businessman, but he is a wonderful guy.'

Mourinho must make at least one change for the next game against Norwich, with Bridge replacing Carvalho. The Portuguese centre-back will be out for two to three weeks with a broken toe and, with Robert Huth still injured, Gallas moves to partner Terry at the heart of the defence.

SATURDAY, 18 DECEMBER 2004
CHELSEA 4, NORWICH CITY 0

Chelsea ensure they will be top at Christmas, with a performance of speed and finesse that swamps the visitors and has the game safe by half-time. 'It was pure counter-attacking football,' says Mourinho. 'We had good dynamics and speed and took up good positions. In fact we could have scored just the one in the first half and three in the second, because we were scoring from counter-attacking. The present system with Arjen Robben in the team suits my players' qualities and we can control the game.'

Mourinho pays Norwich the dubious compliment of fielding what has come to be regarded as his strongest team. Norwich settle quicker and for a time look as though they can give Chelsea a test. But Thomas Helveg and Gary Doherty hand Chelsea a comfortable two-goal lead. The first blunder comes in the 10th minute when Helveg's attempt at a backpass goes straight to Duff. The Irishman storms forward and curls a low shot into the net.

Norwich then suffer another blow when striker Mathias Svensson limps off after falling badly and twisting a medial ligament. He is replaced by Leon McKenzie, who is lucky to avoid giving away a penalty when he clearly punches the ball in his own area. But Chelsea do not have to wait long for a second goal and it is Doherty who obliges in the 34th minute. The former Spurs defender crazily flicks the ball out of his area to Robben, and the Dutchman's square pass sets up Lampard to power a stunning shot into the top left-hand corner. John Terry's programme notes prove prophetic as he jokes that he will have to buy Lampard some vaseline to rub on his chapped lips for Christmas as the midfielder kisses the badge on his shirt so often.

A minute from the break, Robben drifts in from the right flank and finds Lampard in the box who flicks the ball to Tiago. The Portuguese player's back-heel falls to Robben, who completes the sorcery with a ferocious smack that gives Rob Green no chance.

Asked what could stop Chelsea winning the league, Mourinho shrugs and says, 'A better team than us. At the moment nobody is better than us, but you never know. If we keep our present mental and tactical strength, I think nobody can stop us. We have to lose matches in the second half of the season but at this moment no one is better than us. In the future, I don't know. Maybe Arsenal or Manchester United can jump to a different level or maybe we can slide into a lower level. We could have injuries and players could lose form, but at this moment my confidence of winning the league is big.'

> **Team**
>
> Cech, Ferreira, Gallas, Terry, Bridge, Tiago (Parker), Makelele, Lampard, Duff, Gudjohnsen (Drogba), Robben (Kezman).

Sol Campbell's stunning late strike at Portsmouth lifts Arsenal back within five points, and Arsene Wenger warns Mourinho that Chelsea are not unstoppable. 'We are back in the race,' says Wenger. 'We are very hungry and we have talent and the ingredients to make the race interesting.'

Celestine Babayaro turns down loan moves to Crystal Palace, Middlesbrough and West Brom to fight for his place. The Nigeria left-back has made just one Premiership start under Mourinho, but is hopeful of extending his stay at the club he joined seven years ago. Babayaro is Chelsea's longest serving player and wants a new contract when his current deal expires in the summer.

There is bad news for Scott Parker who will be out for several weeks. An X-ray shows a broken metatarsal bone in his foot. The player admits he may have caused some of the damage himself. 'I went for a one-two with Damien Duff but the pitch was poor and my foot buckled and I heard something pop. I went straight over to the physio when we scored and the manager wanted me to come off, but I just wanted to carry on and impress. It just made things worse.'

Mourinho responds to Sir Alex Ferguson's suggestion that Chelsea will drop points when they have to play up north by saying, 'I know that Manchester United will lose points in the south – because they already have done. They lost three points at Stamford Bridge, three points at Portsmouth and two at Fulham. For sure, they have a problem in the south. We will have to wait and see whether we have a problem up north.'

With the busy and vital Christmas period up next and the transfer window after that, Frank Lampard insists the squad is in perfect shape. 'You are always wanting to strengthen the squad but we have a really steady ship at Chelsea and we're going well.' After a session at the club's new training ground in the Surrey countryside, Mourinho says the chequebook will not be coming out more than once, and only then because of the injury to Parker. 'Scott has been important for us over the last two months and was becoming a regular. I don't need a top, top player. Forget Joaquin, forget Defoe, forget all the other names you could speak about. If we do something it will just be a player to help us. Anyway, to get better midfield players than we have got already, I wouldn't know where to find them.'

But with four matches in the next ten days, starting at home to Aston Villa, and with Carvalho, Huth and Babayaro all on the injury list, Mourinho knows he needs his whole squad to be ready. 'January and February are months when I need everybody and I have only 16 outfield players fit. I cannot give the players days off. Everyone is selected,' he says. The only concession to the Christmas holiday is letting his players start training on Christmas Day a few hours later than usual.

But David O'Leary's troubles put Mourinho's situation in perspective. He is struggling to fill his side's bench, as his squad is decimated by injuries and he is unable to field Carlton Cole because of his loan deal with Chelsea. O'Leary says, 'I have got 14 fit players and two goalkeepers. It doesn't give you a lot of options.'

SUNDAY, 26 DECEMBER 2004

CHELSEA 1, ASTON VILLA 0

Damien Duff's goal is enough to beat Villa and Mourinho insists he is more than happy to grind out 1–0 wins for the rest of the season if it means winning the Premiership. 'It is not our target to be winter champions,' he says. 'The aim is for us to be champions at the end of the season. At the moment we have a five-point advantage and this result was important to keep that distance. This result puts us in a comfortable situation and the question now is simply whether our lead goes up to eight points or down to two. The fans believe we can win the title and they understand that when you are playing to be champions you cannot afford to lose points in stupid circumstances. Everyone speaks of all the 4–0 wins we have had lately but the clean sheets we have achieved are just as important. The aim is always to play good football, score early and win easily. But when you get to 75 minutes with the score still at 1–0 it becomes a case of rolling up our sleeves, playing with our hearts and fighting to keep the lead. Today we have done that.'

O'Leary insists, 'The goal aside, it was an even game. It was never our intention to just come here and defend. It was all I could do to name five on the bench today and there is always the chance that you can come here and get a drubbing. But I didn't want to sit back and wait to get hammered. We gave it a go and Chelsea were pretty nervous towards the end of that game.'

For the sixth time in his last nine games Duff opens the scoring to set his team on the road to victory. On the half-hour a Villa attack breaks down just inside the Chelsea penalty area and Lampard's pass immediately feeds Robben for a run from inside his own half. Villa's defence backs off the advancing Dutchman and, as Gareth Barry comes inside to cover, Robben slips the ball out to Duff, who

Above: Mourinho in his trademark grey overcoat shouts orders to his team in the Carling Cup Final.

Below left: One of Mourinho's signings, Didier Drogba, clashes with Liverpool keeper Jerzy Dudek.

Below right: Captain John Terry celebrates with his Chelsea team mates.

Above left: John Terry fought off stiff competition from fellow team mates Frank Lampard, Petr Cech and from Liverpool's Steven Gerrard to be crowned PFA Player of the Year 2004/05.

Above right: Frank Lampard was also named Football Writers' Player of the Year following a fantastic season.

Below: A photocall before an all important match. From left to right, back: Gudjohnsen, Cech, Terry, Carvalho, Gallas, Lampard. Front: Kezman, Makele, Cole, Ferreira and Duff.

Above: John Terry and Didier Drogba in action against Liverpool's Sami Hyypia in the Carling Cup Final.

Below: Mourinho and Lampard celebrate. Mourinho is often seen hugging each of his players before every game. The respect and admiration is evident between the Chelsea players and coach.

Above: Gudjohnsen, Lampard and Terry are jubilant at winning their first piece of silverware – the Carling Cup.

Below left: Mourinho consoles Steven Gerrard after Chelsea beat Liverpool in the final to become Carling Cup Champions. Rumours have been rife all season about a possible move from Merseyside to West London for the Liverpool player.

Below right: A very happy manager. Jose guides his team to their first champion success.

Above: The triumphant players celebrate with their first trophy of the season.

Below: Jose Mourinho holds the Carling Cup high as he celebrates with his assistant Steve Clark on the right, and physiotherapist, Rui Faria, left.

Above: Frank Lampard and Eidur Gudjohnsen celebrate their win at Bolton. Chelsea's 2-0 victory clinched them the premiership title.

Below left: As the actual trophy was to be presented to Chelsea at Stamford Bridge against Charlton, Joe Cole had to make do with this souvenir premiership trophy instead.

Below right: A very happy Mourinho watches his team win the league for the first time in fifty years. After congratulating his team and staff, Jose was seen calling his family from the touchline.

Lampard and Terry – who played in almost every match – celebrate in front of the lucky fans who travelled to Bolton to see Chelsea win the league.

Above: In a packed Millennium Stadium, Makelele clashes with Arsenal's Jose Antonio Reyes at the Community Shield final, leaving Thierry Henry standing.

Below left: Mourinho appears to point a finger at Wenger as Chelsea beat Arsenal 2-1. And there would be more finger pointing as the new season unfolded.

Below right: An exhausted but jubilant Terry with the Community Shield.

cuts inside Liam Ridgewell and beats Thomas Sorensen with a low shot inside his near post. It is a goal that has been coming for some time. Terry has already headed just over from Lampard's deep free-kick and another Duff left-footer has grazed the far post. Yet Villa stick to their gameplan and refuse to blindly chase the game as they seek to deny Chelsea their first Boxing Day victory since 1999.

Petr Cech says, 'It fills me with so much confidence playing behind such great defenders as John Terry, Ricardo Carvalho and William Gallas. They make life so much easier for us, because we all know that if we score one goal, that is often enough. We win 1–0, the game is finished and we have another three points.'

Team

Cech, Ferreira, Gallas, Terry, Bridge, Tiago, Makelele, Lampard, Duff (Smertin), Robben (Johnson), Gudjohnsen (Drogba).

Thierry Henry hits his 20th goal of the season in Arsenal's 2–0 win over Fulham at Highbury, lifting him up to joint second alongside Ian Wright in the all-time list of Arsenal's league scorers with 128. He says, 'I didn't care what Chelsea did. We only need to think about what we need to do. If we didn't believe we could catch them we might as well give up now and go home. We have to believe we can do it. I didn't ask for their result after the game, we just concentrate on our job.' Wenger also insists his side are not worried about Chelsea, 'There is so much time to go that what is most important is we focus on our quality. We don't have to worry about anyone else. If we win our games then I'm ready to count at the end of the season. It's too far away to even speculate about a slip by Chelsea. I do not worry about results of other teams. What can we change about them? Nothing.'

Mourinho is named as coach of a 2004 fantasy team by French sports daily *L'Equipe*. He ends a magical year with his Chelsea side on top of the Premiership after winning the Champions League and the Portuguese title with former club Porto. Two Chelsea players – central defenders John Terry and Ricardo Carvalho – are also named in the team.

Mourinho's first taste of the English festive football calendar is not to his liking. 'I understand Boxing Day is an important day for your football culture and I accept that we have to play on 26 December,' he says. 'But it makes no sense to play again on the 28th. And if some important players get injuries during these matches then we really have to think about this programme. The fact is we have just 24 hours after the Villa game to train and travel to Portsmouth for our next match. I know it is the same for every other team and we must all play under the same circumstances. But to have just one day's rest makes the circumstances so difficult. Speak with the specialists in energetic systems, the biochemists and the physiologists and they will all tell you that it is completely impossible for a player to recover from a Premiership game in 24 hours.'

He already faces a defensive headache as William Gallas has picked up a hamstring strain during the Villa victory. With Huth crocked and Carvalho not one hundred per cent, Mourinho has few options. 'Maybe we will see a lot of goals on the 28th but that will not be because the teams are good but because the players will be broken by the physical intensity.'

Smertin, who spent last season on loan at Fratton Park, warns they must keep Patrik Berger and Aiyegbeni Yakubu quiet if they want to beat Pompey. The Russian midfielder says, 'It is going to be something special for me to go back there. I like Portsmouth's supporters because they are very loyal and they like me as well. Portsmouth play with a big spirit. Yakubu is a great player and very strong. He is hungry and motivated. Their best player is Patrik Berger. He is very dangerous and we have to watch him.'

TUESDAY, 28 DECEMBER 2004

PORTSMOUTH 0, CHELSEA 2

Mourinho is full of praise for the way Chelsea hold off a pumped-up Pompey, who give them the run-around for 45 minutes. 'Portsmouth made it very difficult for us and showed why they had beaten Manchester United at home and were unlucky against Arsenal.

But we got ourselves in a good position after half-time. It is a really big victory for us.

'I told my players at half-time this was not a day to dribble or play wonderful possession football. But it was a day to show how to be champions – which we did. Only top players can fight like we did today. From a mental point of view we have overcome a great obstacle by winning at Christmas. Six points out of six shows we do not have a jinx. There are still some hard tests ahead but my players have shown they have the desire to win the title and they know they have the ability.'

Mourinho is unhappy on two accounts. 'Yes, you can play two games in two or three days but it is still not correct. You can smoke three boxes of cigars and still be alive but that doesn't mean it's right or healthy.' He is also upset that the Gunners have an extra day's rest over the busy holiday period before facing Newcastle. 'They always seem to have two or three days' rest in which to recover,' he says. 'Perhaps it's something to do with the TV schedule. All my players are tired – especially John Terry. He has had to play two big games one after the other but at least he has a few days to get ready for Liverpool on Saturday.'

Robben celebrates the opener by whipping off his shirt and is booked and substituted all within two minutes. He laughs all the way to the dugout, pausing only to shake hands with referee Alan Wiley. An added-time goal from substitute Joe Cole confirms an eight-point lead at the top of the Premiership. Robben's eighth strike could well be seen in retrospect as one of the defining moments of the campaign. With just 11 minutes remaining, a move involving Cole, Duff and Gudjohnsen ends with Robben having a clear shooting chance on the right of the box. He strikes it well enough, but a deflection off Matthew Taylor makes sure Shaka Hislop is finally beaten.

Cole comes off the bench to add spark, invention and the killer second goal, which he drives home from the edge of the area. 'We just seem like a machine at the moment,' says Cole. 'I can imagine that what we were saying about Arsenal last year is exactly what they're saying about us now. What we've done defensively is amazing. The strikers and midfielders have been grabbing the limelight but if you look at the back five with the goalkeeper, and no matter who comes in, it's the same story. That's fantastic. Petr is looking like the best keeper in the world. The big man is keeping Carlo Cudicini out and we all know what Carlo can do, so to have two of them can be the difference in the title race. The one thing we have to avoid is complacency and as long as we steer clear of that I don't think we will have a blip.'

The Chelsea celebrations are tinged with relief, as they hardly look potential champions for the first 45 minutes. Pompey come at them with the sort of passion and non-stop aggression that has seen them beat Manchester United and almost hold Arsenal at Fratton Park. Cech somehow gets a hand to a magnificently struck 30-yard swerver from Nigel Quashie. Half-time brings an abrupt change – just as it did against Fulham, Newcastle and Arsenal. Pushing up much further than they did in the first half, Chelsea play Pompey at their own game and pressure them out of possession.

Glen Johnson sees his header from Robben's corner scrambled off the line before Gudjohnsen, who has replaced Drogba, flicks the loose ball over. Hislop denies Gudjohnsen only with a well-timed save at his feet after good work by Robben. But with time running out Robben once again inspires his team to victory.

Didier Drogba's uninspiring comeback is the downside of the win. Mourinho says, 'We know we have to be patient with Drogba. Steve Clarke had the same operation in his career and says it might feel like it is better but often it is not completely and you need more time. We will try to give him this.'

Since their lone league reverse at Manchester City, the team have dropped just four points out of 33, with Cech and his backline amassing 14 clean sheets in 20 Premiership outings. Although Mourinho admits it will be impossible to have a more 'perfect' year personally than 2004, his new club still have every target in front of them. Mourinho says, 'It was a good year for the club – but they didn't win anything and in 2005 we have to start bringing titles to the club. Unless we go and win trophies, what we've done so far will mean nothing. We have to be top still in May to win the trophy and the Premiership is the trophy we really want.'

Portsmouth coach Joe Jordan says, 'It was terrible to lose to Chelsea after playing so well, but at the end of the game you had to acknowledge you had been up against something special, something you don't encounter so often these days. Chelsea have great talent and resources, but you have to admit they have something else, something put there by Jose Mourinho.'

Team

Cech, Johnson, Terry, Gallas, Ferreira, Makelele, Smertin (Cole), Lampard, Duff, Robben (Geremi), Drogba (Gudjohnsen).

Manchester United make it seven wins and a draw from eight games with victory at Villa, but still can't close their nine-point deficit on Chelsea. 'We are getting in and around the teams behind Chelsea now,' says Sir Alex Ferguson. 'It's getting to Chelsea themselves that is the problem. They are on a great run but we know that when they stumble, as long as we have kept our consistency going, we will go very, very close. All we can do is maintain our form. If we keep playing the way we are playing, we will get our rewards.' Arsenal also maintain their challenge with Patrick Vieira's 20-metre volley enough to give them a 1–0 win at Newcastle.

CSKA Moscow, the Russian club Abramovich sponsors, are reported to have rejected a move by Chelsea to sign Czech international midfielder Jiri Jarosik. Jarosik joined the club in the summer of 2003 for a then Russian record of £2m and faced Chelsea in the Champions League. Chelsea see him as a short-term solution to their injury troubles.

Mourinho is relatively busy wheeling and dealing as he allows Celestine Babayaro to be sold to Newcastle for £1m, with speculation that Toon defender Olivier Bernard will end up at Stamford Bridge. Newcastle United record their thanks to everybody involved at Chelsea for their cooperation and goodwill. Babayaro won the FA Cup, League Cup, Charity Shield and European Super Cup during his time in London, but has increasingly found himself in the wilderness since Abramovich's millions allowed first Ranieri and then Mourinho to invest heavily in new talent. He played 197 times for Chelsea.

Mourinho comments, 'It was a decision made in the interests of the player, not for us. It was not a selfish decision by me or the club. It was a decision taken in relation to the player's future and the best for his career. We had several offers for him but none like the one from Newcastle. Their offer gives him a fantastic future. We will miss him both as a player and a person. Our decision to cooperate with him was, I think, very fair. They are a big club and they play for big things.'

Birmingham cancel Mikael Forssell's loan contract. The Finnish international was signed on loan for a second season but a serious knee injury ruled him out for almost the entire season. City execute a get-out clause in the loan agreement and Forssell returns to London to undergo rehabilitation on the injury following an operation.

Mourinho describes John Terry as 'the best central defender in the world'. 'Since the first minute I arrived here he's played at the same level. Not up and down, no mistakes. Not more committed against Man United and less concentration against West Bromwich. It's not like he prefers to play against tall and strong strikers and has it difficult against fast ones. For him every game is the same, every opponent is the same, the level of his performance is the same. He leads the team. He is an important voice on the pitch, where I'm not. He's absolutely amazing.'

Terry is a key influence within the team, both on the field and in the dressing room where he often gives fiery speeches ahead of games. Mourinho adds, 'In some clubs the captain is the captain of the manager. In other clubs he's the captain of the players. In another club he's the captain of the club because he's been at the club for ten years. John Terry is everything here.'

Mourinho is also clear in his admiration for Lampard. 'Frank is improving every day. Like Steven Gerrard he is one of the best in the world. It's difficult to say who is the best because some midfield players are more defensive, some more offensive. I would say Frank Lampard and Steven Gerrard can both do things. They are great players.'

Gerrard remains top of Mourinho's wanted list, but Liverpool manager Rafael Benitez says, 'If we play well and win I'm sure Steven will think we can beat any team in the Premiership. I want him to stay and he knows that.'

Chelsea are 15 points ahead of sixth-placed Liverpool going into their match at Anfield. Yet Benitez insists his team can win. 'We are a better side since Chelsea beat us 1–0 at Stamford Bridge in October. We have a better mentality and we possess more confidence. It is true that Chelsea have the strongest squad in the Premiership and they have a lot of very good players. But I also believe we are capable of beating them. They have spent a lot of money over the last two or three years on players, but that doesn't worry me particularly. When I was at Valencia it was a similar situation, because Real Madrid and Barcelona had more money yet we still won the title.'

SATURDAY, 1 JANUARY 2005
LIVERPOOL 0, CHELSEA 1

Chelsea's victory is steeped in good fortune as Liverpool dominate and the referee misses a certain penalty. And, like at Portsmouth, the breakthrough comes from a deflected shot. Chelsea have to get back to attacking in a fluent fashion. Gudjohnsen is off colour, while Drogba has still to regain his confidence and power. Chelsea count on the excellent Cech, whose uncanny reflexes enable him to pull off a close-range save when Tiago smashes the ball against Antonio Nunez.

Mourinho takes pride in his side's resilience in the north, which Sir Alex Ferguson had put into question. 'I am proud of my players,' says Mourinho. 'We needed some luck, but luck has a habit of turning up for the champions at the right times and at the right places. We have proved to Manchester United and Arsenal that they will have to really fight for this title, but I think it will now be very difficult for them to catch us. I feel sorry for Liverpool. I didn't see the handball they claimed against Tiago, but sometimes these things go for you – that is football. My players fought and fought and in the end they deserved some luck. But I felt Liverpool also played very well and a draw would have been a fair result.'

Cole follows up his goal at Portsmouth on Boxing Day by crashing home a late winner. Much of Chelsea's first-half struggle hinges on the way John Arne Riise exposes Glen Johnson. But with 76 minutes gone Mourinho sends on Cole for Duff – and is rewarded almost instantly. Robben's corner is headed towards the edge of the box by Johnson, and Cole fires home a low shot that heightens an already rampant sense of injustice fuelled by referee Mike Riley's decision to reject two justified penalty appeals from Liverpool. Undaunted, Chelsea hold out to the end.

Having broken the ankle of local favourite Xabi Alonso with a foul, Lampard has a quiet game. He also earns a one-match ban by picking up his fifth booking of the season for the challenge. He says, 'Me missing one game is nothing compared to Xabi being out for so long. I never intended to hurt him. Obviously, I will say I'm sorry for what happened.'

There is no doubt that Liverpool should have a penalty when Tiago palms the ball from the head of Nunez, and probably another when Makelele bundles over Florent Sinama-Pongolle. Benitez says Cech is Chelsea's finest player. He makes an outstanding save one-on-one from Djimi Traore in the 15th minute, another from Nunez after 42 minutes and pushes a Gerrard free-kick away with four minutes remaining.

Robben should score after springing the offside trap in the 18th minute, but hesitates, cuts inside and is charged down by Jerzy Dudek. Gudjohnsen should also be quicker to a 50th-minute Duff cross.

But this is a day for defenders as the Blues complete their first league double over Liverpool for 85 years. Benitez snaps, 'We lost the game because of two things – the injury to Xabi Alonso, who we have now lost for five or six weeks, and the referee's failure to award us a penalty.' Jamie Carragher also raps the ref. 'He has got it wrong in the two big games he has refereed this season and those two decisions could prove the difference between Arsenal or Chelsea winning the league,' he says. Riley gave Wayne Rooney a hotly disputed penalty in the Manchester United v Arsenal showdown ten weeks earlier that helped end the Gunners' unbeaten 49-match record. Carragher adds, 'If Arsenal had got the right decision at Old Trafford, who knows what might have happened then? Top games need top refs. And with those mistakes the FA have to ask whether this referee should be up there. He was in a great position to see what happened in our game. He was putting his whistle into his mouth and I don't know if he lost his nerve or what.' Even Claude Makelele admits, 'It was a penalty.'

> **Team**
> Cech, Ferreira, Terry, Gallas, Johnson, Lampard, Makelele, Tiago, Duff (Cole), Gudjohnsen (Drogba), Robben (Kezman).

Arsenal and Manchester United both win later in the day to keep up their challenges, but Chelsea are on course to beat United's 91-point Premier League record. Czech international Jiri Jarosik signs for the club and says, 'I am delighted. It is the greatest chance of my life.'

Chelsea's interest in Rio Ferdinand prompts Manchester United to consider opening new contract talks with the defender to keep him at Old Trafford until 2010. Abramovich, who has long been an admirer of the England star, is reported to be preparing a £6m-a-year deal to lure him to Stamford Bridge in the summer. Ferguson tells his club they must move now to prevent Ferdinand leaving, even though he still has two and a half years left on his £70,000-a-week contract. The prospect of linking Ferdinand with Terry could make Chelsea an even more formidable force.

Steve McClaren, boss of Chelsea's next opponents Middlesbrough, believes Chelsea have to keep John Terry fit to maintain their charge. 'I worked closely with John at Euro 2004 and he impressed me immensely' says McClaren. 'But if Chelsea lose Terry or Frank Lampard it will hit them hard. They are Chelsea through and through – talk about the heartbeat and core of a club. They were that last season and have matured and developed since.

Chelsea are going well but if they lost one of those two it would hurt. Their key players are Terry, Lampard, Makelele, Duff and Robben. If they get injuries it could change.'

TUESDAY, 4 JANUARY 2005
CHELSEA 2, MIDDLESBROUGH 0

Didier Drogba's double sends Chelsea seven points clear as title rivals Arsenal and Manchester United both slip up at home. Drogba signals his return to sharpness with blistering strikes in the 14th and 17th minutes.

Already favourites, the leaders are installed as champions-elect by Sir Alex Ferguson. 'Chelsea can only throw it away,' the Manchester United manager says after his team's 0–0 draw at home to Tottenham Hotspur. At Highbury, after a 1–1 draw against Manchester City, Wenger is a little more defiant. 'To give up and say they have won the title would be criminal and totally unprofessional.'

From the moment Drogba latches on to Lampard's pass to slip the ball past Mark Schwarzer, there is only ever going to be one outcome. Drogba then uses his head to connect with Lampard's free-kick and beat Schwarzer again. On both occasions the Ivory Coast star shakes off marker Gareth Southgate. Little wonder Mourinho made little effort to keep Jimmy-Floyd Hasselbaink. The former Blues goalscorer is presented with a commemorative medal by one-time strike partner Eidur Gudjohnsen before the game, marking his four seasons at Stamford Bridge. But that is all he has to show for a fruitless first return.

Cole, making his first Premiership start since October in place of Tiago, is lively, while Alexei Smertin does not look out of place as a makeshift left-back. When Smertin succumbs to illness, Johnson takes his place. No matter how Mourinho shuffles his pack, he always seems to come up with a winning hand.

Schwarzer twice spills low shots from Robben with no one on hand to convert the follow-up, and Duff sends another drive tantalisingly across the face of goal. Drogba pulls a huge Cech clearance out of the sky but his shot on the turn is straight at Schwarzer. And Duff rattles the bar with a fierce 57th-minute left-footer. Even Ferreira has a go, racing on to Lampard's pass but scooping his shot just over. Lampard has another shot blocked by Schwarzer, but the best move of the game comes in the closing minutes when he shoots just wide after an irresistible move of 20 passes.

The only blemish is Robben's fifth yellow card, which rules him out of the first leg of the Carling Cup semi-final with Manchester United. It takes McClaren around an hour after close of play to emerge from the dressing room to share his thoughts on the pummelling his side have taken. McClaren has no complaints about his team. He is pleased with them for 'not folding'. If the manager of the sixth-placed side in the Premiership will settle for a two-goal defeat by Chelsea, then you shudder at what those below him will accept.

Team

Cech, Ferreira, Gallas, Terry, Smertin (Johnson), Cole (Tiago), Makelele, Lampard, Duff, Robben, Drogba (Kezman).

Jiri Jarosik reveals he would have been caught up in the tsunami disaster had he not cancelled a holiday in Asia for talks with Chelsea. 'I was set to go on a break to Sri Lanka over the Christmas period but because of the transfer negotiations I cancelled the trip. Someone up there must love me.' Jarosik was initially thought to have moved on a six-month loan, before details of his improved contract emerged and a fee of £2.5m. The versatile schemer has been likened in style to Patrick Vieira and will provide cover in central midfield with Parker sidelined by a broken foot.

Jarosik stresses that it was Blues manager Jose Mourinho, not Abramovich, who was the driving force behind his move. 'Mr Mourinho was the one who wanted me to join and that was important. He told me he wasn't interested in signing a stuck-up superstar but wanted an experienced and hard-working player. He told me I had a chance to get into the team straight away.'

CSKA coach Valeri Gazzayev is infuriated by Jarosik's departure, maintaining a stony silence, but privately asking friends how the club can have let it happen. The answer, as with many Moscow mysteries, lies with Abramovich, close friend of CSKA president Yevgeny Giner, and his oil company Sibneft, bankroller of the entire club.

Mourinho has used Geremi as an example of a faithful squad player, but now the Cameroon international wants to leave to find first-team football. The £6.9m buy from Real Madrid urges Boro to re-sign him after his 33-game loan spell there in 2002-03. Geremi says, 'I'm not satisfied at Chelsea because I am not playing. Mourinho is not giving me opportunities and I do not like being on the bench. I would prefer to leave and the option of Middlesbrough is excellent, because I have great memories of my stay there.' Geremi is the first player to demand a move and says he preferred life under Claudio Ranieri. 'Mourinho is a good coach but makes few changes,' he says. 'Ranieri made more rotations than Mourinho. This way the players were more satisfied. I am good enough to play in the Premier League and I have demonstrated it in the last two seasons – but in this one I cannot. I don't regret coming to England because in my time here I have learned a lot. But I want to play.'

Steve Clarke says none of Mourinho's squad will be leaving, and that includes the unhappy Geremi and defender Robert Huth, who is interesting Bayern Munich. Chelsea agree a £10m fee with Feyenoord for their 19-year-old striker Salomon Kalou. The Ivory Coast-born marksman will not move to Stamford Bridge until the summer because he must wait at least three months to obtain the Dutch passport vital to his involvement in English football. Arsenal are monitoring Kalou's progress and hope to snatch the player over the delay with his passport. Kalou is widely regarded as the most talented young striker in European football, and his all-round game has been compared to Thierry Henry's. Holland boss Marco van Basten has almost guaranteed Kalou a place in the national side when he attains his passport.

Adrian Mutu signs a five-year contract with Juventus and could even play for Italy's Serie A giants in the Champions League final against his former club as his seven-month ban ends a week before it on 18 May. Juventus announce Mutu's signature as a free transfer as he is technically a free agent, but Chelsea demand a transfer fee to offset the loss of an asset valued at £13.7m. The club still hold the player's registration and it will not be released until after his claim for wrongful dismissal is heard by the Premier League. If they fail to extract a transfer fee from Juventus, Chelsea could pursue compensation through the courts. A senior Chelsea source says, 'Our position hasn't changed one iota. We definitely feel we deserve some compensation from the player or his new club. You don't just wave goodbye to a £13m asset.'

Martin Jol, whose Spurs team Chelsea face next, says he believes Robben can become the best player in the world. The Dutchman says, 'Johan Cruyff is a huge phenomenon in Holland. I said three years ago that Robben is a small phenomenon but he will be big – very big. In England you don't understand how big Cruyff is. So when I say Robben is a small phenomenon, it is a big compliment. In Holland we all think Arjen is the best winger in Europe. When I argue Johan is the best player ever, I'm told it was George Best. I appreciate that but Johan Cruyff played for 18 years and, although George Best was unbelievable, he only played seven or eight years. There is a big difference. But Robben can do the same. Even at 16 when he broke into the Groningen first team he was playing as well then as he does now. When Robben played against my teams in Holland, he always punished us. If we went 1–0 up, he would get it back. I never had any success against him at all. The argument went that maybe he could take on and beat five or six players in the Dutch League but he could never do the same in England. But here he is doing exactly that.'

SATURDAY, 15 JANUARY 2005
TOTTENHAM HOTSPUR 0, CHELSEA 2

Thanks to a double from Frank Lampard, Chelsea become the first Premiership side to keep six consecutive clean sheets while winning every game. Sitting in for Mourinho, Steve Clarke says, 'It was a difficult game for us, so obviously the celebrations at the end told you how much it meant to us as a club. I don't think there is a better midfielder than Frank Lampard. He's been very consistent in his performances and England are lucky to have Frank and Steven Gerrard available for central midfield. He showed his quality when he took the penalty as there was a lot of pressure on him and he also showed great energy to get there for Eidur Gudjohnsen's cut-back in the last minute.'

Lampard snaps back at a spectator dishing out abuse as he walks off for half-time. His crime is to have converted a disputed first-half penalty. Alexei Smertin goes down over Ledley King's outstretched leg prompting vehement Spurs protests. But Lampard coolly smacks home the spot-kick. Tottenham's decision to replay the incident in super slo-mo on the giant video screen is regrettable, and the normally placid Lampard reacts to some fairly vicious abuse as he leaves the pitch for the interval.

Earlier, Robben is clearly nudged by Noe Pamarot as he scampers into the penalty area in familiar style. 'I thought that was a penalty, the one before was a penalty, plus another one we should have had in the second half,' says Clarke. The fourth official signals four injury-time minutes, before Lampard finally ends Spurs' stubborn resistance and gives the score-line a gloss that is harsh on hard-working Tottenham. But this is Chelsea's 14th match unbeaten and it is 601 minutes since Cech conceded – a statistic that is testimony not only to the Czech's prowess but to the defensive qualities of the entire squad. No other central defensive pairing enjoys the sort of cover given by Makelele.

A parry from Jermain Defoe's deflected shot is all that Cech needs to do to extend his run beyond the nine-hour mark. Smertin comes closest to beating his own keeper with a wild miskick that misses the far post by inches at a Tottenham set-piece.

Jol insists the penalty should not have been given. 'I can see why the referee gave it from his angle. But when you see it from a different view Alexei Smertin stamps on Ledley King's foot. He was running very fast and maybe I would have fallen over too – but I am

48 years old. It was a shame as at that time we were the better team. I said after the Manchester United game these things even out, but I am having second thoughts on that.'

Pamarot is also incensed. 'There were many Chelsea players diving during the game,' he says. 'I don't think anyone thought it was a penalty – except for the referee. But it was not just the penalty, Robben was doing it as well and I don't think it's fair. He is great player, but he was diving all the time, so you can understand the fans being angry about it.'

The key flashpoint in Pamarot's row with Robben is a first-half penalty claim before the Smertin incident. Robben falls inside the area under pressure from the Frenchman. Heated words are then exchanged between the two players.

Despite scoring both goals, Lampard says it is his team's defence that should be praised. 'William Gallas and JT give us a lot of confidence at the back. They are fantastic together. A lot has been said about John and rightly so because he has been fantastic. But he and William complement each other so well. John's all-round defensive game is brilliant, and with William's pace next to him they are a very difficult pair for any team to play against. Add to that the fact they have a great goalkeeper behind them. I can't speak highly enough of all of them. They have been superb all season.'

Lampard revels in the frustration he knows Chelsea's pursuers must be feeling from his experience of never quite being able to catch Arsenal a year ago. 'Arsenal set the standard last year by playing the way they did. It's not nice when you keep getting good results and they keep getting good results too. And then eventually you slip up and they still get a good result. That's what it was like when we were chasing Arsenal last season. But we are the ones that have been doing that recently, leading from the front, and that has to continue if we are going to win the league. We know that. And with the spirit we have got and the confidence we have got, there's no reason it can't continue. There's a lot of spirit round here. We celebrate every game we win because we know how important each game is and this one at Spurs felt special.'

Even Joe Cole has shed his reputation for failing to track back. As a second-half substitute, he makes three important tackles, each visibly applauded from the bench by Mourinho. 'I think we took a big step towards winning the title today,' says Cole. 'You could see afterwards that the boys were loving the result. It was hard-fought, but we deserved it again. The close games are the ones that taste best. They are the great victories. The boss asked me to come on and make sure I kept it tight. I could do that and it was good. The result puts the pressure on Arsenal. We know how it feels from last year, when they just kept on winning. It's up to them to keep getting the right results.'

Clarke's message to Chelsea's rivals is the bleakest of all. 'Other people talk about us having a blip. Well, maybe we have had our poor run already when we drew either side of our defeat to Manchester City. Maybe we've had our blip already.'

Team

Cech, Johnson, Gallas, Terry, Ferreira, Smertin (Jarosik), Makelele, Lampard, Duff (Cole), Drogba (Gudjohnsen), Robben.

In the evening Arsenal lose 1–0 at Bolton to extend Chelsea's lead to a formidable ten points plus a vastly superior goal difference. United lie a further point behind after winning at Anfield.

The Gunners overcame a nine-point deficit to beat Manchester United to the title in 1998, but, just as in April 2003 when Arsenal blew a two-goal lead to draw 2–2, the Reebok Stadium has become the graveyard of their title aspirations.

What is most shocking about Arsenal's third defeat of the season is the resigned way they seem to accept it. It is hard to believe that these Gunners are the same team hailed as 'The Invincibles' just three short months ago when they went a record 49 games unbeaten. Wenger reflects, 'Chelsea are a strong team and they have a lot of experience in different departments of the team. But it would be an easy excuse to say that we lost to Bolton because we are young. Chelsea have improved each year and they have bought great players like Drogba, like Robben, like Tiago, like Carvalho, like Paulo Ferreira, like Cech and that makes the difference. But that does not irritate me that they can improve their team because they have the money. It does present us with a problem, but their money does not mean that we have to lose to Bolton. It's not Chelsea's fault or their money, it's down to us.'

Mourinho combines a scouting mission to check on Champions League opponents Barcelona with the chance to run the rule over Barca's brilliant Brazilian Ronaldinho. Ronaldinho would cost a cool £6om. The door is open for an offer after the Brazilian said only last month, 'Any great player would want to be part of the sensational Chelsea team. They are amazing and I can see myself living in London one day.'

Sir Alex Ferguson warns Mourinho would be 'foolish' to think the title will be Chelsea's if they can stretch their lead. 'In the past Newcastle were 12 points clear, we threw a 12-point lead away once, and Blackburn almost threw a 13-point lead away. So we know it can happen. Chelsea would be foolish to think it could not. If they hit a blip, the key is how they recover. Look what happened after Arsenal lost to us at Old Trafford. They dropped nine of their next fifteen points. Arsenal and ourselves have to hope that does happen to Chelsea. And the only thing you can do is be patient. I also think an injury to one of their important players: Frank Lampard or John Terry, maybe Arjen Robben or Damien Duff, would slow Chelsea down.'

Roy Keane backs his manager, convinced Chelsea may yet crumble under the weight of expectation. 'We've been in Chelsea's position before, but a lot of their players haven't had the experience of being there. That's why it is important to put them under pressure. They've answered all the questions so far but we'll see what happens from now.'

Mourinho says he is so relaxed that he no longer watches Arsenal and Manchester United and is amused by the escalating war of words between Sir Alex Ferguson and Arsene Wenger. 'They can say what they want,' he says. 'It doesn't interfere with what I think. There is no pressure at the top. The pressure's being second or third. When you lead you can forget about the other teams. I don't see Arsenal and Manchester United's matches on television; I'm not listening to the radio waiting for their results. If we win, then our job for that week is done.'

Didier Drogba hits back at critics branding him a waste of money with just nine goals in 22 games. 'People talk about my fee all the time,' he says. 'They don't call me Drogba, but the £24m man. When they look at me they are more wide-eyed about the price than my qualities. Despite the critics, I am satisfied with my first six months in England and I don't feel I am suffering because of the price tag.'

Abramovich faces formal legal action in a Swiss court. The European Bank for Reconstruction and Development (EBRD) – partly funded by the British taxpayer – says it is seeking to recover $17.4m (£9m) through proceedings in the Fribourg court against Abramovich and a colleague. Abramovich's side accuses the bank of 'negligence' and warns he might bring a defamation case if certain allegations against him are repeated by the EBRD. The Fribourg case centres on a loan apparently given to a Swiss oil trading company, Runicom SA, which was said to be controlled by Abramovich and Eugene Shvidler, chief executive of Russia's Sibneft oil company. A spokesman for Abramovich says suggestions that Chelsea assets are at risk are 'far-fetched'.

Mourinho wants to beat Liverpool to the signature of Scott Carson but Rafael Benitez plays upon the fact that the 19-year-old keeper might find an easier route into the first-team at Anfield as Cech is in such fine form. Mourinho tells Chelsea TV, 'We don't need another goalkeeper. We have a great group of keepers, but the reality is that we need the best players in the country, especially English ones. If a very young goalkeeper is available, we can think about it for the future of the club, instead of having Lenny Pidgeley as the [only] young goalkeeper. We could have both of them and maybe send one on loan.' Chelsea make a £450,000 bid but Leeds, desperate for money to pay their tax bill, prefer to sell Carson to Liverpool for £600,000. Chelsea are reluctant to increase their bid for an unproven youngster even though Cudicini is set to leave in the summer.

With one eye on the upcoming Carling Cup semi-final second leg, Sir Alex Ferguson heaps unprecedented praise on Mourinho. 'Jose has done great since coming here,' he says. 'He has a confidence about him that has seeped into his team. He has got an assuredness and determination about them. He has been good for the Premiership. He has a wit and a humour about him. He comes across well and I get on OK with him. We had a spat last year but ...'

Chelsea pay £24.5m to end their sponsorship deal with kit-maker Umbro as they line up one of the biggest shirt contracts in world football. Umbro have supplied Chelsea since 1995. In 2001 the west London club signed a further ten-year deal with Umbro, which was worth around £50m. The contract will now end in June 2006, five years ahead of the original date. Umbro release a statement to the Stock Exchange saying the deal has been terminated by 'mutual agreement'. Peter Kenyon is busy securing a lucrative new sponsorship deal, rumoured to be with adidas, to fit the club's higher global profile. Manchester United currently have comfortably the biggest kit deal in British football. Kenyon, then at United, agreed a £300m 15-year contract with Nike in 2000 after also dispensing with the services of Umbro. Chelsea have already announced that their four-year £24m deal with shirt sponsors Emirates will end this season.

Chelsea may also have to write off a further £11m to offload Argentine striker Hernan Crespo. AC Milan, where he is currently on loan, want to sign him, but for just £5m. But Crespo is back on form in Serie A, blaming injuries and cultural differences for his failure to succeed in London. 'I just couldn't assimilate. The Italian way of playing suits me better than the English one, but it didn't have anything to do with that. I was happy enough with my scoring record.'

SATURDAY, 22 JANUARY 2005
CHELSEA 3, PORTSMOUTH 0

Didier Drogba's brace takes him to 11 for the season, overtaking Gudjohnsen as top scorer. But it is Robben who inspires this victory in the opening 39 minutes.

Robben says, 'With our defence we know when we score one goal we win. But we don't just want to win 1–0. We know everyone on the outside wants us to lose but that's not a pressure. I don't sense any pressure in our dressing room. We're playing with a lot of confidence and enjoy every minute of every match. To other people, it seems like we're unbeatable.'

Having resisted the temptation to go down after being fouled, Robben crosses for Drogba to score the first before hitting the target himself shortly afterwards, again staying on his feet as he stumbles past the keeper. Robben takes the opportunity to again refute diving insinuations. He says, 'If you saw the two moments, they were just two penalties and that's it. No diving. Today I kept my feet for the first goal and I went round the keeper for the second.'

Drogba scores his second, converting a free-kick won by Robben. The Dutchman is deservedly given a standing ovation when he is substituted late on.

There are changes in defence, with Bridge returning and Ferreira moving back to the right side. Cole is given a place in the midfield three for the third time in four home games. Portsmouth make early inroads, with Matthew Taylor's cross-shot saved by Cech, but Chelsea are untroubled and simply wait for their moment to pounce. That takes just 14 minutes, and referee Mike Riley intelligently ignores his assistant's well-intended flag for a foul on Robben as he speeds past Gary O'Neil. Robben rides the mistimed tackle and cuts the ball back invitingly for Drogba to sidefoot home from close range.

Six minutes later Chelsea have victory in their grasp as Lampard plays a skilfully weighted ball through for Robben to chase onto and the Dutchman skips around keeper Jamie Ashdown and clips the ball inside the post from a tight angle.

Portsmouth squander their only chance after Lampard's careless pass leaves Terry under pressure from Yakubu. The Nigeria international clips the ball past Terry and bears down on goal, but his shot rolls inches past the post with Cech beaten. That is as near as Portsmouth come to making a game of it. Two minutes later Robben is upended in full flight on the edge of the penalty area by David Unsworth, and Drogba strikes a fierce free-kick past Ashdown. Game over.

The second half is something of a procession, with Mourinho removing Drogba, Duff and Robben, but showing his strength in depth as Gudjohnsen, Kezman and Tiago come on. O'Neil strikes a 20-yard free-kick that Cech tips over, but it is Chelsea who come closer to scoring when Cole gets on the end of a cross and shoots straight at Ashdown.

Steve Clarke warns Arsenal and Manchester United that Chelsea will not get complacent. 'The first thing to do is to win the game and we put ourselves in a position to do that in the first 45 minutes when our performance was electric. It was an easier 45 minutes in the second half.

'It doesn't seem to be strange to be in this position. It seems to be what we deserve for the hard work we've put in this season. Obviously, after a game like that, you think we didn't look like losing that match but there will be difficult matches along the way. We're under no illusions. It's hard to see a danger at the moment. But we won't become complacent.'

Team

Cech, Ferreira, Gallas, Terry, Bridge, Lampard, Makelele, Cole, Robben (Kezman), Drogba (Gudjohnsen), Duff (Tiago).

Boro boss Steve McClaren has three bids for Geremi turned down but finally agrees a £3m deal with Chelsea, only for the midfielder to reject a three-and-a-half-year contract. While the media focus is on allegations of tapping up Ashley Cole and Steven Gerrard for summer deals, John Terry speaks out for Wayne Bridge. He says, 'Wayne's been fantastic all season. He's been in and out of the side but in particular the last five or six games he has been one of our best players. He had the same problem last summer when there was talk about Roberto Carlos coming here, but he came back for pre-season really sharp and he dealt with that. He knows he's up there with Ashley and Roberto so he'll deal with it the same way.' Terry is much liked within the dressing room for expressions of public support such as that. But in reality Bridge shares the same agent, Jonathan Barnett, as Cole, so would be under no illusions about his position at the club.

Mourinho is voted the best club coach in the world in 2004 by the International Football Federation of History and Statistics, finishing well ahead of Arsene Wenger and Didier Deschamps. He now plans to finish well ahead of Wenger and Sir Alex Ferguson in English football. Wenger enjoys a tribute night in his honour at The Savoy hosted by the Football Writers Association, only to discover the Premiership trophy draped in blue ribbons, although Arsenal are still technically the champions. Wenger gracefully accepts the explanation that sponsors Barclays colours are blue!

Mourinho responds to comments from Wenger claiming that Chelsea are merely an 'effective' team, who lack the flair of Arsenal. 'In the beginning we were called boring Chelsea,' says Mourinho. 'After that we couldn't score goals. After that we were top but would not be for long. After that, when Christmas arrives, we will lose matches. After that it is Boxing Day and Chelsea never win on Boxing Day. After that they said we cannot win in the North. After that they said if we lost the Carling Cup semi-final, the blip would start. If they really believed we are not strong enough to win this competition, they would not speak about us. They speak about us because they know we can win.'

Wenger missed out on signing Cech from French club Rennes and concedes he is a player who slipped through the Highbury net after they monitored his progress at previous club Sparta Prague.

At the Czech club he went over a thousand minutes before conceding a goal in any competition – attracting Arsenal's interest. Wenger says, 'We wanted to take him before he went to Rennes but we could not get a work permit. At the time he had not played the necessary amount of games for his national team.

'Yes, we missed out, but these things happen. He is not the only player we have missed out on. And when he moved to France we still had David Seaman and we had Jens Lehmann. But Cech is doing well and he is developing well. He has what you need to play in England.'

Chelsea's season continues serenely as they complete a Carling Cup semi-final victory over Manchester United and then beat Birmingham to reach the fifth round of the FA Cup. Next up is a league game with Blackburn, but before that Mourinho knows that one of Chelsea's closest challengers in the league will suffer a further setback with Arsenal set to take on United at Highbury. 'It's a good game for us,' says Mourinho.

Sol Campbell makes no secret of the win-or-bust scenario. 'Everyone at Arsenal has been waiting for this game. We're up for this one. We know we have to win. A draw does nothing for us – or them.' Campbell winces at the transfer of Arsenal's 'invincible' tag to west London. 'We had that strength last season and now it's their turn. It's frustrating. Unless something dramatic happens it's hard to see Chelsea blowing it.'

Gary Neville is in agreement, 'Whoever loses from our game with Arsenal are going to find it very difficult to get back into the race, and it's hard enough to do that already. But there will be twists and turns left in the championship race. And I have a sneaking feeling the team that wins between us and Arsenal could put a lot of pressure on Chelsea.'

In the end it is United who take the points as they win another tasty encounter between the two 4–2. Wenger says, 'The championship is too far for us now,' and Arsenal suffer another blow as Sol Campbell sustains a serious ankle injury. Henry identifies Arsenal's lack of strength in depth as the main reason for their surrender of the Premiership crown. 'The turning point was when we lost the likes of Edu and Gilberto Silva and other players through injury,' he says. 'Without talking bad about anyone, look at our bench. Look at the bench of Manchester United, look at the bench of Chelsea.'

Mark Hughes, now in charge of Chelsea's next opponents Blackburn, was part of the Manchester United team that won the double in 1994 and went within a game of landing an unprecedented domestic treble. He feels it is easier for Chelsea to succeed as referees have made the game less physical by clamping down on tackling. 'That Manchester United side I was involved with was a fantastic side. It was a side for that era and we had to cope with the physical challenge in the first 20 minutes, half-hour of games. I don't think with the way games are refereed today that teams can do that any more and that makes it easier for the good teams.'

WEDNESDAY, 2 FEBRUARY 2005

BLACKBURN ROVERS 0, CHELSEA 1

After completing their hard-fought victory, Chelsea's players take a few seconds to comprehend Mourinho's tugging at his trademark grey overcoat; then they pull off their shirts and vests and hurl them to their travelling fans. 'This was not a football match,' Mourinho says afterwards, 'it was a fight'. So much for Sir Alex Ferguson's jibe that Chelsea would struggle in the North.

Robben scores the only goal after five minutes before Cech brilliantly saves Paul Dickov's penalty to help Chelsea open up an 11-point lead at the top. Cech sets a new Premiership record for not conceding a goal; it is now 781 minutes since he has been beaten, surpassing Peter Schmeichel's 1997 mark. Cech says, 'Schmeichel was one of my greatest idols. That is why I enjoy my record even more. I wish that my career would go on as successfully as Schmeichel's did.' He has not yet equalled his own personal record while at Sparta Prague.

But it is not all good news for Chelsea as Robben is forced off with an injury after just 12 minutes and sits on the bench with crutches beside him and a hospital appointment for X-rays and a scan the next morning on an injured foot.

Hughes' tactics were to unsettle Chelsea from the start, stationing combative South Africa captain Aaron Mokoena in front of the back four, with Robbie Savage at the heart of the team. Mokoena makes his intentions clear by trying to wrestle Lampard to the ground as they wait for a corner. Only five minutes have gone when Chelsea burst into the lead. Lampard spreads a long ball for Gudjohnsen to flick on to Robben, who turns Lucas Neill and unleashes an angled drive that dips under Brad Friedel. But then Robben tries to win possession to launch another attack, but Mokoena catches him late and the Dutchman limps off to be replaced by Cole.

Blackburn gain confidence from Robben's misfortune and in the 33rd minute Savage tumbles under a challenge from Ferreira and wins a penalty from Uriah Rennie. Dickov hits the penalty low to Cech's left but the giant goalkeeper flings himself across his goal to parry. Cech then hurls himself at the loose ball and takes a hefty kick in the ribs from Dickov, provoking one of many ugly scenes. Mourinho is furious and his mood is hardly improved when Dominic Matteo cuts Cole down right in front of the Chelsea bench.

When Dickov takes yet another slash at Cech a few minutes later, catching the keeper on the knee, Chelsea's players snap. Terry grabs the Scot by the throat and a melee erupts. The game is in danger of veering out of control with Savage charging around looking for trouble. After the interval Savage launches himself at Duff and Mokoena chops down Lampard. Terry gains a measure of revenge when he clatters into Dickov and is shown the yellow card. Dickov is finally booked for shoving Terry in the face. How it took so long is a mystery!

Despite getting his chance to impress as a replacement for Robben, Cole spends the match being chastised by Mourinho for drifting out of position, and the substitute is substituted with 11 minutes to go. It is so clearly a punishment that Cole does not bother to wait on the bench to watch the closing stages.

Mourinho accuses Blackburn of trying to kick his side off the pitch. 'I think they felt they couldn't beat us at football so they tried to beat us with a different kind of football,' he says. 'I'm not saying they tried to get players injured, but they were nasty, and they tried to intimidate our players. We gave a big answer here tonight; we showed we can deal with that tactic. We fought fantastically well, everyone battling for the same cause. The blond boy in the middle, yes, Robbie Savage, made 20 faults and no yellow card. It's difficult to control emotions. They were direct for every ball. They were aggressive, hard and nasty.'

Mourinho also alleges dirty tricks by Blackburn before the game. 'During the afternoon it rained only in this stadium – our kitman saw it – they tried everything. There must be a microclimate here. But we coped with the heavy pitch well and the Blackburn game left me confident about what we can do if we go to another stadium and face the same conditions. That is another sign that we can adjust to every situation.'

But Blackburn manager Mark Hughes is also incensed by Mourinho running on to the Ewood Park pitch at the final whistle to celebrate with his players, rather than shake his hand. 'I'm upset that the opposing manager was not gracious enough to shake my hand. Sometimes you have to be gracious in victory as well as in defeat. The best way to play them is to knock them down a peg or two and we did that. Chelsea know they have been very fortunate to leave here with three points. They are not the best team in the country – at least not on this showing.'

> **Team**
> Cech, Ferreira, Gallas, Terry, Bridge, Tiago, Makelele, Lampard, Duff, Gudjohnsen (Kezman), Robben (Cole (Jarosik)).

The tapping-up row over Ashley Cole rumbles on relentlessly. Arsenal vice-chairman David Dein says, 'We will see what the quality of the evidence is and take it from there. Ashley Cole is committed to Arsenal and under contract until 2007.' A Chelsea statement reads, 'The club has an established policy on stories linking it with players, whatever the circumstances. We have not commented in the past, do not intend to comment now, and will not do so in the future.' The Premier League say they will only launch an investigation if there is a complaint, which has so far not been forthcoming from Arsenal.

Ironically, Mourinho describes Cole as 'the best English defender' in an article in the Portuguese newspaper *A Bola*. Talking of his future transfer targets, Mourinho says, 'We'll buy two – one left-sided defender, because I only have one – and another player. The defender has to be good to join our squad. About the other, it has to be a great player. We are already scouting half a dozen of them, who are the best in the world, because only they have the ability to join a super, balanced squad like ours.'

Wenger maintains Cole will still sign a new contract at Highbury, 'I am one hundred per cent sure Ashley Cole will extend his contract as he is part of the bunch of players who are the core and heart of the team. Ashley said he is fed up with that story. He is completely committed to the club and he doesn't want to know about it.' Wenger calls on Chelsea to make a categorical denial that Mourinho and Kenyon attended a secret meeting with Cole. 'Before we complain, we must have evidence the meeting has happened but I don't know how so much assertive evidence comes out in a newspaper [if it is] just being invented. It looks to me like, yes, it has happened, although I don't know [for sure]'.

Cole himself says, 'Arsenal fans will want to know what's going on, but I'm signed here for two years and we have just got to see how it goes. I just to want to get back to playing football and trying to win the league.' Bookies William Hill offer even money Cole will be a Chelsea player by the first day of the next Premiership season.

Sheffield Wednesday complete the signing of Chelsea midfielder Craig Rocastle on a free transfer. The 23-year-old signs for two and a half years. Rocastle, who arrived at Stamford Bridge from Kingstonian in August 2002, has been on loan at Hibernian since August, making 14 appearances for the Scottish Premier League side.

Chelsea have major concerns about Robben after scans of his damaged foot are inconclusive due to the amount of swelling and bruising. Mourinho says, 'There are no conclusions for the moment. The only conclusion is big, big pain. Arjen cannot walk, he cannot put his foot on the floor and he is immobilised.'

Blackburn and Chelsea are charged by the FA with failing to ensure their players conduct themselves in an orderly fashion. The charge relates to a mass confrontation after Morten Gamst Pedersen tried to head the ball out of the hands of Cech. A number of other players on both sides joining the melee.

Mourinho, whose contract is worth more than £4m a year over four years, says he hopes to stay at Chelsea for a long time. 'I signed an extraterrestrial contract and the intention is here to sign a new one and ideally it would be from four to eight years. Improving the four-year one makes no sense, because I knew what I signed and I know that I'll abide by it. I'm happy with my conditions and I'm completely committed to the growth of the club in many different levels. I like English football a lot; I like to live in England a lot. Therefore I can't see myself anywhere else. I mentioned, it's true, that I'd like to coach in Italy and also the national squad, but I see this day as very far away.'

Next up for Chelsea are Manchester City, the only team to have beaten them in the league all season. City manager Kevin Keegan is fulsome in his praise for Mourinho. 'He was very gracious when we beat them at our place earlier in the season,' he says. 'What I find most remarkable is within weeks he turned a set of talented individuals into an exceptional team.'

But Chelsea will have to face City without Robben, who fears he has broken his foot again and could be out for the rest of the season. Whether it is a break or not, Robben is resigned to being sidelined for some weeks. He says, 'This is a disaster – everything was going so well. It is a massive blow and comes just at the moment when I was in top shape and very fit. But now it is worthless and I have to fight back for the second time this season.'

SUNDAY, 6 FEBRUARY 2005

CHELSEA 0, MANCHESTER CITY 0

Manchester City frustrate Chelsea again, with David James somehow keeping out Lampard's close-range volley in the last minute. Mourinho is in a prickly mood after seeing his side's lead at the top of the table cut to nine points. 'I prefer to say my players in finishing situations weren't lucky and they had in David James a goalkeeper who made incredible saves to get them the point,' he says. 'Only one team had chances to score goals, but we couldn't score and they fought a lot, defended a lot and had a good goalkeeper. They were lucky.'

Those comments do not sit comfortably with Keegan, who says, 'Jose has got to learn to give other teams credit. He has to be careful not to get frustrated and say things he will regret. This might be a big point for Chelsea because they could have lost. Chelsea will get a lot more of this before the end of the season. There's only Manchester United and Arsenal who will come here and take them on. It would have been a travesty after the work we put in if David James hadn't made that save. We had a plan and it worked.'

Chelsea miss the influence of striker Drogba and especially Robben. Early on Kezman almost creates an opening for himself when latching onto a poor headed clearance 25 yards out. But after knocking the ball past outstanding centre-back Richard Dunne, he then theatrically goes to ground, and can count himself fortunate not to be cautioned by referee Howard Webb.

Duff finds enough space on the left-hand side of the area to test James with a low drive. The keeper gets down well to parry and Kezman fails to turn in the loose ball from no more than a yard out.

The City goal is leading a charmed life, with Paul Bosvelt somehow scrambling Gallas' header off the line in the 38th minute. Just before the break the visitors then have a gilt-edged chance themselves when Shaun Wright-Phillips chases a long punt across field and turns Gallas, enabling him to pull the ball back across the six-yard box. Terry slips at the vital moment, handing Fowler a free header, but the former Liverpool striker sends his diving header wide.

In the second half Tiago replaces Jarosik, and Cole then comes on for Kezman, but Chelsea are still unable to beat James in the City goal for the second time this season. After the game Cech hails James as the best goalkeeper the team has faced in England. He says, 'David James saved his team and put in a great performance and was the only reason we didn't win the game.'

> **Team**
>
> Cech, Bridge, Ferreira, Terry, Gallas, Jarosik (Tiago), Makelele, Lampard, Kezman (Cole), Gudjohnsen, Duff.

Before the match the Premier League announced they had received a formal complaint from Arsenal and would convene a commission into the Cole tapping-up allegations. The hearing will take place before a three-man panel made up of a QC and two other commissioners.

Mourinho reacts with contempt for the Premier League's decision. 'I know nothing about it, I don't know and I don't want to know,' he says. 'I'm not a lawyer; I'm a football manager. What matters to me is to train to get the best results. When I win I am happy and when I don't I am not.'

The club issues a statement saying, 'Chelsea can confirm it has been in discussions with the Premier League over the last few days and we will be cooperating fully with the inquiry announced today. It would be inappropriate to make any further comment until the inquiry is completed.'

Terry and Bridge pull out of the England squad to face Holland through injury, but Lampard is picked for the game. Lampard also picks up the England Player of the Year trophy as voted for by fans on the FA's official website. Lampard picks up 40 per cent of the vote ahead of Wayne Rooney (16 per cent) and Steven Gerrard (10 per cent).

Chelsea's hopes of landing an unprecedented quadruple are dealt the biggest possible blow with confirmation that Robben has broken his foot. Once the initial swelling around the injury had subsided scans revealed a double break that could keep the Blues star sidelined for up to two months. Robben will miss the Carling Cup final and the first leg of the Champions League last-16 clash against Barcelona.

Physio Mike Banks says, 'One is a chip on the side of his foot, the other is a small break on the third metatarsal. But this is not the traditional metatarsal that has become so famous since the last World Cup and which has kept Scott Parker out for two months. The fractures are tiny and he could be playing next month.' Robben's injury is linked with the surprise announcement that doctor Neil

Frazer has quit after five years at Stamford Bridge. Frazer allegedly left following a string of clashes with Mourinho, who wanted Robben fit for the Carling Cup final.

Lampard argues that although Robben will be missed, Chelsea are far from being a one-man team. 'Of course we will miss Arjen,' he says. 'He has such great pace and he has given us so much since he's come into the team. People have made a massive thing of him though and we're far from a one-man team. We were pretty much top of the league before he played for us and we have got to carry on without him.'

Damien Duff shows that he could be the man to lift Chelsea in Robben's absence with a mesmeric performance against Portugal on his 50th cap for the Republic of Ireland. Mourinho witnesses the display as Duff inspires the Irish to a 1–0 win.

After the match Mourinho hugs Duff before seeing him into a black Mercedes to be whisked away to Dublin airport – along with Ferreira and Tiago – for a private jet back to London. Last September Mourinho attended the Republic of Ireland's World Cup qualifier against Cyprus in Dublin and left without even speaking to Duff. That upset the 25-year-old, who feared at that time that Mourinho did not want him, having seen Robben arrive at Chelsea. Against Portugal there is an edge to Duff's performance, and Mourinho, to his credit, has made Duff a better, harder, fitter player. Mourinho may not have had him in his plans when he arrived – there has been continued speculation over wingers such as Joaquin – but he has revised his opinion.

Mourinho stands to earn a £4.2m bonus if Chelsea win the quadruple. Winning the Premier League title will earn him a £1m bonus – double what Ranieri would have received – with more than £2m extra if he then wins the Champions League. Again that is double the bonus that would have been paid to Ranieri. In all the bonuses effectively add up to an extra year's salary for Mourinho, who will then be by far the highest paid football manager in the world.

Abramovich has been paying the players an extra £4,000 for every Premiership game they win, and £1,500 for a draw, on top of their lucrative salaries. Abramovich has also been handing over 50 per cent of all prize money from the Champions League to the players. Last season that meant the squad shared £3m – £200,000 each if they were in every squad. The players negotiated their deal when Abramovich bought Chelsea, but the system of payments per game has been dismantled by Mourinho, who does not agree with appearance money and has rolled it into lump-sum bonuses to be paid to the squad at the end of the season depending on what they win.

SATURDAY, 12 FEBRUARY 2005

EVERTON 0, CHELSEA 1

James Beattie helps make a difficult trip much easier with a senseless red card after just eight minutes as Chelsea record their ninth 1–0 win in the Premiership. Joe Cole provides in insight into the enormity of the victory. He says, 'People looked at us without Robben and Drogba and probably doubted us but we came to perform. This was a big win, as important as the ones at Spurs and Liverpool. You looked around the dressing room afterwards and you could see how determined everyone had been not to give Manchester United and Arsenal anything to bite on. Wherever we go to play – Manchester, Barcelona or Timbuktu – it doesn't matter to us. We feel we can win every match we play.'

Beattie's moment of madness costs Everton dear when he chases a long ball down the left with Gallas obstructing his run. First the striker pushes the Chelsea defender and then moments later he butts the back of his head. Beattie is defended by David Moyes, who says, 'I don't think it was a sending-off. First there was a push and then Beattie just runs into the back of him. The centre-half went down far too easily. I was a centre-half and I would have been embarrassed to have gone down like that. Not in a million years would John Terry have gone down in the same way.'

Beattie himself comments, 'We were chasing a ball into the corner and William Gallas was looking over his shoulder and blocking me off. He was stopping as we were running and I said to myself, "If you're going to stay in my way I'll go straight over you." Our heads barely touched. If I'd done it deliberately he'd have stayed down a long time.'

Everton's ten men put up a long, brave fight until a second-half Gudjohnsen tap-in breaks the deadlock. Chelsea return to their 4-3-3 formation, with Cole on the right and Duff on the left, and they dominate the early possession. Everton barely have a decent touch of the ball before they are reduced to ten men.

The home side's work-rate underlines their approach to the whole season, but they tire in the face of Chelsea's persistent attacks and eventually concede after 69 minutes. Ferreira's low cross fizzes into the box, Gallas hits the bar from close range and Gudjohnsen has a simple tap-in.

But it is Everton who apply the pressure towards the end, with Chelsea defending in depth as the crosses start to rain in. Mourinho responds by sending on extra defenders in Johnson for Tiago and Carvalho for Duff, while Jarosik has already replaced Cole to counter the aerial threat of Duncan Ferguson. Chelsea finish with six defenders in a line across their area and Everton even send goalkeeper Nigel Martyn up for set-pieces, but they cannot prevent another victory for Mourinho's men.

Gudjohnsen hails the win as 'massive'. He beams, 'I'm sure many people sitting at home were wishing us to drop points, but we bounced back from last Sunday. Nigel Martyn pulled off some fantastic saves but in the end we managed to get the goal and the points and that's what counts most at this stage of the season. We concentrate on our own results to begin with and then that puts the pressure back on Manchester United and Arsenal. This is a massive three points for us today.'

Mourinho leaves it up to Steve Clarke to give his version of events. Clarke says, 'It's a difficult place to come and we are delighted with the win. But I think the sending-off changed the game. The way it started, it looked as if it was going to be an open, entertaining match, which would have suited us. But once Beattie was sent off they shut up shop and it was down to us to try and break them down. At half-time we said to keep patient, to keep passing and to make the most of the extra man and then it would come. And we managed to edge it, although you have to say it could have been more as their keeper made some great saves.'

Team

Cech, Ferreira, Gallas, Terry, Bridge, Lampard, Makelele, Tiago (Johnson), Cole (Jarosik), Gudjohnsen, Duff (Carvalho).

After having more time to study replays of Beattie's red card, Moyes admits he was wrong. 'My first comments came immediately after the game and at that time I'd had the opportunity to see a quick rerun. Having had more time I believe I should set the record straight by conceding that Beattie's sending-off was correct.'

Manchester United beat Manchester City 2–0 for their 13th win in 15 league outings, but such form is immaterial with Chelsea's consistency. Sir Alex Ferguson brands the Premiership leaders 'lucky'. He says, 'Chelsea aren't playing as well as they have been and they've been lucky recently. There's no doubt they're getting all the breaks at the moment and we're not. I couldn't believe that sending-off at all. That was a real kick in the teeth for us.'

Gudjohnsen is arrested for alleged drink-driving after police spot him driving suspiciously. The 26-year-old is flagged down by police at 5.20 on Sunday morning after celebrating with team-mates. A breath test shows he is fractionally above the drink-drive limit. Traffic police drive him to Battersea police station where he is given a second breath test, which is said to hover on the limit of 35 micrograms of alcohol per 100 millilitres of blood. He is then given a blood test. The father of two is bailed after three hours in custody pending the result of the blood test. 'It is touch and go whether he will be charged,' a police source says. Gudjohnsen is also cautioned by Mourinho after being in breach of the club's 2am curfew.

There is no doubting Mourinho's admiration for Gudjohnsen, who he regards as an intelligent and versatile footballer. Gudjohnsen was the first Chelsea player to be handed an improved contract by Mourinho and is one of his trusted confidants, sitting on the players' committee with Makelele and Cudicini.

The quest for the Premiership is on hold for three weeks, but the squad face three cup ties in eight days. First Mourinho's men go to Newcastle in the FA Cup, from where they will flew direct to Barcelona for the Champions League last-16 clash three days later. Four days after that, Chelsea face Liverpool in the Carling Cup final at the Millennium Stadium.

Chelsea pull off a clean sweep of the Barclays awards for January. Mourinho is named Manager of the Month for four straight wins, Terry is Player of the Month, and there is a special merit award for Cech keeping ten clean sheets in a row.

Chelsea's Premiership break starts badly, with back-to-back defeats in the FA Cup and away to Barcelona in the Champions League. Patrick Vieira says it could derail Chelsea's season. Arsenal endured a similar test in 2004 when they lost their FA Cup semi-final to Manchester United and then crashed out of the Champions League to Chelsea three days later. 'We must wait and see how Chelsea respond,' says Vieira. 'They have lost a big game and there's still so many games for them to play – for us as well. There's still a really long way to go. We are a little bit behind but I don't think we're out of the title race.'

Chelsea are linked with a succession of transfer targets, from the usual suspects to Theo Walcott, a 15-year-old schoolboy winger, rated by one respected scout as the best of his age group in Europe. Chelsea are willing to pay £2m before he has even taken his GCSEs, but he turns down the riches on offer at Stamford Bridge. The boy already has an agent and a boot deal. The west London club lead a pack that includes Liverpool, Manchester United, Arsenal and Real Madrid. But the boy plans to commit to Southampton, where he has progressed through the academy.

A goalscorer tops Chelsea's list, with everyone from Michael Owen to European Footballer of the Year Andriy Shevchenko being linked with a move to Stamford Bridge. But the AC Milan and Ukraine striker stresses that he is not prepared to join Mourinho's foreign legion, even though he holds both coach and Abramovich in high regard.

Inter Milan's Brazilian Adriano is Mourinho's choice, but the Italian club have already turned down £50m from Real Madrid. Joaquin also remains a possibility. Mourinho says, 'He is a very good player and I admit there was contact. We asked and the other party replied. Nothing has been discarded with regard to him. We could try and sign him in June or December.' The 23-year-old winger remarks, 'I came close to joining Chelsea in January for £30m but the deal collapsed. I don't have a preference between them and Real Madrid but it would not be a problem living in London.' His dad, Aurelio Sanchez, who acts as the player's agent, insists the clubs have agreed a fee and the winger is ready for talks. Sanchez says, 'Chelsea are going to offer more than £20m for Joaquin and Betis president Manuel Ruiz de Lopera is convinced by that. Now they will have to convince Joaquin.'

Liverpool skipper Steven Gerrard or Lyon's highly rated Michael Essien are contenders for the midfield slot, while Mourinho dismisses the idea of signing Ronaldinho, 'Barcelona don't have to be worried about us coming in for Ronaldinho,' he says. We won't be back for him because we have totally different qualities. Ronaldinho could play in any team in the world – there's no manager so stupid as to say he wouldn't take him. But it's a policy of building a team. Our team is still forming and developing, in spite of the results we have achieved. It's not a team which has found its full potential.' With Ronaldinho beginning talks over a new contract at Barca, his agent has been talking up Chelsea's interest. But Mourinho adds, 'We know very well what we need to improve the squad but I'm very happy with what we have. I value the players who are already at Chelsea. We're not going to spend, spend, spend and buy and sell every year. The time must come for stability.'

Everton and Birmingham continue to be linked with a summer move for Scott Parker. Mikael Forssell meanwhile rejects a move back to Birmingham to fight for his place at Stamford Bridge, as he is 'looking forward to the chance to impress the right people'. Carlo Cudicini is lined up for a move to AC Milan. His agent Federico Pastorello says, 'It's not a good thing being on the bench after having been named the Premiership's best goalkeeper two consecutive times.' Arsenal and Manchester United are also interested.

Mourinho appoints the doctor who guided Kelly Holmes to her double Olympic success to help Chelsea win gold this season: Dr Bryan English from UK Athletics.

English played a key role in getting Holmes fit to win both the 800m and 1500m in Athens and his record of getting athletes back to fitness quickly is the reason Mourinho has got him on board.

Eidur Gudjohnsen discovers he will not be charged after his arrest for drink-driving, but Glen Johnson is banned after being found speeding at 112mph on a motorway with five friends packed into his car. He loses his licence for a month after answering a call to pick up pals whose car had broken down on the M25.

With Chelsea preparing for the Carling Cup final, Manchester United scrap through against Portsmouth to close the gap at the top to six points. But Arsenal's pursuit is dealt a blow when they are held 1–1 at Southampton. Chelsea end their testing week by getting back to winning ways and claiming their first bit of silverware in the Carling Cup final. Mourinho escapes any FA sanctions after being ordered out of the dugout during the match. It has been a feisty week of cup football before a return to the Premiership.

Mourinho vows not to change but promises there will be no repeat of the controversial 'silence' gesture. 'I know I cannot do that gesture in England. If I do it, the police come and put me in the dressing room and because I don't want to go to the dressing room again, I cannot do it. It is as simple as that – what I can do and what I can't do.'

Manchester United blow their chance to close the gap at the top to three points. Playing ahead of Chelsea, United are held to a 0–0 draw by ten-man Crystal Palace. So Chelsea's lead stays at a healthy five points, with Norwich away the first of two matches in hand to come.

SATURDAY, 5 MARCH 2005

NORWICH CITY 1, CHELSEA 3

Chelsea require two goals in seven second-half minutes from Kezman and Carvalho to silence relegation-haunted Norwich after Leon McKenzie dares to threaten an upset. In the end Chelsea merely underline their claim that the Premiership crown is theirs for the taking.

Mourinho deliberately chooses not to tell his players about United's earlier draw at Palace. 'We don't think about them – they think about us,' Mourinho says. 'I always like my players to be under pressure. Because Manchester United dropped points, it could influence my players in a negative way – so I did not want them to know.'

Mourinho adds that Robben may be able to return in the all-important Champions League second leg against Barcelona after more than a month out with a broken foot. 'He has a chance – maybe not to play 90 minutes – but he has a chance.'

Cole does everything possible in his man-of-the-match display against Norwich to prove Chelsea can survive without the Dutchman. Cole's performance, only the second time he has completed 90 Premiership minutes for Mourinho, is not just about his splendid goal. There is also a brilliant pass that Drogba contrives to miss, excellent movement and a growing awareness of when to perform the tricks and when to keep it simple. Mourinho says, 'Earlier in the season I saw Joe doing fantastic things but sometimes disappearing a bit from the game. But recently he's played very well. He was good in difficult circumstances in Barcelona, very good against Liverpool, and this was his most consistent performance. At the moment he's very confident, he's playing well, showing his talent and at the same time he's showing he is a team player, so I'm very happy.'

From the start the pressure is relentless. There are just seven minutes on the clock when Jason Shackell makes a heroic recovery to keep the champions-elect at bay after a lovely midfield move. Drogba drops deep to lay the ball back to Lampard, whose little chip over the top sends Duff clear with only Rob Green to beat. Duff dinks the ball towards goal and Chelsea's travelling fans let out a mighty roar, only to find it strangled in their throats as Shackell gets back superbly to head the ball off his line.

In the 12th minute Ferreira plays a tidy ball back to Lampard, whose shot dips viciously inches over the bar. From the next attack, Norwich crack. Makelele plays a through-pass to Cole, who is caught in possession and seems to have lost the ball as he crashes to the ground. But Cole jumps to his feet and is first to the loose ball. He strides on two paces and unleashes a left-foot shot that simply flies past Green.

True to form, Cole manages to waste one only half as difficult six minutes later and is then booked for a foolish tackle on Darren Huckerby.

But when McKenzie gets in front of Ferreira to head in a Huckerby cross – Norwich's first genuine chance of the match – it looks as though Chelsea have squandered two points. Cech's record run without conceding a goal finally ends at 1,025 Premiership minutes. Mourinho immediately springs into action, introducing Kezman and Gudjohnsen. He is instantly rewarded, with both substitutes involved in what proves to be the vital second. A Cole cross is deflected into Gudjohnsen's path, and he picks out Lampard with a half-volleyed forward pass. Lampard touches it past the keeper but it needs Kezman to guide it into the gaping net.

Carvalho grabs his first goal for the club, a header from a Lampard corner in the 79th minute, to end the contest.

If anything sums up Chelsea's iron grip on the Premiership it is the almost total lack of celebrations. Brief hugs and grasped hands sum up a team already focusing on the next task with mighty Barcelona. As Mourinho predicted, the Carling Cup triumph makes his men more relaxed and able to play with conviction.

Mourinho comments, 'I try to show the players every day, every match, my experience and my confidence, just by saying to them, "How can we be under pressure when we have a six-point advantage with a game in hand?" I try to motivate them by saying one weekend that we need eight victories, the next that we need seven. Now we need six.'

> **Team**
>
> Cech, Carvalho, Johnson, Ferreira, Terry, Cole, Duff (Jarosik), Lampard, Makelele, Tiago (Kezman), Drogba (Gudjohnsen).

Mourinho reveals the players dedicated their win at Norwich to Wayne Bridge, who will be out for ten months, missing much of the start of the next season, after breaking his ankle in the FA Cup loss at Newcastle. Already linked with one left back, Mourinho will need two.

Mourinho is fined £5,000 and warned about his future conduct by an FA disciplinary commission for accusing Manchester United players of diving following the Carling Cup semi-final first leg tie against Manchester United. Mourinho is so angry at being fined for his 'cheat and cheat' comment that he considers reducing his cooperation with the FA on England issues. He has welcomed Sammy Lee from the England coaching staff to the training ground and is uncertain whether to remain so accommodating after being punished for words which he says were misinterpreted. But he will not withhold players from Eriksson.

In back-to-back hearings Chelsea and Blackburn are fined over the brawl that marred the end of their Premiership clash. The Blues deny a charge of failing to ensure their players conduct themselves in an orderly fashion, while Blackburn admit the same charge. Chelsea are fined £15,000 and warned about their future conduct by the FA's disciplinary commission, while Rovers are given a £10,000 fine and a future conduct warning.

A goodwill mission is lined up for the next international break with Mourinho off to the Middle East to a soccer school in Israel with Jewish and Palestinian kids. He says, 'This invitation makes me feel very honoured. It will be my modest contribution to strengthening the ties of understanding and friendship between the two peoples, who, like myself, want peace.'

In a meeting with the Premier League's lawyers Denton Wilde Sapte, Peter Kenyon states that a meeting has taken place with himself, Ashley Cole, Cole's agent Jonathan Barnett, Jose Mourinho and Pini Zahavi. However, Chelsea refute Arsenal's claims that they approached the England international while also rebutting reports that they have opened provisional negotiations with Cole on a £90,000-per-week contract. Chelsea's testimony is that the player and his agent contacted Zahavi to request a meeting. Zahavi then arranged and paid for hire of the Royal Park Hotel's Green Room to hold the meeting, at which Cole and Barnett aired their frustrations at stuttering contract negotiations with Arsenal.

Nick Fitzpatrick, who is conducting the inquiry, requests telephone records of the relevant parties to help to decide who made the first approach. If Chelsea's claims are upheld by the inquiry, Cole will be in breach of the Premier League's rule K5, stating that, 'A contracted player, either by himself or by any person on his behalf, shall not either directly or indirectly make any approach [to a club with a view to negotiating a contract with that club] without having obtained the prior written consent of his club.' Cole would also be in breach of his contract with Arsenal. Chelsea face a charge under rule K3, which forbids unauthorised approaches for other clubs' players.

The Cole camp admit they asked to meet Zahavi as part of their strategy after contract talks with Arsenal turned sour. But Barnett declares, 'I am happy to confirm on the record that the accusations levelled at Ashley are entirely false. For it to be suggested that I cynically set up a meeting with Chelsea and dragged them to it almost against their will is ludicrous.' Cole is dropped to the bench by Arsene Wenger for Arsenal's FA Cup win at Bolton.

Mourinho gives evidence to the Premiership lawyers on the same day Cole turns up to present his side of the story. Mourinho backs up Kenyon's claim that Chelsea did not make an illegal approach. The Blues manager, like Kenyon, argues they merely attended out of curiosity, listened to what Cole and his agent had to say and then left. Mourinho insists Cole was not enticed to quit the Gunners and that no offers were made. In his evidence, Cole is adamant he never had any intention of discussing anything with Kenyon and Mourinho. He tells the inquiry he was having a meeting with Barnett in his office when Zahavi called and told them he wanted to talk at the nearby Royal Park Hotel.

Mourinho is reported to have said, 'I never dreamt I could consider signing you. You are already the best left-back in the world but I want to see it in your face that you want to play for us. Join us and you can win everything – the Champions League, the Premier League … everything.' There are also strong hints that Cole was actually told he would be teaming up with Gerrard next season. Liverpool make it clear they are not lodging a complaint.

Bryan Robson, manager of Chelsea's next opponents West Brom, warns Mourinho and his players that they should keep quiet until they can back up their actions with more trophies. 'Chelsea have that tag of wind-up merchants and, until recently, they had not won anything for years. They seem to have done it to people from different walks of life, too – refs, officials, fans, players, journalists. If you win doubles and trebles you can talk about yourself a bit more. But they will be the first to fall flat on their faces if they do not get results.'

Mourinho attends a reception at The Butcher's Hook pub, opposite the ground, to mark the centenary of the club. Claudia Schiffer, Gordon Ramsay and Bernie Ecclestone add the glitz. The eatery held Chelsea's first board meeting, chaired by Gus Mears on 14 March 1905 – only this time there is Russian caviar on the menu.

Ken Bates says Claudio Ranieri's contribution to Chelsea's current success should be recognised. 'I was disappointed he wasn't invited on Monday night,' says Bates. 'I'm sure Claudia Schiffer, Bernie Ecclestone and Gordon Ramsay have made a significant contribution to Chelsea's history. They just haven't been given proper recognition by the Press. Ranieri is entitled to recognition for laying the foundations of what Chelsea have now. He should get credit for taking the team to an FA Cup final in 2002 and the semi-finals of the Champions League last season. It happens quite a lot in football that a manager walks into a club, takes over someone else's team and makes them better. I'm not knocking Jose Mourinho. He has changed tactics and the players praise him highly. He has played a part. But Claudio was always a long-term builder.'

TUESDAY, 15 MARCH 2005

CHELSEA 1, WEST BROMWICH ALBION 0

Mourinho collects an award from the League Managers Association but, facing charges from the FA over the Ashley Cole affair and UEFA following comments after the Champions League clash with Barcelona, he has the worried look of a man at the centre of several storms. When Drogba scores he rushes over to his manager insisting he joins in the celebrations.

One young fan holds aloft a homemade poster reading 'Mourinho Is Innocent'. It is hardly the flourish of the spectacular against Barcelona but Drogba's first-half clincher sends them 11 points clear with just nine games to go.

Steve Clarke says, 'Jose is only worried about winning trophies. We have one trophy already with the Carling Cup, we are through to the last eight of the Champions League and 11 points clear in the Premiership. We aim to add those two as well, so what more can we do? It's not won yet, but it's another big step on the way, with another three points. That's what we wanted before the game and that's what we got.'

Bryan Robson fumes that Geoff Horsfield had two 'goals' ruled out for offside. 'I'd like to see his second again. It looked perfectly good to me. I still don't know why it was disallowed.'

Terry marshals his defence impeccably and almost gets the home side off to the perfect start as he heads Duff's corner goalwards in the first minute. Gudjohnsen tries to deflect the ball in, but only succeeds in heading it wide.

Drogba should break the deadlock in the fifth minute but his shot on the turn from six yards is weak. Drogba then sends a free-kick by Lampard over the bar.

Cole causes all sorts of problems down the right flank and

provides two crosses that Drogba and Gudjohnsen fail to get on the end of. Soon after Duff is inches wide with a left-foot pile-driver from the edge of the box, which again Drogba just fails to convert with a cheeky flick. After Drogba fails with yet another chance, even he cannot miss Duff's inch-perfect cross in front of an open goal after 24 minutes. Lampard carves open the defence with a perfectly weighted pass and Duff sprints clear before delivering a low cross for Drogba.

Before half-time Cole sends Drogba clear again, and although he rounds keeper Russell Hoult the ball is cleared. In the last 12 minutes Drogba is guilty of two more glaring misses. First he heads wide from Cole's cross and then he blasts the ball over the bar from six yards.

Terry insists Chelsea are taking nothing for granted despite their commanding Premiership lead. 'It's not in the bag yet and there's still a long way to go. Manchester United are pushing us all the way, Arsenal are still there and all we can do is to keep winning our games and putting more pressure on them. We are a bit disappointed because we had the chances in the first half but three points was what we came for. It was hard to get the points against a team desperate to stay up.'

Team

Cech, Ferreira, Terry, Huth, Gallas, Cole (Kezman), Makelele, Lampard, Gudjohnsen (Jarosik), Duff (Smertin), Drogba.

Wayne Bridge reveals he has had plenty of well-wishers as he begins his recovery from his broken ankle. Bridge says, 'Mr Abramovich and Mr Mourinho plus most of the other players came to see me in hospital, which was great. Alan Shearer popped in, too. Everyone's been brilliant. So many people have tried to keep my spirits up. Since I've been out of hospital the lads have been round every day. I can't believe how much support I've had. I think they know how serious my injury is and they feel for me. They know I'm missing out on the rest of the season and they've promised to win the title for me. I personally think it's already in the bag and I can't wait to get my hands on my medal.'

Bridge explains the full horror of his pain. 'They had to wait for the swelling to go down before they operated. I had no idea what I had broken but it was even worse when they finally sat me down to tell me what had happened. I had broken two bones in my right ankle, ripped the ligaments and broken the fibula in my leg. By the time they came round to operating on me I was on morphine because the pain was so unbearable. The operation took two hours. I saw the boss and he told me to take a holiday for a few weeks so I can get my mind right for the work that will be needed.'

Despite all their disciplinary problems with Europe's governing body, Chelsea are in line to win the Fair Play League! The table is not merely determined by bookings and red cards. A UEFA spokesman says, 'Other factors are taken into account such as the behaviour of team officials towards the referee, the behaviour of the team and also the crowd behaviour.' The marks are only given to teams during Premiership matches, which is why Chelsea are top.

Mourinho chooses to concentrate on the next assignment against Palace rather than worry about drawing Bayern Munich in the Champions League quarter-finals. He says, 'This is a time to remember we have not won the league. Chelsea have not won it for 50 years and this Chelsea side hasn't won it yet in 2005. We want to win the league and we want to win it properly. It is over a year since Chelsea have lost at home and that includes all the time I have been here. Our home record is good but it can still be even better. There's five more home league games and we're aiming at two more Champions League home games, so we can go as high as 24 home wins in one season. I believe we can achieve this.'

SATURDAY, 19 MARCH 2005

CHELSEA 4, CRYSTAL PALACE 1

Spring is in the air, Robben is back, and on a scorching afternoon Mourinho sports a scarf! Joe Cole responds to the long-awaited return of Robben by inspiring Chelsea to a convincing victory as Mourinho's side take another major step towards the title.

Palace commit the cardinal sin of allowing Lampard far too much space outside the penalty box. Still 25 yards out from goal, he takes aim with 28 minutes gone and powers a superb drive into the corner of the net. Chelsea continue to threaten, with Johnson striking the side netting, Drogba volleying just wide and Lampard failing to make proper contact with a diving header. Palace make Chelsea pay for an uncharacteristic defensive lapse just before the break. Chelsea fail to deal with a weak, low corner from Wayne Routledge, with Lampard missing his kick at the near post. The ball speeds across the turf to Aki Riihilahti, whose shot from just six yards out deflects slightly off Carvalho and into the net.

Gabor Kiraly produces a fine reaction save to tip Drogba's overhead kick around the post, while Carvalho also heads narrowly wide. Andy Johnson scuffs his shot wide when presented with a clear opening from Gonzalo Sorondo's mishit cross-shot.

Cole has profited from Robben's injury-induced absence and his vital 54th-minute strike is proof of his renaissance. The midfielder scampers downfield as Chelsea counter-attack and, despite initially tripping over, he hauls himself to his feet and times his run perfectly to race onto Gudjohnsen's pass. Cole briefly weighs up his options before striking his shot into the far corner, leaving Kiraly helplessly rooted to the spot.

Mourinho initially turns to Tiago to shore up his midfield as Drogba comes off, but Robben is finally brought on with 17 minutes left. Significantly, it is Duff – not Cole – who makes way.

The Dutchman is immediately involved in the third goal, although there is little obvious danger until Kiraly's blunder allows Kezman's shot to slip through his grasp.

Robben almost scores himself in the closing stages, and Kezman rounds off the scoring from close range in the last minute after a scramble in the Palace penalty area.

Cole is man of the match and he can hardly contain himself as Chelsea remorselessly close in on the title. 'I'm just so excited,' he says. 'I can't stop looking at the fixture list and thinking if we win this game, this game and this game, then ... But it's important to check yourself and just think about winning the next game. I don't know whether it's the best form of my life, but it's certainly the most I've enjoyed my football as we're winning games week in and week out.'

Palace are left to reflect on Johnson's missed chance just before half-time. Iain Dowie says, 'With a 2–1 lead at half-time it would have been better, but Andrew has done well for us this season, so I'm not going to blame him for that miss. The score-line was probably harsh but you can't defend like we did for the second and fourth goals. We shouldn't have let Joe Cole get in there for their second goal. Manchester United, Arsenal and Chelsea are all good sides but Chelsea are capable of beating you in different ways. Now the other two have everything to do to catch them.'

Team

Cech, Ferreira, Terry, Carvalho, Johnson, Makelele, Cole, Lampard, Duff (Robben), Drogba (Tiago), Gudjohnsen (Kezman).

The board of the FA Premier League charges Chelsea, Jose Mourinho and Ashley Cole with breaches of their rules over the tapping-up affair.

An FA Premier League statement reads, 'The board will be asking for a formal response to these charges within 14 days and have begun the process of appointing a three-person independent commission, in accordance with their disciplinary procedures, to determine this matter.

'The board wish to state that they have so far received cooperation from Chelsea FC, Mr Mourinho and Mr Cole and expect this to continue.'

However, the statement adds, 'As licensed agents, Mr Jonathan Barnett and Mr Pini Zahavi do not fall within the jurisdiction of the FA Premier League for the purposes of this matter. The board will be forwarding information gathered during the inquiry to the Football Association with a view to considering whether further steps should be taken in relation to their actions.'

World Cup qualifiers mean another Premiership break but little rest for Chelsea's squad of international players. Joe Cole's sparkling club form convinces Sven-Goran Eriksson to start with him in England's game against Northern Ireland and the midfielder makes the vital breakthrough just after half-time and is inspirational throughout in a 4–0 win. Lampard completes the scoring with a shot that beats Maik Taylor after glancing off Colin Murdock.

'There are not many better central midfielders than Frank Lampard, I'm quite sure about that,' Eriksson says. 'I don't want to say he's the best in the world, as it's not fair, but I wouldn't change the four midfielders that I had there with anyone.'

Steven Gerrard uses the international break to stress his commitment to Liverpool. He says, 'I held a press conference last summer to say I was staying and the situation hasn't changed since then. There's no deal for me to go anywhere and I've not even been thinking about that. There has been a lot of rubbish written about me this season and it's getting ridiculous. There are people out there whom I've never even met assuming they know what I think.'

But the internationals bring bad news for Chelsea when Arjen Robben limps out of Holland's 2–0 win in Romania after setting up the opening goal for Phillip Cocu. 'It is difficult to say how many weeks I will be out, but it is clear that it is not good,' says Robben. 'Armenia and Bayern are out of the question in any case.'

Mourinho spends part of the international break in Tel Aviv, invited by former Israeli Prime Minister Shimon Peres. 'Coming here makes you realise that football is not the most important thing. My world of football is very different to theirs. Football has a magical power in social terms. I am happy to be able to use that power to help this cause. Professional football does not always set the best example. I admit and accept that. When I have finished with football there are many things in the world that will make me feel happy. This is one of them. From now on, if there is anything I can do to help, I will. If they want my support they can count on me.'

Mourinho takes presents from Chelsea and hands out medals to the youngsters. He joins in a game against Israel's five-a-side champions – a team from both Palestinian and Israeli backgrounds. 'The power we have to change the world through football cannot be ignored,' he tells them. He adds that he plans to retire from football management at the age of 55 after spending another ten years with Chelsea and three years in charge of his native Portugal.

Chelsea are dealt another major injury blow as Paulo Ferreira suffers a suspected fracture to his right foot during Portugal's World Cup qualifier against Slovakia. He is expected to miss the remainder of the season. Ferreira is immediately flown back to London by private jet for an assessment and scans. The injury leaves the squad severely stretched giving Johnson his big chance, but Mourinho only has five fit defenders and no cover at all for the full-back positions. Terry has a sore back while Carvalho has only just recovered from a broken toe.

Reports in Portugal claim Mourinho may consider walking out on Chelsea at the end of the season. Chelsea immediately dismiss the story – which started on the privately owned Portuguese SIC television station – as nothing more than an April Fool.

But the station has a close relationship with the Chelsea manager, who is due to start presenting his own chat show on the channel in May. The reports claim Mourinho was angered by Chelsea's refusal to appeal over the two-match touchline ban handed to him by UEFA for comments about the referee in Chelsea's Champions League tie with Barcelona.

Mourinho, the reports claim, took his own legal advice – contacting lawyer Jean-Louis Dupont, who handled the Jean-Marc Bosman case – and was told any appeal against the ban would succeed. It is claimed that Mourinho held meetings with Kenyon and complained about the stance taken by club chairman Bruce Buck, a lawyer himself, who counselled against any appeal. Mourinho, so the reports claim, said that Chelsea should stick together more over the issue.

Sources in Portugal confirm there is truth in the reports that he was beside himself with rage over the UEFA ruling and Chelsea's reaction.

SATURDAY, 2 APRIL 2005
SOUTHAMPTON 1, CHELSEA 3

On the surface it is business as normal for Mourinho as Chelsea outclass Southampton on their home turf, where they have not lost since September. But with the dust still settling on his UEFA ban Mourinho dodges the post-match media conference and beats a hasty retreat to the team bus.

Chelsea appear to be saving themselves for the Champions League clash with Bayern Munich as they play well within themselves. A dubious free-kick goes Chelsea's way and Lampard's thumping effort takes an outrageous deflection off Rory Delap on the end of the wall to confound Antti Niemi. Home fans are not enamoured with some of Mark Halsey's decisions, and when he gives Chelsea another free-kick after what looks like a good challenge by Nigel Quashie on Gallas, they chant 'have you bought the referee'.

In the 39th minute Johnson's penetrating run past a series of half-hearted challenges ends with a subtle pull-back for Gudjohnsen to drill past Niemi for 2–0.

Kevin Phillips gives the Saints hope just three minutes after coming on when he fires a left-foot shot from Delap's cross past Cech after a lapse from Gudjohnsen.

But with eight minutes left Chelsea unfurl the kind of smooth passing move that is the hallmark of a great team. It culminates with a slick pass from substitute Drogba to Gudjohnsen, who turns the final pass into the corner.

The strike, which confirms Chelsea's lead at the top will stretch to 13 points after Manchester United's home draw with Blackburn earlier in the afternoon, is his 14th of the season, taking him past Drogba as the club's leading scorer. 'The manager put me on in midfield in the Carling Cup final and said it gave him another option,' says Gudjohnsen. I played there against Barcelona, and in the last three league games it's worked well. It's slightly different for me because I have defensive responsibilities, but I am happy with that.'

As for Mourinho's mood, Gudjohnsen observes, 'It's three wins to the title now and this was a big step forward. It was a difficult one because we were up against a team who have been playing well recently. We were focused, especially when we heard that Manchester United had slipped up. I'm sure the manager has a smile on his face.'

Saints manager Harry Redknapp reserves praise for his nephew Frank Lampard. 'I knew Frank was always going to be a top player because of his attitude and the way he worked at his game,' he says, 'but I didn't know how good he'd become. I've never seen anybody work so hard on the training ground as Frank – except for his dad. But he's different class now and has taken his game on. He's become the complete all-round midfield player. I get real pleasure out of seeing him play because I've seen him grow up since he was a baby. He's fantastic and I'd like to see him become player of the year this year. There are only two candidates: him and John Terry.'

Team

Cech, Johnson, Huth, Terry, Gallas, Makelele, Lampard, Cole (Tiago) Gudjohnsen, Duff, Kezman (Drogba).

Mourinho once again declines to attend the pre-match press conference ahead of the home game with Birmingham, but *The Times* prints an interview given to a Portuguese paper in which he describes Lampard as the most complete midfield player in the game, and launches an outspoken attack on managers-turned-pundits who have dared to describe him as 'arrogant'.

He writes, 'The best job in the world is to be a sacked coach. You get up at 10.30, take breakfast, go for a jog followed by a sauna and a calm surf of sporting sites on the net. Lunch with friends, a siesta, a walk, a meeting with your adviser to see how the markets are doing, a visit to the bank to weigh up the interest rates, or to see if the salary the club is still paying you has cleared the account. Return home, have a great meal with the family. That still leaves time to criticise people you don't know. There are so many coaches in this world who want to work but can't and there are those dashing blades who, through their quality and prestige, could work but don't want to, because life as a parasite fulfils them professionally and economically. Get to work you idle scoundrel! And if you don't want to, let others work in peace!'

Mourinho has no doubts about his best performer of the season: Frank Lampard. 'From August to June, always consistent – the quality of passes, whether passing for possession or depth, short or long, with right or left foot, strength of kick on a static ball or while on the move, fast and constant pace, impressive in defence, in recovery, under high pressure, in one-on-ones or in free space. For me, and I don't say this just because he's mine, he is the most complete player of today.'

SATURDAY, 9 APRIL 2005
CHELSEA 1, BIRMINGHAM CITY 1

Chelsea find it difficult to get to grips with a tenacious City side that deny their midfield time and space to weave its usual brand of free-flowing magic. In the end Chelsea need a late strike from Drogba just to rescue a point, and Arsenal's victory at Middlesbrough cuts the lead to 11 points.

Mourinho leaves Gudjohnsen and Drogba in the dugout with him at the start but it is a strategy that does not work. Kezman returns, while Tiago and Smertin are added to the midfield mix with Makelele rested. Smertin, taking the Frenchman's holding role, ends up being substituted at half-time along with Kezman.

Gudjohnsen and Drogba are the replacements, but it is Birmingham who break the deadlock in the second half when Cole gives away a free-kick with a foul on Emile Heskey. The free-kick is moved forward ten yards after Cole kicks the ball away, and Jermaine Pennant's ball in is for once misjudged by Cech, allowing Matthew Upson to head across goal for Walter Pandiani to slam in a shot from ten yards.

Mourinho puts on Jarosik for Johnson, going with three men at the back, but has to wait for the equaliser. Cole feeds a ball in from the left and Lampard turns to set up Drogba for an easy finish.

Mourinho says he is content with a 'positive point', but admits, 'It was a bad performance in the first half. It looked like a friendly in August. Not enough ambition to win the game.'

It is Mourinho's first words in public for two weeks, which, for a man who can pack a lifetime's worth of controversy into a single press conference, is a stupendously long time.

Mourinho adds that the rumours suggesting he is unhappy at the club are wide of the mark. 'We are fantastic,' he says, 'we could not be better. We have a trophy, we are top of the league by 11 points and we are in the quarter-finals of the Champions League and won the first game. We could not be better. I am happy. The only reason I am not happy is that we did not get the three points against Birmingham.

'In the second half it was a game and we did everything OK except concede a silly goal. But we showed a good reaction with a goal. We put a lot of pressure on them and played to win. We were strong but they fought a lot and defended well. It was a silly goal for us to give away and after that they believed they could get a result. They deserved to go home with a point. It would have been very hard on them if we had scored again near the end.

'Maybe this season has been better than everybody could dream, including me. I always thought we could win the league but to have an 11-point lead with a month to go is better than I thought we could do. It was always likely that there would be a bit of a reaction to the games we're playing now. It's three games in six days and Saturday was the first of two in four days. That's very difficult. We are 11 points in front of Arsenal and it is a comfortable distance. We just have to control it and get the points we need to be champions. For me, being champions today, next week or two weeks' time, away or at home, doesn't matter. I just want to be champions.'

Steve Bruce spends five minutes eulogising on the merits of Mourinho, conceding he can hardly find a fault. 'I think I speak for all managers when I say we've got huge respect for Mourinho,' he says. 'He has been a breath of fresh air for us all. We were getting a bit sick of Wenger v Fergie all the time. There's another one on the block now. Apart from Blackburn once, the Premier League has been contested by Manchester United and Arsenal, and we've got one more in there now. It's taken a hell of a lot of money for Chelsea to get there, but, let's be fair, Mourinho's made some big decisions very quickly. You look how he sent out Hernan Crespo and Juan Sebastian Veron on loan. We are all trying desperately to beat him and we can't – it's as simple as that.'

Team

Cech, Johnson (Jarosik), Huth, Terry, Gallas, Smertin (Gudjohnsen), Lampard, Cole, Duff, Tiago, Kezman (Drogba).

A rare moment of dissatisfaction in the Chelsea camp occurs when William Gallas reveals he is fed up playing out of position at left-back. 'I will continue in this position until the end of the season, but after that things will have to be very clear,' he says. 'I do not like playing left-back. I am not comfortable in that position and it is going to have to change at one time or another. I am sacrificing myself for the team but I am suffering. I know that with the injury to Wayne Bridge and also that of Paulo Ferreira the manager has no other solution than to play me on the left for now. I accept that for the moment but, I repeat, it is becoming increasingly difficult for me.'

Ken Bates drops his £2m legal feud with the club. A Chelsea statement says, 'This settlement has been agreed by Chelsea to avoid wasting more management time and to avoid incurring ever increasing legal fees as a result of the forthcoming trial. In reaching this settlement, Chelsea have not admitted any liability. We are pleased of course that this litigation is now concluded and we wish Mr Bates well in the future.' Chelsea are happy to avoid Abramovich and the club facing scrutiny in the High Court.

Chelsea dominate the nominations for the PFA Players' Player of the Year award with Terry, Lampard and Cech all on the shortlist, along with Thierry Henry – winner in 2004 – Crystal Palace's Andy Johnson and Steven Gerrard.

Chelsea are also represented in the shortlist for the Young Player of the Year award, with Arjen Robben nominated with Wayne Rooney, Cristiano Ronaldo, Jermain Defoe, Stewart Downing and Shaun Wright-Phillips. PFA chief executive Gordon Taylor says he thinks it is 'neck and neck' between Lampard and Terry for the main prize.

Lampard comments, 'I've had a remarkable season with Chelsea. It's difficult to take in the transformation here over the last two seasons. I don't know that I have surpassed the likes of Patrick Vieira and Roy Keane because they are the best and they have been the best in the business for a long time. Vieira is a fantastic player. Every time you play against him you can see what a complete player he is, and Roy Keane has been fantastic over the years. I'm a big, big fan. For me he has been the best in the world – the most complete midfielder I have seen for many, many years. To a certain extent you have to say Steven Gerrard falls into that bracket as well. I know what Jose said but he's my manager and people will rightfully say he's slightly biased.'

After completing their Champions League quarter-final victory over Bayern Munich, Terry has an ultrasound scan on the right thigh he damaged in a clash with Bastian Schweinsteiger. The injury is not as bad as first feared. The scan reveals severe bruising and Terry returns to Cobham for treatment, while other players are given two days off, with Mourinho returning to Portugal for a family holiday.

Terry says the powers of concentration that helped him attain the PFA nomination are down to coaching sessions from Gianfranco Zola. 'Franco used to spend a couple of hours a week working with me when I was in the youth team,' he says. 'He'd say, "Watch the ball. It doesn't matter where my feet go as long as the ball doesn't move." He'd have ten one-on-ones with me and score ten. Then I got better – and he would score nine! But whether it's a winger or a striker, it's crucial to let him know early that you're there. There are always little bits of off-the-ball stuff going on. When I first got into the Chelsea team, opponents would try to pinch your nipples when the ball was up the other end of the pitch. They would also grab your nuts at a set-play or stand on your toes when it was freezing.'

Next up for Chelsea is the showdown with Arsenal, and the good news is that Thierry Henry is out injured. But Terry feels he knows how to handle the Frenchman. 'You've got to get his back to goal and keep moving him away from goal,' Terry says. 'As soon as he gets the ball played into him, get tight to him – but not so tight that he can roll off down the side of you. Keep an arm's distance away, so that if he turns you can get an arm across and give him a nudge. But if you're caught on the counter-attack and it's three against three, you drop off until other players get back.'

Terry adds that he has more trouble with Dennis Bergkamp, and is thankful for Claude Makelele's defensive qualities. 'Bergkamp is so clever at pulling out,' says Terry. 'And if you go with him, the other centre-half is left one against one with Henry. At Chelsea we are lucky to have a defensive midfielder like Claude, who can pick up deep strikers. If Bergkamp drops off to the right, I yell "left shoulder", and if he drops to the left, it's "right shoulder". I think that's all the English Maka knows!'

Arsenal were the last team to beat the Blues at Stamford Bridge – 35 games and 14 months ago. Gudjohnsen says, 'I scored and got sent off in that match, which we lost 2–1. We have moved on since then and are closing in on the title. We are hard to beat and we will keep our form going. We want Stamford Bridge to be a fortress and for us to stay unbeaten for the season.'

Ashley Cole warns that Arsenal have no intention of allowing Chelsea to use them as a stepping-stone to the title. 'If they are going to win it then, fair enough, and good luck to them. But they haven't won it yet, and we don't want them winning it by beating us on the way. We still want to win the league ourselves. Chelsea have to win their games and we are not going to give up. We are on a good run at the moment. We had a tough game at Highbury against them, which we thought we should have won, and we are going to Stamford Bridge without any fear. We are going to go there to try to win the game.'

After the Cole tapping-up affair, Sir Alex Ferguson's reaction to the news that Rio Ferdinand met his agent Pini Zahavi and Peter

Kenyon in a London restaurant is expected. Kenyon insists the meeting was a coincidence but Fergie snaps, 'It may be somebody else's view that the meeting was unfortunate, but it is not my view. My concern is our supporters and I just want to let them know that we are not happy with this. When the chief executive of a Premier League club – with the history they have got in recent times – still sits in a restaurant ... whether it is contempt or just thumbing his nose at us, it is ill advised at the very least.' Ferdinand stresses that he wants to remain at Old Trafford.

Arsene Wenger admits Chelsea have had an exceptional season. 'After 32 games there is no coincidence. You have to respect what Chelsea have done on the pitch. They are 11 points better so that means there was a gap this year. But it is not over yet, we have a chance to close the gap and then there are five games to go.'

There is no comment from Mourinho, but in his place Steve Clarke says, 'We are the top team in London. We beat Bayern Munich, who Arsenal couldn't beat. The league table doesn't lie and the club which has been most consistent is the one which wins the title. Arsenal and Man United have dominated over the past ten years and it is good for football that we are challenging that. The fact people talk about us most weeks tells you we've made it. It's because we are top. When you consider we finished 11 points behind Arsenal last season it's been a good turnaround, and it shows how focused we've been all season.'

WEDNESDAY, 20 APRIL 2005
CHELSEA 0, ARSENAL 0

Wenger shakes hands with Mourinho at the end and finally says, 'Of course Chelsea will win the title now. I always felt that if they didn't lose this game they would be champions – unless someone puts a bomb here! But they are worthy champions because they have been remarkably consistent and that is most difficult in top sport. I can only say congratulations for what they have achieved.'

Clarke claims, 'I thought it was a good game between two top sides. The fans have to be patient and look forward to us being champions. Jose is happy – it was a good result for us and keeps the gap at 11 points. It is going to be difficult for anybody to catch us now. The manager is happy and so are the players. We will set out to get another three points against Fulham on Saturday and then concentrate on the Champions League. We didn't expect Arsenal to roll over but I thought we created the better chances on the night. They started well but we settled down and matched their possession.'

Cheeky Blues fans make Ashley Cole feel at home by holding a placard saying 'Welcome Home'. But Cole doesn't have much to say to Mourinho, who even more cheekily gives him a high-five as the Arsenal defender leaves the field – just as he shook Steven Gerrard's hand after the Carling Cup final!

Without Freddie Ljungberg and Sol Campbell as well as Henry, Arsenal start well. With just two minutes gone Jose Antonio Reyes wins a header against Glen Johnson and Robert Pires thunders a volley against the underside of the bar. Pires wastes an even better chance when he drags his shot wide of the far post after John Terry's attempted clearance is blocked and falls kindly for the winger.

Then Chelsea break and Duff slips the ball to Drogba, but Jens Lehmann saves with his legs. Soon afterwards Drogba slightly overhits a cross that would have set up Joe Cole for a certain goal.

Lampard tackles Pires inside his own box, then at the other end fires just inches wide after Drogba's clever dummy, while the striker produces a clever turn from Duff's cutback but shoots inches wide.

Both sides make changes, with the arrival of Robin van Persie and Jeremie Aliadiere proving Arsenal's need for victory, while the combative Tiago demonstrates Chelsea's resolve as he comes on for Cole. Kezman also comes on for Duff. But neither side can make the breakthrough as the game ends goalless.

Wenger says, 'We knew we'd have to come here and take the initiative because Chelsea like to play deep and hit you on the break. It was important for us to score an early goal and my big regret is that we couldn't take our chances because that would have changed Chelsea's plan and made them come out and play. In the second half Chelsea dropped even deeper, became more cautious and more worried. But we lacked the penetration to finish them off. I will leave it to others to compare the two teams but I can take great satisfaction from the quality of this display and the quality of my team.'

With the title now in touching distance, Lampard already has his sights on sustained success. 'The title is almost there but the hard thing now is to back it up,' he says. 'It's well documented that the second title is harder to win than the first and next season we'll start all over again. Arsenal haven't backed it up but have been a dominant force for the past few years. This year we're the best team. We have to make sure that we're not just the best team this year but the best for future seasons. We're all hungry and are not going to settle for one title. We want to win everything we're involved in and we will play with the same attitude next year.'

> **Team**
> Cech, Johnson, Carvalho, Terry, Gallas, Makelele, Gudjohnsen (Jarosik), Lampard, Cole (Tiago), Duff (Kezman), Drogba.

With the Champions League semi-final first leg against Liverpool looming, Chelsea want to rest players without jeopardising their Premiership assault. Clarke insists, 'We're going to put out a team against Fulham that can win the game as we need three points. That would put us very close to the title and then we'd see what happens.' Robben is back in the squad, giving Mourinho the option to rest Cole or Duff.

Mourinho admits he has made errors during the season but says what matters is the final outcome. 'My life in football is about being popular and loved by my team's supporters – and being hated by the opponents' supporters. That's the way I want to carry on because it means we're winning things. Of course I've made mistakes. I can analyse a situation and have the wrong point of view. Of course there will be fights. I can't say I don't like a fight because that's my nature. But sometimes maybe I must be in control of a situation and not react. I always try to do the best for my team. What matters is my club and my players. When we have the cups in our hands we will forget everything.

'I think it is great for English football that a club who has not been champions for 50 years becomes the champion. It is good to run away with this. I can tell you that in Portugal we have been looking for something like this for a long time.'

Mourinho eulogises about his 'Magnificent Seven' – the band of players whose consistent excellence has driven Chelsea to within touching distance of the title. 'Over the season we have had seven players without injuries or suspensions, without bad moments in performances. They have been the big spine of the team: Petr Cech, William Gallas, John Terry, Claude Makelele, Frank Lampard, Eidur Gudjohnsen and Damien Duff play almost every game. The best compliment I can pay Claude is that he has nothing to learn from me. Claude knows everything. He is 32 but because he is out of the French national team, he still has two or three perfect years to give to Chelsea.'

In an especially frank frame of mind, Mourinho then shows his compassionate side by saying, 'Cudicini's situation hurts me. He is fantastic every day in training. He is responsible for Cech performing so well.'

SATURDAY, 23 APRIL 2005

CHELSEA 3, FULHAM 1

It is 50 years to the day since Chelsea last lifted the title and the captain of that side Roy Bentley, now 81, returns to mark the occasion. Robben destroyed Fulham in the game at Craven Cottage and Chelsea are labouring until he replaces Cole. Robben's match-winning display moves Chelsea within two points of just the second title in their history.

Cole gives Chelsea the ideal platform when he swivels onto Drogba's pass and sends a scorching shot past Edwin van der Sar with 17 minutes gone. Drogba squanders two other half-chances, while Cole misses his kick inside the penalty area, and Fulham gradually haul themselves back into the game. Just before half-time Carvalho is guilty of an uncharacteristic error in allowing Collins John to latch onto Luis Boa Morte's pass before finishing. The equaliser comes just seconds after van der Sar races out to deny Duff after the Irishman is sent hurtling through by Drogba.

Robben comes on at the interval and changes the game instantly. Jarosik also comes on for Huth, leaving Duff to drop in behind him at left-back. It is something not even Ranieri managed to come up with, but it gives Chelsea a tremendous threat down the left.

First Robben finds Gudjohnsen but the 'goal' is ruled out for offside, then the Dutchman fires in another shot that flashes wide. Finally he speeds past Moritz Volz and expertly picks out Lampard to score.

Cech tips a fierce drive by Tomasz Radzinski over the bar and foils John's deflected free-kick. But Gudjohnsen makes certain of victory with just four minutes left as he is put clear by substitute Tiago and notches his 100th goal in English football.

Mourinho moans about the Blues' 'ridiculous' midday kick-off. 'A team that plays at 8pm on Wednesday night and then has to play at 12.45pm on Saturday... it is too much. Over the 90 minutes Fulham didn't deserve to lose. They had the fresher legs. I think the result we got is incredible and magnificent and down to the players' character, because at half-time they were dead. I said to them that the only chance was for them to play to their full potential. You have to be super-human to play a huge game on Wednesday night and then again on Saturday morning, and our players are not super-human. It was down to sheer character that we got a fantastic and magnificent victory.'

Mourinho assesses the season so far and says, 'It's not about the treble. The Carling Cup is not such a big thing, but at that time for Chelsea to win a trophy was very important, be it a small or a big competition. But to win the championship after 50 years is very big. Fifty years ago and the fans have not forgotten – this year they will not forget either. Whether it is the players, the staff, the managers ... whoever. Roy Bentley is rightly remembered as the captain of that team and so too will John Terry be of this one. Nobody forgets their names.'

Team

Cech, Johnson, Carvalho, Terry, Huth (Jarosik), Cole (Robben), Makelele, Lampard, Duff, Drogba (Tiago), Gudjohnsen.

Chelsea chairman Bruce Buck says Roman Abramovich is committed to the club for the long haul. 'If you had seen the tears in his eyes in the dressing room in Monaco, you would know this is a committed supporter. You would know how much he cares about the club. His Russian personality is generally to be reserved, but he is hugely excited. I don't see it stopping. I don't see why Roman would sell. If it was the case that he was going to win the European Cup and disappear, why spend £25m on a training ground that wouldn't be built for two years?

Buck also says the spending will slow down. 'We appreciate that the £250m-plus is a lot of money, but we are just playing catch-up. If you look at what United, Arsenal, Newcastle and Liverpool have spent in the last ten years, and then us more recently, by and large we are all similar. If the tag that we have bought success exists, so be it, but I don't believe it is true. I think that money does help and it gets you a long way there, but it doesn't get you over the goalline by a long shot. The answer is to build our academy and bring up more of these younger players, and that is our intention. To bring more John Terrys up the ranks.

Mr Abramovich has invested a lot of money, but I emphasise the word investment. And, on top of that, we have changed our business model, brought in the right sponsors, changed the kit company, the management team, the structure. We have done a lot more than Mr Abramovich throwing money at players and I am not sure we get the credit for that. Although it is difficult to convince people, we are very careful about what we spend, whether it is

£24m on Mr Drogba or £1,000 on pencils. We are careful about every 10p. You have seen the transfer spend go down just in one year and you will see it keep going down. You will see several players come in this summer but also several go out.'

The announcement of a new club sponsor to replace Emirates is part of the realignment. Chelsea are negotiating with Samsung, Siemens and Nokia and the deal will be a Premiership record, eclipsing the £9m a year that Manchester United are paid by Vodafone. The intention is for Chelsea to stand alone from their wealthy benefactor by 2010 and, by 2015 to be eclipsing all their rivals on and off the pitch.

John Terry's remarkable season is recognised as he receives the PFA Player of the Year award from Alan Shearer. Terry says, 'It is unbelievable and the ultimate accolade to be voted for by your fellow professionals whom you play against week in and week out. We have got the Champions League semi-final coming up against Liverpool and are just one win away from the Premiership, so hopefully I am going to be lifting a few more trophies. For Petr, Lamps and myself to be voted in, it was important that one of us won it. It has been a real special season with Chelsea and this just adds to it. I want to thank all of my team-mates. It is my first year as captain and they have helped me a lot, on and off the pitch.'

Terry clutches his precious silverware and refuses to put it down as he discusses Mourinho. 'Jose has been fantastic; I can't speak highly enough of him for what he's done for me personally. He has given me a lot of confidence, gave me the armband at the start of the season and made me believe I'm up there with the best players in the Premiership.'

Chelsea sign a £50m five-year sponsorship deal with South Korean electronics firm Samsung. The deal makes Samsung the club's official sponsor, and the players' shirts will carry the logo 'Samsung Mobile' from next season. It is Samsung's second biggest partnership deal after its sponsorship of the Olympic Games.

Arsenal have a complex eight-year deal with Emirates, worth a potential £100m including the naming of Arsenal's ground and a shirt deal. Manchester United's four-year deal with Vodafone, signed in 2004, is worth a total of £36m.

Peter Kenyon says, 'Over the next five years the plan is quite simple: to turn the world blue. We needed a company that was recognised globally, especially in the UK, China, Russia and America – countries Chelsea are targeting in the next few years. The marketing opportunities are far more critical than the financial sponsorship. I can see a day when we catch Manchester United – on and off the pitch.'

Paul Smith is Chelsea's business affairs director and he believes the gap is already closing on United. 'United have increased revenues as well, but what has affected them is their early exit in the Champions League. That has a big impact on the numbers and within three years we feel we can get close to them.'

An obvious gap between United and the rest is their Old Trafford stadium capacity just shy of 70,000. Arsenal's new ground will be ready for 60,000 in a year's time, but Chelsea are stuck with their 42,449 capacity unless they do something drastic. Smith adds, 'We can't be closer to their [United's] capacity because of the restrictions and regulations. We won't be considering moving right now. Our natural level is probably 60,000, but it can't be done here. We would have to buy all the houses around the ground and knock down the hotels and that won't happen. We want to be big in London and grow the appeal of the club across the city.'

Chelsea are planning to increase the capacity of Stamford Bridge by squeezing 500 extra seats into the Matthew Harding Stand. They have discussed trying to acquire new sites in the area – one idea was the area around Battersea Power Station – but that has also been ruled out. A less likely scheme is that Chelsea will move, on a temporary basis, to the new Wembley Stadium. This has been dismissed as 'pure speculation' and even if Chelsea were interested it would be very difficult for them to gain permission to do so as Tottenham Hotspur have already found out.

Arsenal make Chelsea wait to clinch the title by beating local rivals Spurs at Highbury. Before the match kicks off, among the pubs that line the Fulham Road and Fulham Broadway near the ground, many huddle in the entrances, glued to televisions that hang from the walls, holding banners proclaiming their support for Chelsea. They applaud when Mourinho wanders out of the Chelsea Village Hotel dressed casually in a black and grey tracksuit to whisk his team away in a bus for dinner at a nearby Italian restaurant. It is a nonchalance that suggests they do not care what Arsenal do against Tottenham. In their own minds they have already won the title.

The players' coach arrives back five minutes after the game ends to loud cheers. Joe Cole says, 'We watched the Arsenal game and it would have been nice to have the title in the bag before facing Liverpool. It's still in our hands. We know exactly what we have to do at Bolton.'

The salesman at Fulham Broadway has an impressive supply of T-shirts and flags proclaiming 'Chelsea Champions 2004/05' packed up for the night at the final whistle. But he will soon be doing a roaring trade.

Mourinho wants to keep his men fresh for the semi-final decider at Liverpool, but also wants to finish off the job of winning the title at Bolton. Gallas, nursing a back strain, confirms, 'We want to win the league at Bolton, but it all comes down to how many players are rested – and it could be quite a few.'

Lampard is worried about Bolton's physical approach. He says, 'They scrapped out a 2–2 draw at Stamford Bridge and are too scared of us to try and play football. Their main threat comes from high balls and getting on the end of knockdowns. Teams are realising that to beat us at football is hard because we have good players.'

Bolton are still chasing a Champions League qualifying spot, four points behind Everton in fourth. Sam Allardyce says, 'It's going to be a massive task to get anything out of the game the way Chelsea are going. It's not beyond us but it will be a hell of a result if we can beat them.'

Allardyce taunts Mourinho by claiming Wenger should be known as the 'Special One'. He says, 'Wenger has been the best foreign manager in this country. He is one of the most successful managers there have been here and he showed the way forward in this country with the players he has brought in. Some of the foreign coaches who have come over here have been a disaster. Jacques Santini at Tottenham this season, for instance, lasted no more than two minutes.' But Allardyce adds, 'Mourinho has done brilliantly because he has grasped it in one year. He has swanned into London and Chelsea and said from the start he was going to be successful. He hung his neck on the line and it looks like he is going to achieve. Chelsea should not only win the championship but there is a big possibility they could win the European Cup. They have one of the best-structured defences in the world. In a straightforward contest, we are out of their league. We can only hope we can take advantage of what they have had to go through this week, and what they will have to go through next week at Liverpool. I thought they looked tired and nervy in the first leg against Liverpool. Hopefully, we can catch them out.'

The morning papers are full of headlines of cracks in the camp, based on Robben's reluctance to start the tie with Liverpool and Kezman's frustrations as a squad player. Terry has delayed an operation on a toe injury so could be rested, while Gallas is plagued by a back problem and Duff is out with a hamstring strain. Suggestions that Robben refused to play when Duff failed a fitness test are wide of the mark, and the winger came off the bench for the last 30 minutes.

Chelsea issue a statement insisting the relationship between Robben and Mourinho is 'excellent' and maintain he is 'working hard to get back to full fitness'. Robben's attitude has not gone down well with team-mates.

Despite Kezman playing the last 12 minutes against Liverpool, he is unlikely to be around for much longer. After starting his Chelsea career with four goals in his first three games, admittedly in preseason friendlies, his confidence was destroyed to such an extent that he was scared to shoot when one-on-one with the goalkeeper. Abramovich took him out to dinner in an attempt to lift him from his depression. Kezman says, 'Abramovich is very close to the group and

I have a good relationship with him. He's a funny guy who, if you didn't know his background, you wouldn't look twice at him. He wears just cheap jeans and a cheap jacket and a normal, casual watch. He understands my problems. Then he calls me and we go out to eat. In everything you can see he is obsessed with football.'

Kezman feels he never received Mourinho's full support and has not been given an explanation for starting just six Premiership games since his £5m move from PSV Eindhoven. He is particularly angry that he was dropped after contributing significantly to the thrilling win over Barcelona. Kezman says, 'It's a pity that Jose Mourinho never stood behind me, never gave me full confidence. I can't score a lot of goals if I am only playing for five or ten minutes. I am number two. Everything I do is not good enough. That's the feeling I have and that's very hard to accept. I respect him because he has fantastic results. From his side he understands my situation but he cannot change anything. He would be crazy to change it. This is the way he works and this is the way he had success the last couple of years. He feels he is the best and he is the most prettiest. You have the world of Mourinho and you have the other world.'

Chelsea fans will toast former vice-chairman Matthew Harding if the team clinches the Premiership title at Bolton. The millionaire businessman was killed in a helicopter crash returning from a League Cup tie at Bolton in October 1996. Rick Glanville, commissioned to write the official history of the club, says, 'More and more fans have said that it would be fitting to win the title at Bolton and then raise a glass to Matthew Harding. I wouldn't be surprised if there wasn't a banner or two among the Chelsea fans tomorrow.'

Harding had big ambitions for the club he had supported all his life and had invested in Chelsea. His widow Ruth says, 'It's a fantastic idea and lovely that the fans still remember him. I don't know what the fans are planning for Bolton but it is a lovely gesture and one which is greatly appreciated by all the family.'

Mourinho illustrates his long-term planning by lining up a deal for Javier Mascherano, the outstanding young Argentina midfield player, who will join them after next year's World Cup finals. An agreement has been reached with Corinthians over the signing of Mascherano, even though the 21-year-old is not scheduled to join the Brazilian club from River Plate until this summer. Suggestions Chelsea have dropped their interest in Gerrard are way off the mark. Mourinho tells his board that Mascherano is potentially a better player than Gerrard and he is also looking at Barcelona's Xavi. But the England player remains high on Chelsea's shopping list along with Joao Alves, a relatively obscure midfield player from Sporting Braga of Portugal. Chelsea are showing exceptionally keen interest in AC Milan left-back Kakha Kaladze. The Georgian has won 35 caps and has been starring in AC Milan's determination to regain their European crown.

Mourinho's determination to dominate for years to come will be illustrated by the next wave of signings. Samuel Eto'o has proved himself at Barca and is again on the wanted list.

When Chelsea last won the title the rest of the country was debating how Britain would cope with the arrival of more immigrants from the Caribbean; the Government promised women working in the Civil Service would have equal pay with men by 1961; Sir Winston Churchill resigned as Prime Minister and Anthony Eden, his successor, quickly called a general election that increased the Tory majority; Princess Margaret announced that she was calling off her wedding to Group Captain Peter Townsend; James Dean was killed when his Porsche plunged off the road in California; in Britain, motorists were being a little more careful, especially when the price of a gallon of petrol rose to 4s 6d.

SATURDAY, 30 APRIL 2005
BOLTON WANDERERS 0, CHELSEA 2

Mourinho takes his place in history as the first foreign coach to win the championship in his first season in English football, and it vindicates the confidence he has had since the day he arrived. Lampard has been immense with goals and performances, and his match-winning brace seals his own contribution to the title as the team's top scorer from midfield. Quite an achievement.

Mourinho's managerial genius combined with hunger, desire and ferocity of spirit are the cornerstones of the title triumph. He immediately expresses his affinity to the club. 'Am I the "Special One"?' he asks. 'No, the whole group at Chelsea is special and no one can say we didn't deserve this title. The players have been fantastic. I am proud of every single one of them and they are worthy champions. But Roman Abramovich, the big boss, also deserves it, and so does Peter Kenyon and his group. This group is really special – that's why I want to stay with them for the maximum time, maybe for longer than the contract I have.'

As his players celebrate in front of the travelling supporters, Mourinho sits in the dugout with his mobile phone. 'I was speaking to my wife and children,' he says. 'They went to Portugal for the weekend but they saw it live and they are happy of course – like me. Football is crazy sometimes. We knew a few months ago we had a lead of some distance but anything is possible – so only now is the moment we really feel we are champions. It's not easy the way we are champions and it was the same story this weekend. This game was the perfect game to be champions because Bolton have a difficult style of play and we had to adapt – and we did. We fought like lions. This squad is incredible. When we play, we play together. When we fight, we fight together. When we suffer, we suffer together. And no one who has any sense of fairness can deny that we deserve the title.'

Lampard says he will remember the moment for ever. 'This is a great feeling and I am proud to have got the goals that have clinched it for us. This is a moment I will enjoy for the rest of my life. I felt I owed the fans one after that miss in midweek against Liverpool. This was the best way to repay them. We wanted to win the league first, now we want to beat Liverpool in the Champions League on Tuesday. It is a great relief after 50 years for the fans and for everyone. Our schedule this season has been so hectic and we have had so many things to concentrate on that we knew it wouldn't be easy. But we always believed we could do it.'

Lampard reveals that Jose Mourinho, within minutes of the title being sealed, has ordered a booze ban on the players. 'We had a little sip of champagne and then the manager got the hump because he wanted us to calm down. Maybe he'll let us have half a glass back at the hotel, but then we will have to be tucked up in bed.'

Lampard also explains why he ignored Carvalho after being sent clear for his second goal. 'When JT won the toss he asked me if we wanted to stay the way we were facing but I just had a feeling that if we are going to score goals and win the title then we might as well do it towards the fans. The first one was great but when I went through for the second I was just thinking to myself, "Don't f*** it up." I think Ricardo Carvalho was with me but there was no way I was going to give the ball to him – he would've put it in the stands! I had tunnel vision at that stage. The first goal was massive for us because we were below par. But it was the second one that really killed Bolton off.'

Lampard also has some words for Arsenal and Manchester United. 'We've proved that the best team wins the league. There have been some harsh words spoken about us not being entertaining and that the best two teams in the Premier League are in the final of the FA Cup. But the best team wins the league and we have done that. You look at Arsenal, who lost at Bolton, and Manchester United, who drew, but we went up there and won. It's time for the others to take a look and know that we are definitely the best.'

Terry reveals how Mourinho – who dashed away from the celebrations to allow his players to take the glory – lost his temper after a goalless first half. 'Bolton probably out-battled us in the first half which didn't please the manager. At half-time he gave us a bit of a bollocking, but we came out and responded well in the second half. The gaffer was fuming. He had a go at everybody, telling us we were 45 minutes from the Premiership and that we had to liven up, that we'd have been better putting him out there than us. And he was right, too. Everybody was under-performing. You're not going to play well every game, so it's about giving 110 per cent. But we didn't do that in the first half. They were first to all the headers and tackles.'

Cole, on as a late substitute, can scarcely believe Chelsea are finally champions. 'I'm a bit dazed to be honest and it will take a few days to sink in,' he says. 'It is the pinnacle of any English player's career to win the league title and we have realised this season just how hard it is. We've got two trophies now and we all want to make it a treble. It's a fantastic feeling. We thought we'd won it after the Arsenal game, but now it's actually happened it's a dream come true for me and all of us. It's hard to believe it's actually happened. There was a stage in the season when I did wonder if I was going to be part of things here. But now, after all that's happened for me in the last few months, it's all worthwhile. I can't see why we can't go on from this to win the Champions League. Why not? We'll be going to Liverpool and we'll be flying now. We just want to get out there.'

Chelsea are set on their way by an inspirational pre-game team-talk from former Bolton star Gudjohnsen, who explains, 'I was very calm for most of it but I did get a bit carried away towards the end of the talk. Nothing crazy – just a bit of shouting. I just said to the lads, "We can make each other champions today." We were all heroes out there, particularly Frank who did brilliantly to get us two goals. He's been such an integral part of the team this year and deserved to get the glory, but it has been a joy to play with all of these lads. Bolton made it really tough for us and we didn't play very well in the first half, so the manager made us fully aware that we were playing for the championship. All of this hasn't really sunk in yet, but together with John Terry and Frank this probably means most to us because we have taken a leadership role in the dressing room as players who have been at the club a few years. All three of us have grown up together and, after the birth of my children, this is my proudest moment.'

Mourinho has to start the match without his two wingers, Duff and Robben, while Joe Cole is left on the bench. There is also a scare in the first minute when Lampard shoots from distance and pulls up, temporarily lame. To the considerable relief of Mourinho and his men, the England midfielder is able to run off the problem. Alongside

Lampard in midfield are the peripheral figures Geremi and Jarosik, who are brought in to add steel to Chelsea's defence of set-pieces. Mourinho learned the hard way from Bolton's fightback to draw 2–2 at Stamford Bridge, and the aerial bombardment immediately resumes. When a long throw-in is not properly cleared, Stelios's snap-shot is held by Cech, while Makelele is booked for his attempts to stop Jay-Jay Okocha's next delivery.

Cech also saves a header from Gary Speed and a shot by Fernando Hierro. The visitors manage only a long-range effort by Lampard in the opening 20 minutes, with the England midfielder shaking off a worrying knock sustained in the process. Then Kevin Davies is left unmarked to meet a lofted free-kick, only to direct his header straight at Cech.

Terry plays on despite having a black eye that restricts his vision in one eye following a clash with Davies just before half-time. Tempers start to fray, especially when Geremi goes down easily under a tackle from El-Hadji Diouf, which earns the Senegal international a booking. Bolton are livid when, from the ensuing free-kick, Chelsea seize the lead against the run of play. Lampard shows great composure in cutting back inside Vincent Candela as he seizes on Drogba's headed knockdown, before picking his spot past Jussi Jaaskelainen. The Bolton keeper is booked for his protests.

Mourinho is concerned with protecting his side's advantage, with the towering figure of Huth soon replacing Drogba. That leaves Gudjohnsen up front on his own, while Chelsea form a five-man defence. But Cech still needs to claw the ball around the post, hurting himself in the process, when Geremi deflects a cross with his head that seems destined for the corner.

Bolton rally once again, but they are caught on the break with 14 minutes left as Lampard races clear. The midfielder has Carvalho bursting his lungs to provide an option to his right, but instead he uses the defender as a decoy before dipping his shoulder and skipping past Jaaskelainen. His finish is assured and sparks delirium on the touchline, with Mourinho dancing for joy and Drogba even seizing an inflatable Premiership trophy from the crowd in expected triumph. He has to wait just 15 minutes longer to repeat the feat, this time for real, as Chelsea's path to the title is complete.

Sam Allardyce is said to have accused referee Steve Dunn of effectively handing the title to Chelsea by failing to spot a perceived foul on Hierro in the build-up to Lampard's first goal. 'The referee has won them this game,' says Allardyce. 'He failed on a major decision, with Jiri Jarosik's foul on Hierro. There was nothing more blatant than that you can see in the game. Hierro was going to win the header but Jarosik just barged into him. The referee waved play on and Frank Lampard got in to score. It's just not on. That's cost us the game, as well as ourselves not punishing them in the first half, when we were hugely on top.'

But Allardyce pays tribute to Lampard, saying, 'I don't want this to overshadow what Chelsea have done over the whole season as they truly deserve to win it. They've been absolutely magnificent and the best player in the world at the moment has to be Frank Lampard. There's no question about that. To play as many games as he does, with the distances he runs and the finishing power he has, it's wonderful. He has been absolutely magnificent all season. You can't take anything out of Frank Lampard. He could play 100 games in a season, that lad. The energy he put in, certainly on the second goal, was amazing. He started in their box when we had the corner and he finished in our box scoring the goal, that's how good he was as well as his quality of finishing. He has to be one of the best players in the world.'

Roman Abramovich parades arm-in-arm with Terry and Lampard on the pitch as the Chelsea pair join the fans singing the owner's name. Abramovich also takes a call from Gianfranco Zola in Italy confirming his job as academy chief next year. Outside the Reebok Stadium, Drogba and Cole hoist themselves out of the skylight in the team coach to dance on the roof in front of fans beside themselves with joy.

Terry is still inside the ground performing his media rounds, gripping a little transparent plastic bag tightly to his side: inside is his shirt from the game, a memento he will treasure for ever. Some of his team-mates threw theirs into the crowd after the final whistle. Others changed into T-shirts with 'Champions' written on them. Terry kept his on his back until he disappeared into the dressing room. 'I've kept my shirt from every game this season and thankfully we've gone and won it. I've kept every shirt and every captain's armband. I'll put them in one big frame. I dreamed of being able to do that when I first started collecting them in the opening four or five games.' It is going to have to be an awfully large frame!

Like Lampard, Terry played in every game of Chelsea's march to the title. He was felled towards the end of the first half by a finger in the eye, and had double vision at half-time because the eye had swelled so badly. Still Terry came out for the second half. 'It feels very emotional,' he says. 'I just want to break down and cry really. I probably will when I get back to my hotel room on my own, when I sit back and watch it on TV.'

Terry finally leaves and takes his place on the team bus. The biggest cheer of all comes when he and Lampard thrust their heads out of the skylight and take the plaudits of the crowd. An hour earlier, the same two players had remained out on the pitch, unable to tear themselves away from the fans.

> **Team**
>
> Cech, Geremi, Terry, Carvalho, Gallas, Tiago, Makelele (Smertin), Lampard, Jarosik, Gudjohnsen (Cole), Drogba (Huth).

Mourinho only gives one interview, to Sky TV, sending a message to journalists that he has no problem with the press but wants the players to bask in the glory.

However, Mourinho tells *Visao*, a magazine in Portugal, 'I made everyone understand you can break with ties to the past where behaviour, preparation of a team and even image go. I helped break several taboos, things that were traditionalist that the English are still hanging on to. They tried to wear down my image, make it more difficult for me to impose myself.' He points the finger at Manchester United and Arsenal, who, he claims, fear and begrudge Chelsea's success. 'It has everything to do with Chelsea: what the club means. First, because the owner is a foreigner and he symbolises external economic power. In addition, the club had not won anything for a long time and now they want to end the successful routine of Arsenal and Manchester United. In other words, everything came together: the Russian millionaire, the arrogant Portuguese, Chelsea as a symbol of the nouveau riche, the institutional power of the two big clubs that are used to winning everything, and who are now scared. They tried to make our success as hard as possible. But our victory in the Premiership could promote a change in attitudes and responsibilities.'

Mourinho's first season has never been dull. Chelsea faced 12 separate disciplinary charges. Two months into the season the club was charged by the FA, along with West Ham, with failing to ensure the proper behaviour of fans during their Carling Cup tie. After the first leg of the Carling Cup semi-final against Manchester United, he described the second half as 'whistle after whistle, fault after fault, cheat after cheat'. Guilty of improper conduct, he was fined £5,000 and warned about his conduct. February was a bad month. Chelsea were fined £15,000 after a brawl in their Premiership match against Blackburn. After the match against Barcelona in the Nou Camp, UEFA charged Chelsea, Mourinho, Clarke and Miles, the club's security officer, with making false declarations about an alleged half-time chat between Anders Frisk, the Swedish referee, and Frank Rijkaard, the Barcelona coach. A £33,000 fine for Chelsea and £9,000 for Mourinho resulted. Mourinho collected another warning for his 'silence' gesture to Liverpool fans during the Carling Cup final, and the affair of an alleged illegal approach to Ashley Cole, rumbles on.

Kenyon hails Mourinho as 'undoubtedly' the best manager in the Premiership and predicts that the 42-year-old will remain in charge at Stamford Bridge for at least another nine years. Chelsea expect to secure his long-term future by finalising the terms of a five-year deal within days. Kenyon believes the coach dreams of building a dynasty that will keep Chelsea at the vanguard of European football for the next decade. 'There's an enormous desire to put Chelsea right up at the top,' he says. 'In order to be a top team, you have to win things more than once and do it over a sustained period of time. That's what attracted Jose to Chelsea. He is a manager that can get us there and I know that is what he wants to do. He wants not to tell everyone that he's the best manager in the world, but to prove that he is.'

Kenyon concedes there will come a time when the club will have to be self-financing. 'We did a lot of activity in terms of getting our squad size right last year, moving 14 players out and bringing seven in. This year it will be a lot less than that. We've a young squad, with an average age of 25, and there's a few selected positions and that's it, so it will probably be about three in to maintain a squad size of 24. We're in a good position and confident we've a squad of players that have not reached their potential, so we will be adding to it in a selective manner, and we've enough in our budget to get the players we want. But it's wrong to say we are going to keep throwing money at the club. We've made a commitment that within five years the club will be profitable and as a consequence of that there are financial parameters. We have invested a huge amount of money – £280m in the last two years on players – and there is a long-term plan in the next five years of recouping on that investment. The team will not suffer in terms of the investment we are planning for it, but we have to move away from the fact we are going to buy anybody and everybody.'

Gallas has expressed interest in joining Barcelona, who contacted his representatives to inquire about his availability, but with two years remaining on his contract he is expected to be rewarded for his loyalty by signing a new deal in the summer. Gallas says, 'Chelsea have the best team spirit I've known in my whole career. Everyone who sees us play must realise how hard we fight for each other. We have absolutely everything. We have great spirit, good players and a manager who gives us the belief that we'll always win. The club have grown up every season and this is good for the future. I want to be with Chelsea and don't want to leave.'

Gary Lineker gives his verdict on Chelsea's season by saying, 'The key moment for me was when Arjen Robben first came into the side as a substitute against Blackburn at the end of October and galvanised Chelsea to a 4–0 win. There is no doubt that they have had their breaks along the way, but when you have as many shots on goal as them you are bound to get deflections and, when you look at the size of their lead, you have to say that those efforts have had little effect on the league outcome.

'People will accuse them of buying the title. But although Mourinho has had a massive budget, you still have to get the right players in and put a team together. If you want proof that money does not give you the right to dominate everything, just look at Real Madrid, who have spent more than anyone and now look certain to finish a second successive season without a trophy. Chelsea have spent big, but they haven't gone out and bought Madrid-style *galacticos*.

'For all his buys, Mourinho has achieved something that untold millions cannot bring into a club: a sense of camaraderie and fierce collective spirit. And although there has been something of a siege mentality inside the club, after all the shenanigans surrounding the Barcelona game and referee Anders Frisk, that consistency and team spirit has been obvious from the early weeks of the season. Of course, when you start well and build up a winning habit, everything is rosy in the garden. But Mourinho had to construct that positive mentality in a dressing room full of new signings and huge egos. That he managed to do so in such a short space of time is remarkable, especially when he was new to the club himself. In fact, managing to adjust so swiftly to the Premiership and all the differing demands compared to other European leagues is perhaps his greatest achievement. Maybe he really is the "Special One".'

Despite his 'special' talents, even Mourinho cannot prevent Chelsea crashing out of the Champions League at Anfield. His immediate reaction is to give the players two days off while he returns to the Bridge to agree a new five-year contract and plan for next season with the vow that his side will come back even better. Mourinho says, 'I am delighted to be signing this new contract. My heart is with Chelsea and the fantastic group of players I have. They have done a great job this season. But the vision of the owner and the board for the future of Chelsea is also one I want to be part of. I'm totally behind this project and their support in achieving it means Chelsea is the place where I will be happiest in my work. I cannot imagine another club or situation where I would be happier.' Kenyon says, 'This is great news for everybody concerned. This deal demonstrates Jose's commitment to Chelsea and also our certainty that he is the best manager to take the club into a new, exciting and successful era.'

Mourinho waited until he knew Chelsea's European fate before agreeing the deal. He adds, 'The new deal is very important for me and I'm very happy with it. I promise we will be even stronger next year. This season we won two out of four trophies and next season we will compete for five because we are also in the Community Shield. We'll be out to win two or three of those. I know what the club want for the future and we want the same. We all know that this season was a good start – not the end, but the start. We want to win more titles and my players are the same. We were very happy with this season but we want more for our lives and our careers. The club and the owner are the same. And to have a five-year contract is very good in family terms. There is now no doubt that our lives are in London and that is important for my children. When my family situation is stable, that is better for my professional situation so I can be completely focused towards Chelsea. I think my players will be happy with the news, as they will be with me for the next five years. It is also good for the fans as I feel we have established a good relationship and they are happy with what I have brought here.'

Chelsea insert a hands-off clause worth more than £5m into his new contract. His new deal is worth £5.2m a year, but the real value could be as much as double that with more success. Mourinho's contract contains a clause stipulating that his next employers must pay Chelsea the value of his contract for a year should he leave within the next five years.

Just as interesting is the personnel he plans to bring to the club: Inter Milan striker Adriano. There are suggestions of a £70m offer for the 23-year-old, who is considered the most exciting hitman in European football, but that is way too high. Even at that level Inter boss Roberto Mancini resists, saying, 'It would be a very impressive offer but a correct one considering that he is an extraordinary player. It is also true that we could use that money to buy a host of players but Adriano is too important for us to sell.'

Mourinho and Abramovich would like European Footballer of the Year Andriy Shevchenko, but the Ukrainian star wants to stay in Italy. But Chelsea begin negotiations to sign Shevchenko's AC Milan team-mate Kakha Kaladze. If they fail there they will switch to Athletic Bilbao's Asier Del Horno. Earmarked to leave are Crespo, on loan at AC, and Veron, on loan at Inter, plus Geremi, Smertin, Parker, Cudicini, Johnson, and Kezman.

But Steven Gerrard hints he might stay at Anfield. 'After the final I will be sitting down with chief executive Rick Parry and gaffer Rafa Benitez to discuss the future. That has been the situation for a while so, from that point of view, nothing has changed.'

If Gerrard commits to Liverpool, Lyon's highly rated midfielder Michael Essien remains the favoured alternative. The Ghanaian was first linked with Manchester United, but Sir Alex Ferguson does not possess the resources to move for the £14m-rated player, who was the inspiration behind the French club's run to the Champions League quarter-finals.

Frank Lampard beats off the challenge of John Terry to land the Football Writers' Association vote as Footballer of the Year, becoming only the second Englishman since Alan Shearer in 1994 to win football's oldest and most prestigious individual award. Teddy Sheringham was the other in 2001. Lampard and Terry poll more than 90 per cent of the votes, with Jamie Carragher finishing a distant third. Gerry Cox, chairman of the FWA, says, 'It was a close-run thing between the two Chelsea team-mates until a fortnight ago, but Frank Lampard ended up winning by a substantial margin. John Terry has been a huge player for Chelsea in what has been a fantastic season for the Blues, but Lampard has clearly convinced our members that he is the best player in the country and right up there with the world's leading players. His all-round game is superb, his fitness phenomenal and the fact that he has weighed in with 18 goals this season makes him something special for any team.'

Lampard was runner-up to Thierry Henry in last year's Footballer of the Year award, as well as coming second for two years running in the PFA's Player of the Year award, which was won by Terry. Lampard becomes only the second Chelsea player ever to win the award, after Gianfranco Zola in 1997. Lampard was on the receiving end of remorseless 'Fat Boy' jibes from his own fans during his last two seasons at West Ham – abuse that did not go away after he made his £11m move across London. 'I took some stick in the West Ham days,' he says. 'But it's all part of the process that's got me where I am now. I'm that much stronger, that much tougher. When I look back to the days when I did take stick and people did doubt me, that's when I get the most pleasure out of football, that I've proven those people wrong.

'I remember at the start of last season, when we went to Prague for a Champions League game, John Terry, Eidur Gudjohnsen and myself were all on the bench. We all looked at each other and we were pretty fearful for our future in a way. We worked very hard from then on and got what we deserved. It would be very hard to say the title means more to me than the players who arrived last summer. But JT, Eidur and me have been mates for four years and we've looked on enviously as teams like Arsenal and Manchester United won leagues and cups. Obviously, the new owner moved us up to their level. I can talk for us three because we're very close and we're very proud of how far this club has come. Life's almost perfect – although it would have been better if we had beaten Liverpool. We're very hungry to continue the success we've had. It's going very well for the team and me personally, but I want even more.'

Mourinho insists that winning the Premiership and not the Champions League was always their top priority. 'I always say, since I arrived here, that the best team always wins the league championship,' he says. 'What I can also say is that there are not many times when the best team wins the Champions League. In the Premiership things can happen, you can make a mistake one day, you will have players missing another day, you will have bad luck or good luck in other days but at the end, when the battle is over, the best team always wins the title. That is why the Premiership was our top target. We wanted to prove we are the best. In the Champions League it is different; it is cup football and an example is Porto when we scored a goal in the last minute to give us the game against Manchester United. This season Chelsea are out of the competition because of a ghost goal. If, in the Premiership, we lose a match to Liverpool through a ghost goal, it is not a problem because you have more matches to recover from that defeat. In our case, though, we are out of the Champions League despite the fact that, as everyone knows, we did not concede a single goal in the semi. That is cup football for you. Last season Porto scored in the last minute and went through. This season, Gudjohnsen could have scored in the last minute to put us through or the linesman could see the same as everybody else and not give a goal. So to win the Premiership and prove we are the best makes me very happy because we are a young group who has worked together just this season. To win two out of four trophies was very good and just what we want at the beginning of a wonderful Chelsea period.

'The priority is to keep the champions – make sure you don't lose the important players. This club has conditions for that. We will keep our group of champions and we will improve it. If we look at the left-back position for example, we have only Wayne Bridge. We can improve on that place before next season. When you look at the attacking players we can say we need another one and in midfield we can keep them all and maybe add another one. We also have a lot of players in the group who have been in England for just one season. It is not easy, in my opinion, to adapt to football here so these players will be better next season.

'My contract is for five years from now. It means the club very much wants me to stay and I also want very much to stay. We are committed. We want to work together for the future of this club. This season was not the end, just the start. To win the championship after 50 years was a fantastic achievement. We must look forward now to win more silverware, not after another half a century but year after year.

'Now I am emotional with my players, but that won't last for ever. I can be in love with my players for what they have achieved this season but if they don't do it again next year I won't be in love any more. I cannot say to John Terry, "You are my captain and the Footballer of the Year and you have been fantastic so I promise you will always play next year." He has got to continue performing. Petr Cech has been absolutely fantastic. But next year he must want to prove again that he is the best keeper in the world. Claude Makelele must look to finish his career at Chelsea with even more trophies. Everyone must be hungry to improve. I will not have anyone thinking their place in the team is already waiting for them just because they have been fantastic this season.'

With the dust still settling on this year's achievements and three Premiership games still to go, Mourinho is already putting in the groundwork for next season. 'There was a scream of victory at Bolton, but this game against Charlton will be the last day for enjoyment,' he says. 'The day after we went out of the Champions League at Liverpool I had a meeting with Roman Abramovich, Peter Kenyon and director Eugene Tenenbaum to prepare for next season. I spoke to my players and told them a lot of people would be jumping for joy because we did something great. But we are not happy. We want much more. Some players in football win one simple, small cup and they are up on the moon. And they can sleep happily with one trophy. But I cannot work with players like that. Winning the Premiership is just the start of the process at Chelsea – not the end of it. I am always looking forward, never backwards.

'We will be back for pre-season training on 6 July and I expect to have all the new signings in place by then. Last year I did not arrive at Chelsea until the end of May and I had just one month to make a lot of changes to the playing and coaching staff. This time I only need to make a couple of changes and I have two months to do it. So it will be much easier. It will be difficult for me to sign any English players because to improve the squad I need the very top players. But the best Englishmen are already with the top Premiership clubs. In Italy it's easy because AC Milan are not afraid to sell to Inter or Juventus. But here Chelsea and Manchester United will not swap players because we're scared they will perform well for our rivals.'

Abramovich pledges his commitment to the club, vowing to make them the biggest in the world in a special address to the fans in the match-day programme for the Charlton game. 'I view this championship as just the beginning of a new era for Chelsea and would like to reiterate my long-term commitment to the club. Much has been said about the financial outlay over the past two years. However, this must be seen in the context of placing Chelsea on a level playing field with the other top clubs in England and Europe for a sustained period. We have made solid investments on the field in players, management, training facilities and an academy that will nurture the next generation of home-grown talent.

'Off the field, a team of executives and senior managers has been put together to grow the business and capitalise on the playing success. All of this is a deliberate, long-term strategy with the aim of building the most successful football club in the world in the next ten years and beyond. Under chairman Bruce Buck, chief executive Peter Kenyon and Jose Mourinho, we have a strong leadership team that shares my vision.'

SATURDAY, 7 MAY 2005

CHELSEA 1, CHARLTON ATHLETIC 0

It's a day of celebration as John Terry lifts the Premiership trophy, 50 years after Chelsea's last league triumph. The players are still on the pitch nearly two hours after the final whistle as Mourinho quietly leaves the stadium with wife Tami and kids Matilde and Jose.

'I am happy, I am tired and I need a holiday,' Jose declares. 'But now we look ahead. Enjoy today because tomorrow we start planning for next season. It's not in my nature to be happy with what I have got now ... I want more.'

Chelsea's unbeaten league run stretches to 27 games. Carlo Cudicini, appearing in his first league game of the campaign, has the satisfaction of keeping the clean sheet that takes Chelsea past the Premiership record of 24 in a season. Mourinho reveals his team started celebrating on 15 January when they won at Spurs and Arsenal lost at Bolton. In his programme notes he simply lists the 102 members of his staff – from captain to cook – and declares, 'These are my champions.'

However much Mourinho and his players are still smarting at their Champions League exit, thousands of fans inside Stamford Bridge do not allow that defeat to spoil their day. They chant for Abramovich and for Mourinho, they 'stand up for the champions' and they hail Terry and Lampard. And that is just before kick-off.

Compared to the celebrations, the match is merely a sideshow. Chelsea wait until the final minute before Lampard is brought down on the edge of the box. The foul looks to have been outside the area and contact is, at best, minimal, but the penalty is still given. The ball is handed to Makelele, whose first effort is saved, but he nets the rebound with a mishit to score his first goal for the club in his 94th appearance.

His team-mates joke that he doesn't even come close to scoring in training: in penalty practice on Friday he missed two out of two! But that doesn't stop the players ushering him forward to the spot. When he finally forces the ball over the line, Makelele is promptly buried under an avalanche of team-mates, a testimony to both his talent and popularity. Charlton just have time to kick off again before ref Mike Riley blows the whistle to allow Chelsea's celebrations to begin.

Mourinho insists his players disobeyed his strict orders. 'I said if there's a penalty – Frank Lampard. If there's a penalty in minute 90 with us leading 2–0, then Makelele.'

But the late winner is deserved, even though it is so fortuitous. Chelsea create several first-half chances, but Lampard directs one free header over the bar and Gudjohnsen volleys another effort wide. Charlton are indebted to keeper Stephan Andersen, who produces one acrobatic save to tip a fierce drive by Cole onto the bar, while he is also out quickly to foil the midfielder as he breaks clear. Cole clips another shot wide of the far post, but Charlton also threaten on the break, Jonathan Fortune lifting one half-chance over the bar and directing another effort inches wide. Charlton's goal continues to live a charmed life after the restart, with Terry rising to meet Johnson's deep cross, only to crash his header against the face of the bar.

Cudicini is required to produce an excellent save to tip Matt Holland's drive around the post. Still Chelsea press and still they waste openings. Lampard clips the ball through to Cole, who fires that chance wide before promptly flashing another effort over the top.

Mourinho needs goals, but instead opts for sentiment, bringing on third-choice keeper Lenny Pidgeley for his first-team debut with nine minutes left. Pidgeley is soon called upon to make an important block, but the real drama is reserved until the last minute when Makelele strikes his late penalty winner.

The Premiership trophy awaits and Stamford Bridge's celebrations can finally begin in earnest. There is an elongated presentation ceremony as all the backroom staff are individually introduced and paraded before the fans and make their way to the winners' podium before the players. Mourinho explains, 'On the pitch I got my entire staff together and said to them, "Enjoy the day because tomorrow we must think about the future."'

Before the 2005 team lift the trophy, 13 members of the 1955 side are brought out with the old Football League trophy. Terry and Lampard hand over the trophy to them that was never publicly presented 50 years ago. It is a wonderful addition to the occasion. Then it is on to the main event. 'Are you watching Arsenal!' and 'Chelsea are back!' are sung with gusto as staff and players are brought out of the tunnel one-by-one. Many Charlton fans sportingly stay behind and clap. Roy Bentley and Stan Willemse, legends from 1955, carry out the Premiership trophy and Terry lifts it to the accompaniment of explosions and streamers.

There are tears and much singing as no one wants to go home. An impromptu football match breaks out between the players' kids in front of the Shed, and Cole is booed when he joins in. Finally the team reluctantly troop off down the tunnel, Lampard, Terry, Gudjohnsen and the trophy the last to leave.

One banner reads 'What blip? Chelsea FC Champions 2005', while another simply states 'Jose Mourinho for Prime Minister'.

Team

Cudicini (Pidgeley), Johnson (Jarosik), Terry, Carvalho, Gallas, Makelele, Cole, Lampard, Tiago (Forssell), Geremi, Gudjohnsen.

TUESDAY, 10 MAY 2005

MAN UTD 1, CHELSEA 3

For the first time in 103 league matches, United are beaten after taking the lead. Goals from Tiago, Gudjohnsen and Cole not only inflict United's only home league defeat of the season, but also allow Mourinho's men to rewrite the record books. Victory means Chelsea break United's Premiership records for points and wins in a season. After going behind to Ruud van Nistelrooy's goal, Chelsea take total control. Those United fans who remain to the end clap Chelsea off the pitch. Sir Alex Ferguson now knows just how far his team are behind Chelsea.

While United's in-house television channel hosts a debate on whether Chelsea are worthy champions, Ferguson lauds Mourinho's 'formidable achievement'. Writing in his programme notes, Ferguson promises 'no cheap Portuguese plonk in the manager's office tonight, but fine wine deserving of a champion.

'For a manager new to the country and the English game, breaking entirely new ground, it is a formidable achievement. We know Chelsea have raised the financial stakes but money isn't the total reason for success. There's still a team to be built, balance to be created, tactics to be applied and spirit generated. All this Jose has done. To come into the Premiership and leave us all standing is brilliant and everyone at Manchester United offers sincere congratulations.'

Ferguson makes his players form a guard of honour for Mourinho's title-winners – a sporting gesture, although possibly done to remind his charges that their standards have slipped. Roy Keane does not look comfortable with the whole plan. The Chelsea team emerge to a chorus of boos from the crowd. Wayne Rooney and Gary Neville scowl. It is one of the more surreal moments of the season. 'Have you ever won the Treble?' comes the query from the Stretford End. Chelsea fans react by chanting 'One Malcolm Glazer'.

Keane is soon cautioned for catching Cole, and is lucky not to walk for upending Lampard. By then United are ahead, with Keane and particularly Wayne Rooney playing their parts in Van Nistelrooy's eighth-minute poacher's goal. From the wreckage of a United corner, Keane lays the ball back to Paul Scholes, whose firm shot is diverted by Robert Huth to Rooney. The England international drills the ball into the box for Van Nistelrooy to pounce from close range with a confident flick. Johnson is guilty of playing the Dutchman onside and failing to react. Chelsea's defence is simply not the same without Terry.

Chelsea respond stylishly to the rare indignity of falling behind in a Premiership game. Within ten minutes the new champions are level. Tiago collects possession 35 yards out and spots the United players are dropping off him expecting a pass, so he lets fly. His beautiful arcing shot rises and dips, leaving Roy Carroll completely bemused in the United goal. Carvalho then denies Van Nistelrooy with a wonderful late interception, while the busy Rooney also goes close. Cole also sends a curling shot narrowly wide in a competitive first half.

After the break Darren Fletcher is unlucky not to match Tiago's attempt as his effort cannons off the woodwork. And it is not long before Chelsea are in front as Lampard feeds Tiago, whose driven low pass is controlled by Gudjohnsen. The Icelander waits for Carroll to commit himself and coolly dinks the ball over the on-rushing keeper.

Gaps begin to appear in the United defence and another Chelsea goal seems more likely than an equaliser for the home side. Sure enough, inside the last ten minutes, Wes Brown's clearance is cut out by Lampard, who darts into the area and cuts the ball back for Cole. There are clear suspicions of offside as he turns the ball home, but the travelling Chelsea faithful are not bothered.

In happier times Sir Alex would pick up the microphone after Manchester United's final home game of the season and deliver a victory speech to the masses. Now Chelsea have established a new order to English football, United's manager is silent. Instead, Old Trafford hears the clanking of emptying plastic seats long before the final whistle. Those who stay see Ferguson's players embark on a lap of 'honour' with heavy hearts. Ferguson is in denial afterwards, pontificating about a 'marvellous spectacle' while neatly swerving any possible criticisms of his team. But there is one brief moment of acceptance that they have come up against superior opponents. 'Once Chelsea's second goal went in they were worthy winners,' he says. 'Chelsea played like you expect champions to play – with authority.'

Mourinho describes beating United's record points total as 'perfect'. 'The record was our motivation,' says Mourinho. 'We wanted to beat it and this is a special moment. It is the perfect way to do it – at a great stadium against a team who in Sir Alex Ferguson have a manager who leads by example in success and fair play.'

> **Team**
>
> Cudicini, Geremi, Huth, Carvalho, Gallas, Makelele, Johnson (Jarosik), Lampard, Tiago, Cole (Grant), Gudjohnsen (Morais).

There is only ever going to be one winner of the Barclays Manager of the Year award. Mourinho's landslide victory in the championship race earns him the required majority in the voting panel's ballot. Only once has the champion manager not been given the award. In 2001 when Ferguson led United to the title, George Burley won it after lifting Ipswich Town to an unexpected fifth place. It was also the year Gerard Houllier won three trophies with Liverpool. David Moyes and Rafael Benitez have valid claims this year, but they are still not going to deny Mourinho.

SUNDAY, 15 MAY 2005
NEWCASTLE 1, CHELSEA 1

Mourinho concedes that he will struggle to surpass this record-breaking season as Chelsea move on to an unprecedented Premiership haul of 95 points and set yet another record for the fewest goals conceded in a season – a mere 15. Mourinho observes, 'The record does make you realise this season has been magnificent. It has been fantastic and that is why I want to stay in this country. It is the best football country in the world. Our objective will be to be champions again and improve in certain aspects, but we know next season will be harder because people know the side and what we can do.'

Newcastle are gifted the lead when Geremi inadvertently diverts the ball in after Alan Shearer rises to head on Charles N'Zogbia's 32nd-minute corner. The home side's advantage is short-lived. Celestine Babayaro misjudges Lampard's through-ball and resorts to fouling Gudjohnsen inside the penalty box. Lampard steps up to beat Given, driving the ball straight down the middle, despite losing his footing as he strikes the ball, for his 19th goal of a memorable campaign.

After the break, Jermaine Jenas miscues from close range and Cudicini does well to palm away Patrick Kluivert's header. Shay Given also excels with a save from Gudjohnsen and somehow claws an effort from Jarosik away at the death.

Mourinho generally takes the biscuit, but this time he takes two – as he is walking away from the press room, Mourinho smiles and grabs a couple for the journey back to London. His Chelsea team, missing eight of their significant contributors this season, have just extended their Premiership points record by one and but for a brilliant reaction save by Given from Jarosik near the end, it would have been three.

Chelsea's record on the road is 15 wins, three draws and one defeat. Their total of 95 points – meaning they finish 12 points ahead of Arsenal – will take some matching. So will the record 25 clean sheets. 'It is an unbelievable record,' says Mourinho with all the modesty he can muster. 'Ninety-five points is a lot of points. The clean sheets gave us a big push to be champions. At the beginning of the season, when we were not so fluent, clean sheets gave us a lot of points. People said Chelsea were boring, but Chelsea were building.'

And Mourinho has not finished building just yet. 'We started thinking about the next campaign a few months ago,' he says. 'It's easy to prepare for next season as we have a group of champions and want to keep them. We want to make two or three adjustments but we have the base.'

Team

Cudicini, Geremi, Huth, Carvalho, Johnson, Cole (Morais), Makelele, Lampard, Tiago, Jarosik (Watt), Gudjohnsen (Oliveira).

The Champions League

'I HAVE TO DEFEND WHAT IS MINE. THE CHAMPIONS LEAGUE IS MINE AT THE MOMENT. I AM THE LAST WINNER AS MANAGER OF THE CHAMPIONS LEAGUE – SO IT IS MY COMPETITION.'

Jose Mourinho

Chelsea's Champions League campaign couldn't start with a more controversial and intriguing draw in Monte Carlo. Jose Mourinho will begin the defence of the Champions League he won with Porto in a group that includes CSKA Moscow, a team sponsored by Roman Abramovich. The other teams in Group H are Paris Saint-Germain and Porto.

Chelsea's Russian owner has ploughed £40m into a sponsorship deal with CSKA – and the multi-billionaire's links to both clubs spark an investigation by UEFA. Ironically, Abramovich was in Scotland to cheer on CSKA as they reached the group stage by beating Rangers in the qualifiers and he was invited into the dressing room afterwards to congratulate the team.

His oil company, Sibneft, is the club's main sponsor and UEFA spokesman William Gaillard says, 'This has to be looked at thoroughly to see whether there is a controlling interest by Abramovich in CSKA because the teams are in the same group.'

After carrying out a week-long investigation, UEFA declare themselves satisfied that Abramovich does not have a controlling interest in CSKA Moscow. A UEFA spokesperson says, 'The investigation is over.'

Anyone who thinks Mourinho cares only for big-money signings should see him on the morning before the Champions League draw. He is watching Chelsea Under-13s from behind one of the goals. 'That's the second time he's been down here in two weeks,' says Chelsea's academy director Neil Bath.

'Jose's produced a document for the [academy] coaching staff and scouting staff which sets out the philosophy he'd like to see,' says Bath. 'He's very clear about the type of player he'd like coming through. He wants players who are physically, technically and tactically capable of playing in the first team and have experienced the systems of play and the typical training methods that he implements. So we have spent time watching his training sessions and reading up on his philosophy.'

As they approach their opening Champions League tie in Paris, Chelsea have kept four consecutive clean sheets in the Premiership. Mourinho says, 'It's important to be strong defensively. It's about being compact and that can be beautiful.'

Striker Didier Drogba expects a hostile reception from the Paris crowd because of his Marseille associations. So far this season PSG have failed to win a single league game and are 14th in the table. Mourinho is even tempted to alter his usual safety-first approach. 'If you start the group stage at home, you have to win. Away, you have to get a point. If we leave Paris with a point, normally it is good for the next stage. But that is not the way we are thinking. We come here to play with a victory in mind. We are not going to play a defensive game.'

TUESDAY, 14 SEPTEMBER 2004
PARIS SAINT-GERMAIN 0, CHELSEA 3

Jeered by PSG fans from the moment his name is announced, striker Didier Drogba has cause to laugh after his two goals secure an away victory that already makes Chelsea's progression to the second round look a safe bet.

In fact, the only real surprise is that it takes Chelsea 29 minutes to take the lead. Joe Cole's clever turn brings the corner that results in the opener. Frank Lampard floats in a cross from the left, goalkeeper Lionel Letizi flaps at the ball and John Terry can hardly believe his good fortune as he nods in. Mateja Kezman is brought down for a free-kick 15 minutes from time and Drogba picks his spot over the wall, leaving the keeper without a prayer.

The game is settled in added time when Tiago wins the ball and Cole instantly releases Kezman through on the left. The Serb, on for Gudjohnsen, shoots straight at Letizi, but Drogba is perfectly placed to stroke home the rebound. Each time he scores the man from the Ivory Coast cups his hands to his ears in mockery of the home fans, mimicking the goal celebrations of their Portuguese striker Pauleta, and blows kisses at them for good measure.

Jeered mercilessly by PSG supporters throughout the game, Drogba walks off bare-chested when the final whistle blows. Drogba admits, 'I did wind them up but they wound me up a bit as well, didn't they? I lost against them three times for Marseille last season so it was important for me to score and for the team to win. We're very pleased. The manager said we could win and we wanted the three points so we could be top of the group because we know we are the sort of team that should be top.'

Mourinho adds, 'People always want to talk about the dark side of football but Didier showed tonight why I pressed my board to bring him to this club. He was the man of the match, scored two goals and respected everybody. He only wanted to show how much he loves both countries. If you love football, even if you're a PSG supporter, you should only be pleased with the performance you saw Didier give.

'We played top-class football and controlled the game from the first minute to the last. Our use of the ball was superb and we were in charge of the tempo and pace of the game while defensively we were incredible again. We could have scored more goals but we made it look easy. That was a measure of how well we played because Paris were not an easy team to beat.'

Lampard too hails Drogba. 'Didier's got pace, power and great finishing ability and can get us 20 or 30 goals this season, like Thierry Henry does for Arsenal. We've been lacking a player with real pace and power and now Didier's doing it. He's very strong, has good feet and is very willing to run for the team. It's nice to have a big figure up front that you can pick out straight away.'

> **Team**
> Cech, Gallas, Ferreira, Terry, Bridge, Lampard, Cole, Tiago, Makelele, Drogba, Gudjohnsen (Kezman).

Mischief in the fixture calendar brings FC Porto to Stamford Bridge four months after Mourinho led Porto to victory in the European Cup. Chelsea are like Mourinho's Porto in that they play a midfield diamond and largely leave the job of winger to their full-backs. Chelsea also guard the ball jealously. 'You can see some of last season's Porto in the way Chelsea now play,' says Tiago. 'Maybe it's in the possession of the ball, maybe in the organisation of the game, especially in midfield, which is tight and quite close together. They had Deco, but apart from that I think we have more attacking options. I don't think you can call us a defensive team.'

Abramovich paid £33m to Porto for defenders Paulo Ferreira and Ricardo Carvalho. Porto also sold Deco to Barcelona and Pedro Mendes to Tottenham. Despite their newfound wealth, Porto are struggling. Going into the weekend, they have drawn all three of their domestic Superliga matches and, in their opening Champions League contest, they could do no better than manage a goalless draw at home to CSKA Moscow.

With six wins and two draws in his first eight matches, the only thing upsetting Mourinho is what he perceives to be persistent and unfair criticism of his tactics. Chelsea are not exactly playing with the panache of Arsenal, but in their ability to retain possession and control the tempo of a game, Chelsea are showing a tactical intelligence that Arsene Wenger and Sir Alex Ferguson have seldom coaxed from their sides.

WEDNESDAY, 29 SEPTEMBER 2004

CHELSEA 3, PORTO 1

The match begins with an unsavoury incident as Jose Mourinho goes over to shake the hands of Porto fans before kick-off and a yob pushes forward and spits on his shirt. Disgusted at what has happened, Mourinho takes a step back and security guards manhandle the idiot out of the ground.

Revenge is not long in coming. After seven minutes, Chelsea score their first goal when Damien Duff flicks the ball over the head of a defender for Eidur Gudjohnsen to hook a first-time cross into the middle where the unmarked Alexei Smertin drives a shot deep into the far corner for his first goal for the club. It brings the former Porto boss to his feet in celebration – not far from the Portuguese fans – which, in turn, produces a warning from the fourth official for Mourinho to cool it.

Didier Drogba, the second most expensive striker in the Premiership behind Wayne Rooney, does his best to give Chelsea fans something to celebrate following the Old Trafford wonder kid's amazing hat-trick against Fenerbahce. With Chelsea coasting on the back of Smertin's opener, he strikes with a header from a Duff free-kick in the 50th minute to reignite the game.

Benni McCarthy then gives Porto a lifeline by netting a 68th-minute rebound after Petr Cech fails to hold a stinging shot from Carlos Alberto that skims John Terry's head. The Chelsea skipper, though, takes just two minutes to respond, diving full length to head home Frank Lampard's free-kick.

After the game, a jubilant Mourinho lavishes praise on a group of players he clearly believes is good enough to bring the Champions

League trophy to Stamford Bridge. 'It's great. We've beaten the European champions, have six points and are in a fantastic position to go through to the next stage.

'I have a fantastic group of players at Chelsea. We have the right personalities, the right characters and for me it's amazing to see the way they fight in every match. At some of the top clubs the big names think more about themselves than the team. But my big players play for the team. That is why no one has beaten us in nine matches.'

Porto manager Victor Fernandez acknowledges the value of Lampard's deliveries from set-pieces. 'One of our problems was Lampard at free-kicks because we were playing against some of the best headers of the ball in Europe.'

Chelsea have now ended a run of four successive Champions League draws at Stamford Bridge. Considering they reached last season's semi-final, it comes as a surprise that this is only their second home win in seven European matches.

It also marks the end of a record-breaking run of 12 Champions League games without defeat for Porto and continues a sorry run in which they have been beaten seven times in eight trips to England. The 1–1 draw, when they knocked out Manchester United last season, was the only point they gained.

Team

Cech, Ferreira, Carvalho, Terry, Gallas, Smertin, Makelele, Lampard, Duff (Tiago), Gudjohnsen (Kezman), Drogba.

Jose Mourinho pens a personal letter to UEFA chiefs begging them not to punish his old club after UEFA announce they will be taking action against Porto following the spitting incident at Stamford Bridge.

Helder Mota, the fan who spat at Mourinho, is a member of FC Porto's fanatical Super Dragons supporters club. He describes Mourinho as an old pal and makes wild claims, fiercely denied by

Mourinho, that the Chelsea manager has been sending his wife saucy text messages. 'When I saw Mourinho, the blood came rushing to my head and I couldn't stop myself. It was everything: the fact that he was texting Luciana behind my back, the fact that he abandoned Porto and the fact that we used to be friends. On Wednesday he didn't even acknowledge me when he came to within feet of where the Super Dragons were to sign autographs. I ran up to him and spat in his face twice. Four stewards threw me out of the ground and I had to watch the match on TV.'

Mota has also admitted making a death threat against Mourinho the night before the Champions League final. 'Spitting at Mourinho is only half of what I want to do to him. I am prepared to go to prison over this.' Mourinho is taking Mota's threats seriously and has informed police. Chelsea will also increase security for Mourinho during the return match in Porto.

Chelsea face CSKA Moscow in a week when plans to make a musical of Roman Abramovich's life are announced at the same time as the Russian government continues to investigate his finances. Mourinho says, 'CSKA are a very good side. They went to Porto and did not concede a goal. That shows how strong they are. If they get points against us at Stamford Bridge or in Moscow, they'll be in a very strong position.'

Mourinho's main worry is the form of Vagner Love, the Brazilian whose goals have taken CSKA to the top of the Russian league, which they lead by one point with four games to play. CSKA bought Love in the summer for £6m, with money provided by Sibneft. With Drogba injured, Mourinho has no choice but to pair Kezman with Gudjohnsen up front. The Serb has yet to score in ten appearances for Chelsea.

Drawing a blank at Manchester City resulted in Chelsea's first defeat under Mourinho at the weekend. Now he expects a response. 'We do not lose much and we did not enjoy the taste. I have no doubts my players will give me a good answer.'

WEDNESDAY, 20 OCTOBER 2004

CHELSEA 2, CSKA MOSCOW 0

Before the match, Jose Mourinho is presented with the European Club Manager of the Year award by Sir Bobby Robson. In the crowd, the contingent of Moscow fans holds up a giant banner with a message to Abramovich written in Cyrillic script: 'Abramovich, give us three points'. But their team begins as though it does not need any help from the man who pays £10m a season to have the name of his oil company, Sibneft, on their shirts. Chelsea are soon on the back foot as CSKA come out fighting.

However, in the ninth minute, Chelsea make the Russians pay when they expose their defensive frailties with a Frank Lampard corner to the back post. Eidur Gudjohnsen rises high above the defenders to nod the ball back across goal and John Terry stoops to head it across the line from close range. It is his third goal of the season and maintains his record of scoring in every Champions League game this campaign. Then there is a scare for the home side. Early substitute Laizans takes a corner that skids across the area, bounces off Gudjohnsen's back and is heading for the top corner until Petr Cech arches his back to produce a fine reaction save and tip the ball over.

CSKA's aerial weakness at the back undoes them again in first-half injury-time from another Chelsea dead ball. Duff swings over a free-kick from the right-hand side of the area and Gudjohnsen runs unchallenged between two defenders and leaps to power his header past Igor Akinfeev. It is only the Iceland striker's second goal of the season but it gives Chelsea a commanding lead at the top of Group H.

Later Mourinho hails goalkeeper Cech. 'The boy is doing fantastic for us. The first half was very difficult for us. They started the game better and had one or two good chances. Our goalkeeper made one or two great saves and the second goal came at the right time for us mentally.'

Chelsea could not have done better than win their first three group matches, but efficiency rather than excitement has been the keyword tonight. The lowest crowd of the season – 33,945 – is a big surprise. These big European nights used to be special, highly charged occasions. Mourinho says, 'I like a full stadium. Maybe it wasn't full because of Chelsea's past record at home in the Champions League. But now that we've beaten Porto and CSKA, maybe they'll all come to see us play PSG.'

However, a win in Moscow will guarantee Chelsea top spot and that would render the visit of PSG largely academic.

> **Team**
>
> Cech, Bridge, Terry, Gallas, Ferreira, Lampard, Duff (Cole), Smertin (Parker), Makelele, Kezman (Tiago), Gudjohnsen.

Former Chelsea manager Claudio Ranieri's honeymoon at Valencia is over after they are thrashed 5–1 at home by Inter Milan in the Champions League. Valencia face an uphill struggle to qualify for the second stage after losing two of their first three games.

Alexei Smertin claims Chelsea are now the biggest team in Russia. Smertin is a hero in his home country, where his popularity is similar in stature to that of David Beckham, Steven Gerrard or Michael Owen in England. 'Chelsea is the most popular team in Russia now. English football is now so big in Russia that they can watch every Chelsea game. Every time I come home they want to know what is happening here.'

Mourinho's side need just a point in Moscow to claim their place in the last 16 of the European Cup and they trail Premiership leaders Arsenal only on goal difference. But he plays down growing expectations of a double by claiming clubs from Europe's biggest leagues cannot conquer the continent as well as their own country. Since United did it in 1999, Porto are the first team to have won their domestic title and the Champions League in the same year. 'I know Manchester United won the title and the Champions League in 1999 but it's really difficult. It happens once in a lifetime. For me it's happened twice in the last two years [with Porto]. I don't think this will be the third consecutive year.'

Mourinho and his players arrive in the Lokomotiv Stadium on the same coach as Roman Abramovich. Conspiracy theorists have been claiming any result other than a Chelsea victory will be 'a fix' to help CSKA qualify. When Abramovich steps off Chelsea's team bus before training, he is clearly relishing the build-up. On Sunday he is also seen mingling in a hotel with visitors who include Sir Bobby Robson. But it comes as no surprise that he does not join Chelsea players and coaches on a visit to Red Square where hard man John Terry braves the cold in shorts and flip-flops.

Mourinho insists this is just another game for Abramovich, which is hard to believe. The Russian is on home soil and, as well as his sponsorship of CSKA, he is also a close friend of the club's president, Evgeny Giner, and has been to at least one of their home games this season.

Mourinho offers an insight into Abramovich's involvement with the squad. 'He's very committed with us. He's not just the owner, he also wants to win like the pros. Every single match since the beginning [of the season] he's been involved ... he feels part of the group and also the group feels he's part of us. We are always very comfortable when he is with us and I think he feels the same among the pros.'

Much interest in Moscow centres on whether Smertin will play. Mourinho says, 'I have to choose not with emotion, with heart, with relations with countries but with what is best for the team.'

Victory will allow Chelsea to turn their attentions to the Premiership. Indeed they face Arsenal just five days after their final Champions League group game, away to Porto, which may be meaningless by then. A result here could make the twin challenge less of an impossible task.

TUESDAY, 2 NOVEMBER 2004

CSKA MOSCOW o, CHELSEA 1

Mourinho hails Arjen Robben as his 'extra dimension' after the Dutchman's first goal enables Chelsea to become the first team to qualify for the last 16, with two games to spare. Robben's sweetly stroked first-half finish is enough to complete Chelsea's perfect passage through Group H.

The build-up to the 23rd-minute goal is elegant as Robben slips through to find Damien Duff's diagonal run before racing into the box to receive the Irishman's back-heel. The finish is sublime, as Robben allows the ball to run beyond the lunge of Sergei Semak before looking up and passing it left-footed into the bottom corner.

Roman Abramovich grants himself a small grin as the ball rolls into the net. Nearby, former Russian President Boris Yeltsin suggests his vodka supply has not yet been entirely cut off as he throws a minor tantrum in the directors' box. The Russian elite are out in force.

By half-time Chelsea have conceded ten corners – the most they have given away in any game this season has been 11, also against CSKA. But the key to their success here is the rapid transition from rock-solid defence to rampaging counter-attacks – the hallmark of Mourinho's Porto. Robben is a particularly useful asset when you play this way.

Chelsea have a close call when Brazilian Vagner Love blasts a second-half penalty high over the bar after Glen Johnson's wild foul on Yuri Zhirkov. Mourinho says, 'Glen has to play these matches to learn from his mistakes. He has to control his position and avoid sliding tackles.' Johnson, making just his second start for Mourinho, travels back to London wondering if he will get another chance.

Chelsea have conceded only four times in 16 matches this season and their performances will have been noted in Madrid, Barcelona, Milan and Turin as well as Highbury and Old Trafford. Today John Terry and Ricardo Carvalho have been all but impenetrable in front of

Petr Cech, while midfielder Scott Parker has shown how determined he is to be considered for a first-team place.

Robben, who linked so brilliantly with Duff before firing home, says, 'It was a great goal to score and I finished it quite well. I knew what I was doing and last year in the Champions League I did exactly the same, going one way and shooting in the other corner. It was a great combination with Damien and a good finish. I'm sure we can play in the same team – I've always said that.'

John Terry believes Chelsea's magnificent Champions League performances have sent shockwaves around Europe. 'Real Madrid and AC Milan may be the best teams in Europe, but the way we're playing at the moment I'm sure we can match them, if not better them. We've looked very solid in the Champions League so far and are sending out a message to the rest of Europe. It was a great performance and four wins out of four is a fantastic start. We've been scoring a lot more goals and have only conceded one in four games, which shows how well we're playing.'

Having now won the group, Chelsea are free to focus on the Premiership until the knockout stages begin at the end of February, though there will be no let-up from Mourinho. He says, 'We will face the next stage against the second-placed team but I promise CSKA that we will play exactly the same way against PSG and Porto. Anyone who thinks we will take it easy is making a big mistake.'

> **Team**
>
> Cech, Johnson, Terry, Carvalho, Gallas (Ferreira), Duff, Parker (Tiago), Lampard, Makelele, Robben, Gudjohnsen (Kezman).

Chelsea lodge an official complaint with UEFA because around 50 of their fans with tickets were stopped from entering CSKA's ground and missed most of the first half. UEFA will also investigate a flare thrown from the crowd at Petr Cech.

After being out for five weeks following a groin operation, Didier Drogba returns to the squad for the encounter with Paris Saint-

Germain. 'The team is improving because of time together,' Drogba says, 'and it is easier to come back into a winning team. I will have to give my best.'

The French club are third in the Group H table with four points and desperately need good results to progress. 'We want to win these last two matches,' says Mourinho. 'I will make some changes and rest some players, but the team I put out will still be a good one. The truth is, though, that my team have done the job in the Champions League while Paris Saint-Germain and Porto have not.'

When Mourinho left the pitch in the Lokomotiv Stadium after victory over CSKA Moscow, he made a promise to Valeri Gazzayev, the CSKA coach. He assured Gazzayev that, even though they were through to the last 16, his team would not be relaxing in their final fixtures against Paris Saint-Germain and FC Porto. 'In the players' tunnel,' Mourinho says, 'I told the Russian coach that he could be sure that my team would be fighting for results against PSG and Porto. If CSKA want to be the second-best team in the group, it is up to them.'

'This is not a dead match,' he insists. 'I told the players that we are better than PSG, but motivation will make the difference. The players have to fight for a position in the team and I look not at their faces, who they are or how much they might have cost. I look for what they can give me in the performance.'

WEDNESDAY, 24 NOVEMBER 2004
CHELSEA 0, PARIS SAINT-GERMAIN 0

Ominously, PSG have failed to win an away game in Europe for seven years. Despite the sell-out crowd at Stamford Bridge, this game proves that dead group matches are a turn-off. The French club have plenty more to play for with qualification between them, Porto and CSKA Moscow still in the balance but the match never catches fire.

Jose Mourinho rests nearly £80m worth of talent in Petr Cech, John Terry, Eidur Gudjohnsen, Damien Duff, Claude Makelele and Tiago. In come Carlo Cudicini, Glen Johnson, Joe Cole, Scott Parker and Mateja Kezman. Didier Drogba returns from injury to sit on the bench but Chelsea still lose their 100 per cent record in Group H. Having already reached the second phase before the game starts, Chelsea do not create a real chance until the 81st minute when Drogba fires straight at keeper Lionel Letizi.

Still the game presents a rare chance for some of Mourinho's squad to press a claim to the first-team in the build-up to their crunch match with Arsenal at Highbury. Chelsea certainly start brightly enough as the lively Arjen Robben probes and presses for an opening, while Kezman looks a constant threat.

Joe Cole, one of the players with most to prove, sets up Kezman but the Serb has rarely shown the sort of goalscoring form which made him such a threat for PSV Eindhoven and once again he wastes a good opening from 20 yards. Ironically the best entertainment comes from the rollicking Mourinho gives Cole from the touchline for being badly positioned at a free-kick just before the break.

At half-time Mourinho proves that not even the in-form Robben is irreplaceable as he takes off the Dutchman and sticks on Duff to try to give his team fresh impetus. But Mourinho's second-choice team do not manage a single shot on target until the 60th minute when skipper for the night Frank Lampard produces an effort on the turn that is easily saved.

The PSG fans are busy barracking Drogba, who comes on in place of Kezman, for his Marseille connections, while Mourinho then throws on Gudjohnsen for Lampard. Drogba's comeback after seven weeks on the sidelines turns out to be the only highlight. He has a chance to gain revenge for the taunts of the visiting French fans just minutes after coming on but his well-taken 'goal' is disallowed for offside.

Mourinho makes no excuses for sending out a much-changed side. 'The fact that I rested a lot of players was good. My attitude will be the same against Porto in the sense that we will try to win. We did not give the match to PSG – they had to fight.

'All my players are playing regularly and for their national teams, so if I cannot give them a rest – we don't really need the points to get through – then I am stupid. We tried to win and had some chances, the last of which was a great one and could have killed the game.'

For PSG coach Vahid Halilhodzic it is very much a case of mission accomplished as his team keep alive their hopes of making the last 16. 'This result puts us in good stead to hold on to second place in the group,' he declares.

Reflecting on the end of Chelsea's perfect record in the Champions League, Mourinho says, 'It's nice to have a 100 per cent record. But the first objective in this competition is to go through.'

> **Team**
>
> Cudicini, Johnson, Carvalho, Gallas, Bridge, Smertin, Parker, Lampard (Gudjohnsen), Cole, Kezman (Drogba), Robben (Duff).

Chief executive Peter Kenyon's appraisal of the manager he's worked alongside for four months hasn't changed. 'Jose has all the traits of someone who's supremely confident in his own ability, has a firm belief in what he's trying to do and, above all, has a minutely detailed approach to the game. He's created a complete team ethic, a squad that's totally together. His methods of coaching are challenging and interesting and he's a natural leader: someone who commands total respect.'

Meanwhile, Jose Mourinho's lawyer asks judicial officials to provide extra security when he returns to his old club Porto. Under Portuguese law, the Porto supporter who spat on Mourinho is barred from the return game. When asked if he needs bodyguards, Mourinho says, 'Yes. If you visit Palermo [Sicily] you probably also need [them].' This remark arouses much indignation on the Italian island. Banners at Palermo's home match against Atalanta read, 'Mourinho – Champion of Ignorance'.

Mourinho relates how his greatest triumph – managing the European champions in 2004 – nearly turned into a nightmare. The evening before Porto beat Monaco 3–0 in Gelsenkirchen, Mourinho took a call. It was from a well-known figure in Porto's underworld. 'The person on the other end told me, "You think you're the best, you bastard. We won't do anything now because you have a final tomorrow. But as soon as it's over, consider yourself a dead man because we'll get you. As soon as you get back to Porto, your fate is sealed. You don't have a chance." I replied, "You must be mad, I don't know what you're talking about."'

Porto president Pinta da Costa adds to the controversy by claiming that Mourinho deserves the threats because of his 'bizarre' behaviour and insists he left the club in a mess by quitting with two years left on his contract.

In these circumstances, Chelsea change their travel plans, bring in private security guards and take police advice on whether Mourinho will be breaking UEFA rules by ducking public appearances. The team will not train on the Porto pitch before the game and Mourinho will skip UEFA's compulsory pre-match press conference.

Chelsea receive a police escort from the airport to their hotel and Steve Clarke admits, 'We are expecting a hostile atmosphere but that is the case in all European away matches. I don't know how Porto's fans will react to Jose. All I know is that, if he won the European Cup for Chelsea and then came back to Stamford Bridge with another club, Jose would get a fantastic reception.'

If Porto fail, the beneficiaries will be CSKA Moscow – the club Abramovich sponsors. Da Costa makes it clear he will not be shaking the hand of Mourinho but the Chelsea coach will find at least one friendly face in the Porto ranks. Defender Pedro Emanuel insists, 'Meeting Mourinho again is going to be very special. He was the person who brought me to Porto and who took a chance on me. I had an excellent relationship with him because of all the good work he did during his time at this club.'

Ricardo Carvalho who, along with Paulo Ferreira, followed Mourinho from Porto, says, 'Porto may have won the Champions

League last season but Chelsea have a better side. I believe Jose, myself and Paulo will get a good reception. Ninety per cent of Porto's supporters will cheer us, I think, because we had such happy times together. But if I foul a former team-mate on the edge of the penalty area as he is about to shoot, they might not cheer me any more.'

TUESDAY, 7 DECEMBER 2004
FC PORTO 2, CHELSEA 1

Ruthless Mourinho shatters any hopes that he will make things easy for his old side when he fields a powerful-looking team. However, Porto are desperate to avoid becoming the first defending champions to crash out of the competition at the group stages and they are also motivated to prevent their ex-coach Mourinho from being the man who knocks them out. They also cling to the fact that, in seven matches on their home turf, they have never been beaten by English opposition.

This, however, is no ordinary English opposition. Chelsea soak up their early pressure, then have the best of the first-half chances. Wayne Bridge sends a right-foot shot narrowly wide of the far post after just three minutes. Didier Drogba then connects with a Frank Lampard cross, forcing keeper Nuno E Santo to push his header against the bar.

Damien Duff strikes on 33 minutes. A solo run is capped by a powerful strike which Nuno lets slip through his fingers to prove exactly why he is normally on the bench when Victor Baia is fit. The Porto game provides compelling evidence that Chelsea function best when playing 4-3-3. As the game progresses the lack of width in Mourinho's midfield diamond, part of tonight's 4-4-2 system, becomes all too apparent.

Diego responds with a stunning goal on the hour. Petr Cech is left rooted to the spot as the Brazilian playmaker sends a 25-yard volley scorching past him with such ferocity that it nearly leaves a hole in the net. Benni McCarthy then strikes with a header to inflict the first defeat on Chelsea in the Champions League and only the second reverse of the season.

In reality, this defeat is more damaging to Mourinho's pride than to his side's long-term prospects. Scott Parker is singled out for particularly harsh treatment, when he is berated at Oporto airport for failing to block Diego's second-half equalizer. Mourinho even goes as far as to question his players' motivation. 'My players were happy with the draw and looked comfortable but Porto had extra motivation.

'The night was a big sensation for me. I worked very hard to detach myself and did my best to win the game. It's a special stadium for me because for two years it was mine. I tried to come here to win and I am frustrated we lost.'

The Blues boss is seething at the defeat but insists it will not affect his build-up for Highbury. 'You can't make any relation between this match and Arsenal. If you could then I'd have played the team that will start against Arsenal – including Claude Makelele and Arjen Robben.'

Before this setback, Mourinho has lost just once in his 24 games in charge. The home supporters further ruined his night by taking out their early frustrations on Drogba and Gallas, who suffered abuse from every corner of the ground, with monkey chants drowned out only by the support of the travelling Chelsea faithful.

The worst came in the 18th minute when Drogba was clattered by Derlei. Mourinho and the rest of the Chelsea bench leapt on to the pitch to register their anger but the home fans responded with the re-emergence of the vile monkey chanting to mar what had previously been a good-natured contest. All in all, a fairly depressing evening.

> **Team**
> Cech, Gallas, Terry, Carvalho, Ferreira, Smertin (Tiago), Lampard, Parker, Bridge, Duff (Robben), Drogba (Kezman).

The possible opponents for Chelsea in the Champions League draw in Nyon are Real Madrid, Barcelona, Bayern Munich, PSV Eindhoven and Werder Bremen. David Beckham claims Europe's elite will be trembling at the prospect of drawing Real Madrid in the knockout phase. The England skipper was instrumental in Real's crucial win behind closed doors in Rome, as Ronaldo's early strike and a Figo double sealed victory over Roma.

For his part, Michael Owen says he would love to face an English club. 'We are very happy to have qualified after winning a very difficult game in Rome,' says Owen, who only played the last five minutes of the encounter. 'I would like to play Chelsea or Arsenal because I think it would be a very attractive fixture.'

Joe Cole meanwhile is hoping Chelsea will be paired with one of the big Spanish sides. He says, 'I'd love to play against either Barcelona or Real Madrid and I'm sure, whoever we play, the games are going to be very tight. Whoever we get, I'd like to think we'd have a very good chance of winning and making it through to the next stage.'

Mourinho is more specific: he wants to be paired with the Catalan giants. After all, he learned his trade at the Nou Camp under Bobby Robson. 'For emotional reasons, I'd like to play Barca. First of all I love the club and the city; I spent four incredible years there. And the second reason is because everyone says they're Europe's best, who play beautiful football. I'd like to play them.

'Everyone is tipping them to win the competition. They play great football and it would be two incredible matches. The Spanish leaders against the English leaders would be a fantastic game – the most powerful tie of the draw. But there are a group of fantastic teams we could play – Barca, Real Madrid, Bayern Munich, Werder Bremen and PSV – and they would all be tough. You always want to play the big teams, the big managers and the big players. But I don't like to play against Italians, so I'm glad we can't face AC Milan, Inter and Juventus.'

As group-winners, Arsenal and Chelsea get to play their first-leg games away. When the draw is made, Chelsea are matched against the 16-time Spanish title-winners Barcelona just as Mourinho predicted.

Barcelona have met Chelsea once before in the Champions League, at the quarter-final stage in April 2000. The Catalans overturned a 3–1 first-leg defeat at Stamford Bridge to go through 6–4 on aggregate after a 5–1 extra-time victory at the Nou Camp.

Mourinho shrugs off the dangers of facing the runaway La Liga leaders by claiming his number one priority is to see Chelsea crowned as English champions for the first time in 50 years. 'Chelsea are a strong team now – but we are in a fight with Arsenal, Manchester United and Everton. We are in a good position. I don't like the word fear in football because I don't believe in fear.

'In their league Barcelona are in an even better position because they have no opponents. Barcelona are alone. Real Madrid and Valencia are too far behind; Deportivo La Coruna have been very poor this season. Barcelona are in a comfortable position so maybe they can prepare for the Champions League in a different way to us.

'At Porto, I could rest eight or nine players before a Champions League game because I had the championship in my pocket by December. In the Premiership we have to fight until the last kick, so maybe they have an advantage. Week after week, match after match, it is harder in England than in Spain.

'I've never won the Premiership and I like to win new things. The Premiership is the ultimate test. It takes a great team to win the Champions League – but the great teams still need luck. There are almost 40 games in England and only the best team wins.'

Mourinho reckons he learned the skills that have made him Europe's hottest boss working under Bobby Robson and Dutchman Louis van Gaal at Barcelona. He left four years ago after helping break Chelsea hearts in that epic 6–4 Champions League quarter-final double bill. He says, 'I go back to Barcelona as European Champion and Chelsea manager. I have a friend in every corner, so it will be a very emotional time for me. But I am keen to play against them because they want to win and play football the pure way. Barcelona is more than a football club; it represents a country. Catalonia is for them a country and Barcelona is its face around the world.

'My son, Jose, was born in Barcelona and has a Spanish passport;

he is a little Catalan, so my blood is speaking here. But he will be supporting Chelsea.

'Chelsea are one of the best clubs in England; we hope they can be the biggest in a few years. Barcelona are a massive club but, as a football team, they are not better than us. When I was assistant manager there, we played Chelsea and they were two great games. Chelsea were a good team then, a young Gianfranco Zola with good players around him. It was Luca Vialli's time and they won a few trophies. We won almost everything at Barcelona.'

Meanwhile, Barcelona star Ronaldinho hints he might be interested in joining Chelsea at some stage in the future. Striker Samuel Eto'o, who has 12 goals for Barca, sets great store by his team-mate and says, 'Ronaldinho is worth half of Chelsea's players. That's our great advantage on the field.'

But Eto'o, who is African Footballer of the Year, insists Chelsea do not always get their man – he knows because Chelsea have missed out on him! The £18m ex-Real Mallorca star says, 'Several times I've been close to signing for Chelsea but the deal was never closed. Now they'll have me on the other side in the Champions League and they'll come out as losers. This is a very special game for everybody involved. The whole world seems to think Chelsea are invincible and the best team in Europe, but I want to help Barca prove that is not true.

'The attack of Chelsea? It does not worry me. For a start, Robben is injured and Drogba is not better than me. Ivory Coast have never beaten Cameroon. I am the best African player, not Drogba. All the world knows that. What has Drogba won? It is fair to say that Chelsea's defence is a very good one but they have not played Barcelona. John Terry, Carvalho and Paulo Ferreira are all good players but they will not be able to cope with my speed or the football of Ronaldinho and Deco. We all know that Petr Cech has not conceded a goal for a long time but then again he has not played against me.

'Playing Barcelona will be a nightmare for Chelsea at the Nou Camp and in London. We must be favourites for the tie because Barcelona are a better team than Chelsea. This game will be the best clash in Europe – the fans just can't wait for the games to start. Let me assure you I am not an arrogant person, but I have been preparing for this round with the maximum concentration. I want to play to 200 per cent because it is a final of champions for me. I dream that we beat Chelsea and then go on and win the Spanish title and Champions League final.'

Mourinho says, 'My dream final would be Chelsea v Arsenal. English football hasn't won enough in Europe; that's not right. It's time to put an end to that injustice.'

Chelsea continue to excel in their quest for the title until 'the blip' finally arrives, but from an unexpected quarter with the loss of one of their key players, Arjen Robben, who was kicked soon after scoring the early winner at Blackburn. Once the swelling subsides, the diagnosis is two cracks in the foot and an absence of at least six weeks. Barcelona boss Frank Rijkaard is delighted that Robben will miss their Champions League clash. 'The injury to Robben is bad news for Holland and Chelsea but excellent for Barcelona. We will not have to face one of the best European players of this moment and it will make playing them less complicated for us. Robben is the best forward Chelsea have – and Mourinho knows it.'

Rijkaard is a meticulous manager and has spent time analysing the way Chelsea play. 'I've seen some matches on the telly, they are a great team. Very functional ...'

That subtle put-down highlights Barcelona's contrasting reputation for playing football rich in finesse and skill. The personal battle of the coaches will be as fascinating as the on-field struggle. Though there are obvious similarities, both being sophisticated, 42-year-old multi-linguists oozing self-worth, there is a plain distinction. If Mourinho's searing ambition is motivated by his failures as a player who never came close to the first rank, Rijkaard will always form one point of a sublime triangle of Dutch talent alongside Ruud Gullit and Marco van Basten. Rijkaard has won the European Cup three times – twice with Milan and once with Ajax – and could become one of the few men to lift the trophy as both a player and manager.

Acknowledging Rijkaard's 'fantastic' playing legacy, Mourinho remarks that, as a manager, his counterpart 'has zero trophies and I have a lot of them'.

'I haven't met him yet,' Rijkaard replies. 'All I know is what we see on TV or read in the papers. Our papers are very interested in him because he worked here once.' Rijkaard is surprised by the possibility of verbal sparring. 'You call them mind games? How do they work?' After hearing a few examples of Mourinho's more cunning jibes, Rijkaard laughs loudly, 'Thank you! Thank you! I look forward to this kind of game. What has he said so far?'

The Dutch manager prefers to remain aloof. 'I didn't have a big reaction when our name came out with Chelsea. Even before the draw I said it doesn't matter who we play. When you're down to the last 16, there's not much difference between Team A and Team B. Maybe it's better we play Chelsea. In a clash between big teams, you know your players will concentrate. They have to play very well against Chelsea to go through.'

He recognises the danger. 'Chelsea have good team spirit and their defence is very strong. They are disciplined but they also have some wonderful players – especially in midfield. Robben is important to them because, when he is fit, he gives them something extra. They are also dangerous because they're being challenged to do great things. You can see they're hungry. So all this makes them one of the best teams in Europe.'

Rijkaard will find it hard to avoid talking about Mourinho. 'I can't say yet if I will like him. How can you really judge a man until you come face to face? Maybe I'll find out what he's really like over these next few weeks. I know he's very successful but we'll learn a little more about both him and his team. He can say the same for me. So, sure, when we finally meet, it could be quite a moment.'

Ronaldinho picks out Lampard as the biggest danger to his dreams. 'Lampard has been outstanding for Chelsea all season. Chelsea remind me very much of Barcelona. They have very good individual players all over the pitch, but it is their spirit that stands out above all else. Chelsea's strength is their defence, but also the fact that they play as a team. They all play for each other at all times. They have many great footballers. We must be aware of every single one of them for this tie.'

Deco takes a swipe at Mourinho's Chelsea for conquering a poor quality league. 'It tells you everything about the Premiership and how much easier it is than the Spanish league that Chelsea have won eight in a row during this season. The Premiership is full of mediocre and, frankly, very poor teams.'

Mourinho prepares Chelsea for his biggest game since arriving in English football. 'I have to defend what is mine. The Champions League is mine at the moment. I am the last winner as manager of the Champions League – so it is my competition. I have to try and fight for Chelsea and I have to try and fight for myself by defending my cup until the last moment. Maybe winning the Champions League enabled me to come to a big football country like this. The competition means a lot to me. At 42, I am very young as a manager. I have 15 more years to work in football. I hope to get that taste of winning the Champions League again. But it is so difficult to win. You can perform well, have a good team and have big ambition. But make one mistake and you are out of the competition – even if you don't deserve to be.'

In another swipe at Barca, Mourinho adds, 'Barcelona have a great club. But in 200 years of history, they have won the European Cup only once. I have been managing for a few years and I have already won the same amount.'

Mourinho feels Chelsea are not as good as his Porto side yet but he is working with better players. His squad are still two years from reaching the kind of technical standards that helped Porto to Champions League glory. Mourinho says, 'We have better players than the Porto squad of last year, but in my third year at Porto we had a better technical team. They knew everything I know. They knew how to adapt, change from system to system, when to press high or to block low.

'Porto won the Champions League in their third year – here at Chelsea it has been seven months. The contract I have with Chelsea is for four years. By the time we get to the third or fourth year then I think you will see my best Chelsea team. We still have a way to go. The beginning of the next season will be very important for us to make steps ahead. There are things I do not want to work on now. I really don't want to mix things before the players are ready on the tactical side. You can't jump phases, there has to be a steady progress, achieving things step by step. So Chelsea have the better players but maybe Porto had the better team.'

Chelsea's fate against Barca depends on how they cope with the absence of Robben. Mourinho's method of dealing with the problem is to ignore the Dutch winger completely. 'I don't want to think about Robben. The best way to face an injury to a very important player is to forget the player. I don't speak with him. When my fitness coach says he is ready to play, I will jump, but at this moment I don't want to think about him. He cannot play so I have to work and support the other players.

'I will never give missing Arjen Robben as an excuse for anything – we have players to work with without him. It's unfair to put more pressure on Damien Duff in Robben's absence. I didn't see Damien play for Blackburn in the flesh but I know the reason Chelsea bought him was because he was playing outstanding football there. But I doubt if he has had a better season than the one he is having. He has been fantastic.'

Mourinho has already formulated a plan he believes will neutralise Eto'o and Ronaldinho and his self-belief is illustrated by his suggestion that his first six months at Chelsea have already begun to transform the face of English football.

Chelsea's preferred 4-3-3 formation has been adopted by Manchester United, other Premiership sides and was tried – unsuccessfully – by Sven Goran Eriksson in the draw with Holland. 'The long-ball tactics still exist, but the traditional 4-4-2 is changing,' he says. 'In two years it will all be very different.'

Meanwhile, John Terry stars between the sticks in a training session at Stamford Bridge but twists his ankle. Terry and his team-mates thrill hundreds of children who have arrived for guided tours of the Stamford Bridge set-up. Despite hobbling, Terry does not disappoint the watching youngsters and signs all their autographs – as do the rest of Mourinho's men. He says, 'Ronaldinho is the one player in the world who stands out at the moment. His all-round game is great, with his skills and his quick feet so it will be good to play against him. But they've got quality all over the pitch: Eto'o looks fantastic and he's full of goals. However, we've got quality in our side too, and we'll be going to the Nou Camp full of confidence.'

Roman Abramovich is pictured next to European Footballer of the Year and possible transfer target Andriy Shevchenko at an Italian awards ceremony, as AC Milan prepare for their big Champions League tie with Manchester United.

After being dumped out of the FA Cup 1–0 at Newcastle, Chelsea fly direct from Newcastle to Barcelona on Sunday night and hold light training the next day at the city's Olympic stadium. Mourinho insists three injured players travel to Spain in a last-minute attempt to get them fit. The problem with Duff's knee and Gallas's groin does not deter Mourinho from bringing them to Barcelona in the belief they can recover in time.

There is also private optimism about Drogba's chances of recovering from a thigh strain in time. He has not played for Chelsea since their Carling Cup defeat of Manchester United and the player is told that he should be prepared to face Barcelona. Kezman is a shock potential starter at the Nou Camp alongside Gudjohnsen after Duff picked up a knee injury against the Magpies. The Blues are also missing Wayne Bridge, who left St James' Park with a broken ankle and lower leg, while Gallas is also struggling.

Mourinho recalls what he sees as the most significant moment from the last 12 months. 'My players are crazy to win something important. When we were in the USA last summer we were together 24 hours a day and talked a lot and exchanged feelings. The message that came over clear from that is that, while it is a club full of stars and rich players who have earned a lot of money, only Claude

Makelele and the ones I brought from Porto have won titles. The others: zero. When I said that to them, they said, "You are right, it's true." So I said, "If I'm right, why didn't YOU win anything? And if I'm right, why don't you try to follow my concepts and projects?" That is what we have done. I now have a very ambitious squad.'

So when Ronaldinho, Deco and co come calling, Mourinho will expect his 'three team leaders' to stand firm. 'Psychologically, the leaders are Terry and Lampard,' Mourinho explains. 'Tactically the leader for the organisation is Makelele.'

Meanwhile, Barca's quest for a first La Liga title since Mourinho was assistant to Louis van Gaal in 1999 comes closer as they open up a seven-point gap over Real Madrid. Deco scores both goals in Barcelona's 2–0 win over Real Mallorca, while Real lose 2–0 at home to Athletic Bilbao. The mood in the Catalan capital could hardly be better ahead of the visit of Chelsea.

Mourinho tells his players there is no room for doubt. 'You must be confident and act like this before this sort of match. I keep saying to the players that when you have a bad result or injuries you mustn't look back and forget what you have to do in the future. I can't say, "I don't have him or him, so we can't expect to get a good result." We must find another way. We still have many good players and have to adapt the way we're playing. We are without Robben and Duff so we have to change. When we go out there, we still have to fight for a good result. You have to think positively and realise there are 180 minutes, maybe more – and that it will not be easy for them in London.'

Mourinho proudly boasts he has *never* lost two games in a row as a manager. 'We are confident,' Mourinho says, before illustrating the point in a barbed answer to a journalist's question. 'In the eight or nine years since I was here I have progressed in life, I've evolved. You haven't.'

He then dispenses with the usual tactic of keeping his line-up plans close to his chest by naming what he believes will be the Barcelona team, followed by his own.

'We have one more session but I think Drogba plays, Gallas plays;

Duff I don't think so,' says Mourinho, before predicting the team Barcelona will field. Then he adds, 'You want to know my team? All right: Cech, Paulo, Ricardo, Terry, Gallas, Tiago, Makelele, Lampard, Cole, Drogba and Gudjohnsen.'

In typically mischievous style, Mourinho attempts to plant an element of uncertainty in Rijkaard's mind by naming his team early. Duff, he says, will not be fit. Yet Duff trains and has not given up hope of making a surprise appearance.

Rijkaard is reluctant to bite back and says, 'There is no need to respond.' But, when the former Dutch star is asked why he has given his players a couple of days off and not sent anyone on a spying mission to Stamford Bridge, while Chelsea are in Spain working hard, Rijkaard cuts loose. He says, 'Chelsea show up three days early, train behind closed doors and then announce their line-up. What was the point of training in secret then? But you can say what you like before the game – the match tells you the truth. Most coaches think that the players deserve to know the team rather than the press. But Chelsea are in an unusual situation now. They've just been knocked out of the FA Cup and Manchester United are closing in on them in the Premiership. Let's see how all that will affect them. A lot of times when people talk before games it's a sign that they aren't at ease with the match to come – not very calm. I'm not worried.'

Mourinho's bullishness during the build-up could backfire. As Ronaldinho observes, 'Chelsea may think they are motivated for the match. But Mourinho says he has never lost two games in a row as manager – and that has motivated us even more. Hopefully, we can make him suffer two defeats.'

WEDNESDAY, 23 FEBRUARY 2005

BARCELONA 2, CHELSEA 1

When the same two teams met in the Nou Camp four years ago, referee Anders Frisk dismissed full-back Celestine Babayaro and awarded Barcelona two penalties as the Spanish side romped to a

5–1 victory in extra-time. Blond-streaked Frisk is widely regarded as one of the top officials in world football, but games he is involved in rarely pass without the 42-year-old Swede leaving a lasting impression. So it proves this time.

Chelsea start off solidly in defence as Barcelona make good use of the flanks. Mourinho springs a major surprise by including Damien Duff – a day after insisting it was 'almost impossible' for the winger to recover from a knee injury. And it is Duff who speeds on to Lampard's pinpoint 40-yard pass to collect with precision control and then flick a cross towards the unmarked Joe Cole, which right-back Juliano Belletti slides in at the near post in the 33rd minute. Then after Belletti's own-goal rocks Barcelona, Didier Drogba misses a golden chance to put the tie beyond doubt a couple of minutes later, shooting wide with only keeper Victor Valdes to beat.

The game erupts in the 55th minute when Swedish referee Frisk dismisses Drogba after a legitimate attempt to reach a back-header in a challenge with Valdes. A series of rash challenges by Drogba leads up to his second-half dismissal – and his reluctance to leave the pitch may prompt a UEFA punishment. Both players go down, but Drogba picks up his second booking, having earned a first-half yellow card for a foul on Rafael Marquez. It leaves the Blues with ten men for the second game in a row. Their sense of injustice is heightened by Barca fans chanting racist abuse at Drogba – monkey chants fill the air as he trudges towards the visiting dugout.

Not long afterwards, Maxi Lopez squirms clear of William Gallas in a crowded area – after a move involving Ronaldinho and Samuel Eto'o – before finding a glimmer of space to angle a right-footer into the far corner. Worse follows in the 73rd minute when Lopez's mishit cross-shot from the right is left by Carvalho as Eto'o emerges from between two Blues defenders to slam home an eight-yard winner.

Mourinho has now suffered two losses in a row for the first time as a manager, but it is the manner of the defeat, the harsh dismissal of

Drogba, and a fracas at the interval and that push the manager into hyper drive.

The London club plans an official complaint about Rijkaard's conversation with the referee at half-time. Mourinho is upset at what he sees as fraternisation between the Swedish referee and Barcelona's manager, plus the fact that Chelsea went down to ten men so soon after the interval. It is a carbon copy of Mourinho's rant accusing Sir Alex Ferguson of attempting to influence referee Neale Barry during the first leg of last month's Carling Cup semi-final. Mourinho is so angry that he refuses to take part in any post-match interview, a violation of UEFA regulations that is likely to result in a fine.

There are also suggestions of a scuffle involving Rijkaard's assistant and Mourinho, in which it is reported that Henk Ten Cate assaulted the Chelsea manager with a kick to the backside. Though Chelsea take no steps to indicate the thrust of their submission to UEFA, they do move to douse these particular wildfire rumours.

There has, however, definitely been a dispute between Ten Cate and Chelsea's goalkeeping coach Silvino Louro as well as their head first-team coach Baltemar Brito. The Chelsea coaches walked on the wrong side of the players' tunnel – where a barrier separates home and away players and staff – precipitating heated words and a minor scuffle. Mourinho also booted Barca midfielder Xavi Hernandez out of the Chelsea dressing room. He refused to shake Xavi's hand.

Later Frank Rijkaard confirms that he did chat to Anders Frisk but insists, 'I was not the cause of the incident. I said, "Hello, pleased to meet you," to the referee. I said something about the game in a very polite and informal way. So the reaction of the Chelsea side was a little bit exaggerated. It is not true that the referee went into our dressing room and I am glad this rumour has come out because now it all seems even more ridiculous to me. Maybe they want to start something and make it worse than it is.'

Defender Rafael Marquez accuses the Londoners of making

excuses. 'Everybody could see who was the better team out on the pitch. Chelsea are just angry because of the defeat. Everyone had talked about Super Chelsea before the game, but I didn't see anything super out there. The only team that played football was us. When a team just waits for their opponents or the referee to make a mistake then it makes you angry. Even when Chelsea scored, we weren't desperate because they had done nothing.'

Ten Cate also weighs in, 'Football is supposed to be for fun. The paying public don't go and buy tickets to go and see the boring football that Chelsea played. They had very few shots on goal while we had many. We could have won by even more goals. The only team playing proper football was us.'

Jose Mourinho's philosophy, which he restates, is that 'when the game is finished, the next one has already started'. The return at Stamford Bridge will be a true test of his managerial mettle.

> **Team**
>
> Cech, Terry, Ferreira, Gallas, Carvalho, Makelele, Lampard, Cole (Johnson), Duff (Gudjohnsen), Tiago (Smertin), Drogba.

The Dutch contingent are ganging up on Mourinho. Johan Cruyff backs up the 'boring' attack by Barca, while Tottenham head coach Martin Jol maintains there is nothing wrong with speaking to officials – it is a common occurrence in European football. Cruyff says, 'I'm sure Mourinho is going to be the best coach in the world but I don't support his type of football. It bores me to sleep. I recognise that Chelsea defend very well but it's not what I want to see. Chelsea are a copy of Porto, a max-mix of English and Portuguese football but playing only on defence.'

Mourinho finally gives part of his version of the row with Rijkaard and Frisk in his media press conference ahead of the Carling Cup final. Mourinho maintains that his Barcelona counterpart and the referee talked 'in a private place' rather than the tunnel. 'Sometimes you can talk to the referee, but usually in a common space. It is different in a tunnel with 20 people around. You can't say you can't communicate or there should be a wall. But it is another thing to talk to a referee in a private place.'

In his weekly column for Portuguese sports supplement *Record Dez*, Mourinho calls for Italian Pierluigi Collina to take charge of the second leg. 'Something was said to me in London, that the referee will be Collina, the best in the world, independent, above all pressures. The perfect referee.

'In Barcelona, the referee was inefficient. It was an adulterated result. When Deco produced a ridiculous dive in the area, the referee didn't show him a yellow card. When I saw Rijkaard enter the referee's changing room at half-time, I couldn't believe it. When Drogba was sent off, I wasn't surprised. When the game finished I breathed a sigh of relief. Drogba wasn't unlucky. Unlucky is when you waste a shot in front of Valdes. The red card was not unlucky. It is a fact. It is wrong.

'In Barcelona the team that played best won. However, they only did that against ten; I think the game would never have been lost if it had been 11 against 11.'

UEFA spokesman William Gaillard says, 'We have made no decision at all on this [who will referee the second leg]. The normal procedure would be for it to be decided at the end of this week. If Mourinho thinks it is Collina, you will have to ask why he thinks this. We have eight excellent referees and eight ties, the only thing we do know is that it will not be Anders Frisk because we never have the same referee for both legs.'

Claudio Ranieri is sacked as Valencia coach just eight months into his second spell in charge of the Spanish champions. The decision is taken at a board meeting brought forward following the club's shock elimination from the UEFA Cup by Steaua Bucharest.

Hours before the Carling Cup final, chief executive Peter Kenyon confirms the club will be forwarding a report to UEFA about Rijkaard's dialogue with Frisk, but the complaint will not be heard until the tie is over.

Medical experts predicted Arjen Robben would be out for six weeks, but Jean-Pierre Meersseman, the Belgian chiropractor who is treating Robben, believes the Dutchman has a chance of facing Barcelona.

Robben has been receiving treatment from the AC Milan club doctor following the personal intervention of Roman Abramovich who phoned vice-chairman Adriano Galliani to request the club's medical coordinator fly to London to see the player. Meersseman says, 'Abramovich asked Galliani if I could treat Robben and I suppose he said yes because I came to London. They are very good friends and Galliani was happy to help. There has been a great relationship between Chelsea and AC Milan for the last couple of years. Abramovich knows Galliani well and the Russians are on good terms with our Prime Minister, Silvio Berlusconi.'

It is highly unusual for one club to provide such assistance to a direct rival and it is a measure of the extent of Abramovich's influence. 'I hope he can be back in time to play against Barcelona and I will try to help him make that happen,' says Meersseman. 'I put everything right with Arjen's foot the last time I saw him 12 days ago. He had a fracture on the cuboid bone and his third metatarsal. I corrected one fracture and we adjusted the bones around it. I also needed to balance the muscles and we worked on his posture too. I know he was pleased with what I did and now he is running again.'

Barca's French star Ludovic Giuly is given the all-clear to play at Stamford Bridge but Rafael Marquez is out. It is a boost for Barca who had said earlier in the week that they did not think Giuly would play.

The pain of the Champions League calamity against Monaco last season still gives Eidur Gudjohnsen sleepless nights. 'Whenever I am reminded of what happened in the competition last year it is something that keeps me awake. First of all we came so close and secondly it would have been a fantastic achievement for me to go into the Champions League final. There was a real feeling among the players that we had a great chance because we were so close.

'We were 1–1 in Monaco with a man advantage on the pitch and when you think back to that night it just looks like a cock-up really.

Then we got off to a flier at home and were 2–0 ahead and we were thinking, "This is it, we just need to see this game out." But they hit us on the break just before half-time and got back into it. It deflated the team a little bit. We had the tie won twice, but maybe it was due to a lack of experience. We should have settled for the draw in Monaco.'

Fulfilling the prediction made by Mourinho, Pierluigi Collina is named as the man in the middle for the Barcelona game. Collina, who handled the World Cup final between Brazil and Germany in 2002 and the 1999 Champions League final between Manchester United and Bayern Munich, will quit in the summer for a desk job as *designatore*, the man who appoints referees for Serie A fixtures.

Frank Lampard calls on Chelsea fans to generate a special atmosphere. 'We have to use our crowd to help get a result in the second leg. What happened with Didier in Barcelona was difficult. We were in a really good position with 11 men but the sending-off changed that. It was a harsh sending-off but at a place like that, with the noise of the crowd, decisions were going to go their way. Now it's our turn. We have to stop them scoring which will be tough with the players they've got, but it's achievable.'

The all-for-one mentality fostered by Mourinho should give Chelsea the edge as Lampard says, 'The pre-game talks we do are really good. We do them in a huddle, with our arms round each other's shoulders and everybody – the physio, everyone – is involved. John Terry's really into it from the start when he does his but I build mine up a bit more. I gave the one before the Barcelona game – there were three or four F-words but not as many as you might get in John's. There were a couple of stutterers at first and some of the lads like William Gallas were a bit shy. But it's a good thing for us – it helps every member of the squad feel important and that they've got a role.'

According to 'Lamps', revenge is in the air. 'There's been a lot of talking from them since the game; they've been giving out stick to our manager, our team and to certain individuals. You can ignore it or say it doesn't bother you, but when I see opponents talking about us, I want to do something about it. That's why I can't wait for them to come over here. I'm certainly surprised that experienced pros like theirs have spoken out halfway through a game like this. They've been a bit premature because they've now got to face us on our own pitch and in front of our own fans and it will be very different to how it was at the Nou Camp. It's all got a bit personal, and that's given the match even more of an edge.'

Raising the stakes further, Ronaldinho suggests Chelsea are a dirty team. 'I was bruised all over after the game and I can count on half of one hand the number of Chelsea players who played the game in a clean fashion.'

As the verbal war intensifies, Mourinho changes the time of his pre-match press conference so he can have the last word. Originally, Mourinho was going to speak at 4.30pm. Now he plans to give his sermon at 7pm, half an hour after Frank Rijkaard's.

In Barcelona it was Mourinho who spoke first before the match and took the unusual step of naming his own side, as well as predicting Barcelona's team. This time Mourinho wants the benefit of hearing Rijkaard's address to the media before he offers his own thoughts. He believes the psychological warfare can have a significant impact on the result.

The Dutch coach is bemused by the change of times for the press conferences but feels to complain would be to play into Mourinho's hands. Rijkaard can't resist a dig when he jokes Robben could line up for Chelsea. When asked to guess tonight's Chelsea team, Barca boss Rijkaard says, 'One, Robben. Two, Robben. Three, Robben.'

Rijkaard attempts to broker a fragile peace, even if Mourinho cannot resist restoking the fire. Rijkaard is in conciliatory mood after a fortnight of squabbling, the likes of which the competition has rarely seen. 'Jose is doing a great job at Chelsea,' he says.

Mourinho provocatively suggests he would prefer Frisk to be in charge. 'If you ask me which referee I would want for the game, I would say Frisk, because maybe he would help us in the same way that he helped Barcelona. Instead we have a referee who will not have a direct influence on the result.'

Mourinho does pay the Spanish club a compliment. Again, though, it contains a sting in the tail. 'Barcelona have great qualities and play such beautiful football, that they should not have to dive so much.'

Chelsea can go through with a 1–0 win. But Robben has lost his race against time to make the bench. Instead Parker is set for a surprise comeback as substitute. After all the mind games and criticisms, Joe Cole expresses Chelsea's hunger for success. 'Victory would be very sweet, with all the controversy and drama that has gone on,' says Cole. 'That's what inspires us.'

Around 42,500 will pack into the Bridge, but the club with ambitions to be the biggest in Europe could have sold another 10,000 seats with ease.

TUESDAY, 8 MARCH 2005
CHELSEA 4, BARCELONA 2
(CHELSEA WIN 5–4 ON AGGREGATE)

Chelsea earn a place in the folklore of the European game with this magnificent victory in a spectacle of explosive drama and swaying fortunes. Having been accused of negative tactics in the Nou Camp, Mourinho bravely fields Mateja Kezman just ahead of Eidur Gudjohnsen. Kezman makes an immediate impact, surging down the right flank after Frank Lampard wins possession before producing an inviting cross for his strike partner. Gudjohnsen's first touch takes him past Gerard, before he lunges forward to power his shot past Victor Valdes with just eight minutes gone. That is, in itself, enough to take Chelsea through, but their tails are up and Lampard volleys over the bar on the turn from just eight yards out.

When Joe Cole's shot is deflected, Valdes can only parry the ball and Lampard is on to it in a flash to finish. 'Boring, boring Chelsea' rings out ironically around Stamford Bridge. Then Cole produces more midfield inspiration, driving a through-ball for Duff to scamper onto and roll underneath the body of the stranded Valdes.

That should be game over. Instead, Barca surge back. Petr Cech denies Samuel Eto'o at full stretch and Ronaldinho rises to direct a bullet header just inches wide from a Barca corner. Then Paulo Ferreira, with his back to the ball, handles unnecessarily, Ronaldinho converts the ensuing penalty even though Cech guesses right and gets a hand to the ball. The tie is transformed. Barcelona only need one goal to go through and, even though Cech again performs acrobatics to deny Deco, Ronaldinho conjures one of the greatest goals ever in this tournament – an all-time classic!

Swivelling his foot and his hips with Ricardo Carvalho in front of him, and with minimal back-lift, he crafts a shot that curls into the far corner, leaving Cech motionless. Eto'o also skims a shot over the bar from Ronaldinho's inspired through-ball, but Chelsea rally and Cole strikes the post, with Duff just failing to convert the rebound as he stretches. And that is all in the first half.

It is so action-packed that Ferreira can be forgiven for believing the full 90 minutes are up when he swaps shirts at half-time with Ronaldinho! Ferreira is withdrawn soon after the restart after suffering a torrid time at Ronaldinho's hands, with Glen Johnson the next to be run ragged by the Brazilian.

However, John Terry and Lampard lead the revival as the match continues to fizz with excitement. Lampard twice comes close, but Cech scrambles Juliano Belletti's long-range effort around the post and then produces an incredible save from Carles Puyol. Valdes is also equal to a thunderbolt from Cole, while Lampard and Gudjohnsen both threaten. Pushing forward, Chelsea leave themselves open to the counter-attack and, when Cech tips Andres Iniesta's shot onto the post, Eto'o fails to punish Johnson's hesitation and blazes over. That is the let-off Chelsea need. When Terry heads home Duff's corner, Barcelona's pleas for a foul on Valdes are ignored.

Mourinho immediately introduces Tiago for Gudjohnsen and

then Huth soon follows amid a frantic final spell as Deco flashes an injury-time free-kick just wide.

When the final whistle blows and Terry's 76th-minute header has sent the Blues roaring into the last eight after a nail-biting tussle, Mourinho dances along the touchline and flings himself into an ecstatic sea of players – later he insists Chelsea's amazing win is sweeter than his Champions League triumph at Porto.

Mourinho says, 'I'm so happy to beat the side supposed to be the best in the world. Even after I won the Champions League final with Porto, I did not celebrate like I did tonight. Tonight the game was changing every five minutes and the result was in doubt right up to the whistle.

'I was just about to put Robert Huth on at centre-forward when we scored, so I put him on at centre-half! Had they scored in the last seconds, we'd have gone out. That's why it felt so good to win. There was absolutely no time to breathe and enjoy the moment but this has been an unbelievable night and a magnificent game. We scored four, hit the post and should have scored six or seven. Barcelona scored two and could have had four or five. But the reality is over two legs we've scored five and they have four.

'That shows the difference between the teams. Over 180 minutes the best team goes through. But the point of the night is not beating Barcelona. The point is getting to the quarter-finals.'

Now it is Rijkaard's turn to feel aggrieved. He accuses Chelsea of lies and insults after being involved in a tunnel brawl following taunts from Chelsea's Portuguese scout Andre Villas. Villas sparked a brawl by blowing kisses at Rijkaard after the final whistle. Rijkaard had to be pulled away by heavy-handed stewards before Eto'o, Ronaldinho and Puyol all waded into the fray.

Rijkaard rages, 'I am always bitter when I lose and tonight I am even more bitter because of all the lies they told before this game and the things they created. Some guy came forward and insulted our bench and I don't want to say what I think of him. I wanted to win this game even more than usual because of all the stuff surrounding the build-up. So it hurts me even more to be leaving after this defeat.'

The club's astonishing victory is marred by ugly scenes and Eto'o claims he was called a monkey by a steward. 'Chelsea going through is a disaster for football,' he tells the Barcelona-based newspaper *El Mundo Deportivo*. 'And if this team wins the Champions League, it would make you want to retire. With so much money and so many players, what they do is not football.'

Steve Clarke has a different viewpoint. 'We think we are one of the best teams in Europe and having a deficit from the first leg made it difficult for us to go through. The boys went out with great belief and got there in the end. We felt a little aggrieved that we lost the first game and set out to put that right. It was a very good start and I think we proved we can be an attacking force if we have to be. We've proved that all season. We are formidable at home and set out to put them under pressure.'

Chelsea captain Terry has the knack of scoring vital goals – but there's been nothing to match his late winner. Terry says, 'What a great feeling. It's right up there with the best. Our pitch is a lot tighter than the one at the Nou Camp and we knew that if we could put them under pressure, they wouldn't like it. I don't care about the things their players said before the game. Today is about Chelsea. That sent out a message to the whole of Europe. There's still a long way to go and a lot of quality teams are left, but I'm sure there will have been a lot of people watching who are afraid of us now.'

Abramovich appears in the dressing room as usual at the end. Gudjohnsen observes, 'Mr Abramovich likes to soak up the atmosphere, see how the lads react. Every win gives you pleasure but this was extra special with the magnitude of a match with Barcelona and all that had been said. You can say what you want in the press, but the real answers are delivered on the football pitch. That's where you answer every critic. Chelsea have gone from a big club to a massive club. The manager has given us a winning mentality. We work together; there are no individuals. There is such a good team spirit that starts with John and Frank. It's important the Englishmen let the foreign players know the culture of English football. I'm also considered English!'

> **Team**
>
> Cech, Ferreira (Johnson), Terry, Carvalho, Gallas, Makelele, Cole, Lampard, Duff (Huth), Kezman, Gudjohnsen (Tiago).

According to Frank Lampard, Chelsea's amazing triumph was inspired by criticism from the Spanish giants. 'A lot was said from the Spanish side before this game but I think we showed a lot of people in Europe that we have the character and ability. The idea that we're boring was shown to be wrong. I thought that all the talk from Barcelona between matches was a bit strong because it was only half-time. I think that's part of the reason why we started so strongly. It gave us an extra edge. Some of Barcelona's possession play was fantastic but the game's not all about possession.

'I was still confident at half-time that we would win the game. We just had to be patient. Barcelona have done a lot of talking but we were clever enough to realise that there were 90 minutes to go. The performance we put in shows we're a top, top team. We're an English team with a lovely mix of English spirit, great foreign players and a foreign manager who is very tactically aware and he got straight into the spirit of the English game. It was one of the most satisfying games I've played in and is up there with the Champions League win over Arsenal last season.'

Of all people, Johan Cruyff is now backing the Blues. 'Chelsea could be European champions thanks to having one fundamental player – Lampard. I looked at the Chelsea team and I thought that Lampard would really fit in well in the Barcelona team. He would make Barcelona stronger in midfield. At the same time he would benefit from playing for Barcelona. He is a very attacking player and Barcelona always play attacking football. He would score far more goals. One other player who would be good for Barcelona is Duff. He is one of the few players who can really play on the wing. Barcelona are a really good footballing team. They are a team who use their wingers, and on the left he would really give them something special. Barca failed in defence because they played too many horizontal balls against a rival that is dangerous in this type of game.

'Mourinho makes his team play defensive all the time. I have no joy in watching Chelsea. It is a shame because I like English football. But Chelsea do not play like the English. They play like the Portuguese: defensive and only looking for counter-attacks.'

With Real Madrid crashing out at Juventus, there are no Spanish teams in the European Cup quarter-finals for the first time in 12 years. But some of the great names of European football still stand between Chelsea and a place in the last four. The quarter-finalists are made up of six former European champions, with the other two places going to Chelsea and Lyon. Clubs from the same countries are no longer kept apart in the draw, so it is possible that Chelsea and Liverpool could meet in the next round in what would be a repeat of the Carling Cup final.

David Beckham is tipping Chelsea. 'Mourinho has been there and done it and will have that experience for his players and his team. Seeing the way Chelsea beat Barcelona and the way they've been performing all season, they have to be major contenders to win the Champions League this season. They're the new *galacticos* because of the way they've been playing. They have the money of Roman Abramovich to keep taking them on as a club. They also have a new young manager and no one has seen anything like him before. Mourinho has got the confidence and the arrogance to keep the pressure off his players and you have to respect him for that. Chelsea have a very good mixture of excellent young English players and talented foreigners who have come in and performed right from the off. People thought it would take quite a while for all their new signings to gel. But they've won trophies straight away.'

Meanwhile, referee Anders Frisk announces that worries over his own and his family's safety have prompted him to quit refereeing. 'The threats toward me have escalated the last few weeks after the Barcelona–Chelsea game,' Frisk says on Sweden's football federation website. Frisk, ironically a big Chelsea fan, says he has received death threats since the match. 'It's not worth carrying on ... My safety and the safety of my family goes before anything else. These last few weeks have been the worst of my life. I still say that what I did in Barcelona was correct.'

Frisk tells the newspaper *Aftonbladet*, 'Chelsea have supporters in many parts of the world, so all of them [the threats] didn't come from England. Soon it will be impossible to referee a Champions League match if the clubs can't accept defeat or a player being sent off.'

Mourinho is blamed by Volker Roth, chairman of UEFA's Referees Committee, for the incidents that led to Frisk's retirement. Roth says, 'People like Mourinho are the enemy of football. It's the coaches who whip up the masses and make them threaten people to death. We can't accept that one of our best referees is forced to quit because of this.' Swiss referee Urs Meier, who suffered a hate campaign by England fans after disallowing a Sol Campbell 'goal' against Portugal at Euro 2004, says, 'It's not OK for a coach to put this much pressure on a referee. He [Mourinho] has to be punished.'

But Mourinho insists he is not to blame. 'Mr Roth, he has only two ways out – he apologises or he will be sued. I regret that Frisk has decided to leave football. If as some people say his decision is associated with the criticism of his exhibition in the match against Barcelona, I find it odd. Every day, everywhere, there are criticisms like these from coaches, directors and players. It is a normal situation. A referee with the experience of Mr Frisk would not take such a drastic decision because of criticism of his performance at Barcelona. If there are other motives I do not know them and I would like them to be known. If it has something to do with the threats – which should obviously be condemned – then it is a police case.'

Sepp Blatter, the FIFA president, calls on football professionals to show greater respect to officials. 'I am appalled by the verbal attacks directed at referees and it is often such extreme behaviour that sparks off trouble among supporters.'

Mourinho faces a ban from the touchline and the dressing room for the quarter-finals if he continues his war of words with UEFA. Gaillard, UEFA's director of communications, confirms that Mourinho's latest outburst has been 'added to the file'.

UEFA distance themselves from claims by Roth that Mourinho is an 'enemy of football'. Spokesman William Gaillard says, 'Roth has our full support and respect but he's not a UEFA employee. He was reacting as a private person, a referee. UEFA have never said Jose Mourinho is an enemy of football. We are looking into respect for referees as a whole. There is nothing in our statement about Chelsea or Mourinho.

'UEFA have never said that Mourinho caused Frisk to resign. This is a big logical jump. All we're saying is that some statements from managers and players are misconstrued by the public at large who are not mentally stable.'

Mourinho's conduct in Barcelona will be considered by UEFA's disciplinary body. 'It was never Mourinho's intention to whip up feeling against Frisk, but we would ask all managers to be careful and refrain from making these statements,' says Gaillard. 'We want to have a good relationship with Chelsea. No one becomes a pariah. When the Chelsea delegation come for the draw tomorrow they will be warmly received by us.'

Behind the scenes, though, friction remains, with UEFA leaking the substance of Chelsea's response as to why they took the field late for the second half – because they were 'too nervous' – and as to why Mourinho failed to attend the mandatory press conference – because he was too upset. A high-ranking source on UEFA's control and disciplinary body lets it be known that 'eyebrows will be raised both about what they did and about their evidence'. Clearly an irate UEFA do not accept Chelsea's version of events: that Rijkaard entered Frisk's room at half-time.

Mourinho maintains he is still anxious to avoid the Italian sides in the draw. 'They are the most difficult teams to play against in Europe, as you can see by their records. Playing an Italian team is not the same as Spanish or French. We must be a team with thinking qualities. You can't play with the heart or by instinct. You need to be clever enough to play with the brain.'

Bayern chairman Karl-Heinz Rummenigge wants to avoid Chelsea, describing them as 'one of the strongest teams in the Champions League. We would prefer to avoid them at this stage. If we are to meet them, then I would prefer it to be one round later.'

In the event, the draw is intriguing, pairing Chelsea with Bayern, AC Milan with Inter Milan and outsiders Olympique Lyon and PSV Eindhoven together. Liverpool play Juventus for the first time since the Heysel Stadium disaster at the 1985 European Cup final in which 39 fans died after a riot by Liverpool supporters.

So it's sod's law for Rummenigge as Bayern get the draw he did not want. It will be the first time the pair have met in European competition. The winners will be matched against the winners of Juventus versus Liverpool in the semi-final.

Bayern Munich boss Felix Magath claims, 'Three months ago we would have had no chance against Chelsea. But the winter break we had in Germany will make a big difference and now is the ideal time to strike against Chelsea.'

The first leg at Stamford Bridge will be Chelsea's 49th game, six more than Bayern, who had a six-week break over the Christmas and New Year period. Chelsea have never lost a tie to a German team. Mourinho says, 'There are no easy adversaries; there are only feelings and facts. Everybody wished for Lyon or PSV, but I wasn't that keen on Lyon because they are an extremely organised team. They are a second Porto. Last season if it hadn't been Porto, it would have been them. They are a true team. Bayern are powerful, they have good players and are a typically German team.'

The Germans are going for a treble of their own and director of football Uli Hoeness is full of bravado. 'Chelsea, with the away game first, was exactly the draw I wanted. Chelsea have a good team but we showed against Arsenal we can raise ourselves to the task. This is a super draw.'

Bayern also take the opportunity to confirm their interest in Chelsea's German centre-back, Robert Huth. Hoeness says, 'We have already spoken with Chelsea and his agent.' Jurgen Klinsmann, Germany's national coach, says Huth must play regularly to be certain of a place at the World Cup. The £5m-rated centre-half comments, 'I've always said I would be interested in playing in Germany. Obviously I have the pressure to play for a club where I will be guaranteed first-team football because I know I need that to stand a chance of playing in the World Cup.'

Huth backtracks within days. 'I'm staying here [at Chelsea], unless the club wants to get rid of me. It's not an issue, even if some people say it is.'

Didier Drogba makes a public apology to referee Anders Frisk. 'I would like to apologise to Mr Frisk if I might have, in any way, prompted him to end his refereeing career,' he tells French television channel TF1. 'I really hope he will change his mind. Soccer needs great referees and Mr Frisk is one of them. Everyone makes mistakes and referees are human, we have to accept that.'

The Swede says he will not go back on his decision despite efforts by UEFA and the game's worldwide body FIFA to persuade him to change his mind. In an interview with the *Sunday Times*, Frisk describes the period after the game in Barcelona as 'the worst 16 days of my life'. Without naming Mourinho directly, Frisk is quoted as saying, 'He violated my integrity. When you attack something that is so important to refereeing and so important to my culture, as well as to this fantastic hobby I have had for the last 26 years, of course you [inflict] hurt.'

Mourinho drops his threat of legal action against Roth and has privately promised not to criticise match officials in public as part of a peace deal between the club and the European game's governing body.

Mourinho is finally charged with bringing the game into disrepute by UEFA. Assistant manager Steve Clarke and security officer Les Miles are also in the dock for 'wrong and unfounded statements' after the tie in Barcelona. A statement is issued by UEFA: 'These charges relate to making false declarations, notably in the complaint sent by Chelsea following the UEFA Champions League match against Barcelona on February 23. By further disseminating these wrong and unfounded statements, Chelsea allowed their technical staff to deliberately create a poisoned and negative ambience amongst the teams and to put pressure on the refereeing officials.'

The trio face fines or touchline bans. In response, Chelsea will only say that they are 'reviewing their position'. Mourinho has blown any chance of covertly getting around any restrictions that may be imposed. UEFA will be wise to certain passages in his authorised biography in which he boasts of using a 'small, sophisticated telecommunications device' to relay tactical messages and order substitutions when he previously faced a touchline ban while manager of Porto.

William Gaillard issues a detailed and highly damaging set of charges, which include 'basically using lies as a pre-match tactic'. He accuses Chelsea of 'trying to qualify for the next round by putting pressure on referees and officials'. He says, 'There is a clear contradiction. They say Clarke and Miles saw the meeting but we know by looking at that, from where they were, they could not have seen anything. Then Mr Mourinho says in a signed article that he was the one who saw it, which again is false. What we do know from the reports from the referee and the venue director is that Mr Mourinho came out of the dressing room and shouted in a quite aggressive way at Anders Frisk, "Can I also come into your dressing room?"' UEFA will even use plans of the stadium at the hearing to prove that Chelsea have concocted their story.

Who saw what in a tunnel is normally a petty issue, but the UEFA hierarchy is furious as Mourinho keeps casting doubt over the integrity of its staff.

After discussions with senior UEFA officials at the draw, Chelsea are prepared for disciplinary action, but the force with which it is delivered comes as a shock to many at Stamford Bridge. After Gaillard's remarks, they can expect no leniency. UEFA are also awaiting reports about the brawling at the end of the second leg at Stamford Bridge.

Chelsea are standing by their original allegations and considering their legal position. Chelsea are also seething at the inflammatory language. Senior figures fear the club have already been found guilty and some are even questioning the independence of the Control and Disciplinary Board.

Chelsea demand that Mourinho gets a personal hearing. Under UEFA rules disciplinary matters are usually dealt with via paper submissions, though in exceptional circumstances they will allow oral evidence. Six of the nine members of the Contol and Disciplinary Body are or have been UEFA match delegates. The chairman of the body is Josep Luis Vilaseca – a Spaniard with links to Barcelona – but UEFA insist members of the panel are neutral.

Whatever judgment is made, Uli Hoeness insists he wants Mourinho in the dugout against Bayern. 'We hope Mourinho is in the dugout for both of the games. We want to meet Chelsea at their best and that means with their coach on the bench. It would be a real shame if he could not guide his team from the dugout.'

To add to a growing sense of the absurd, there are media reports that the visitors' dressing room at the Bridge was trashed by Barcelona's stars and there appears to be photographic evidence that wood panelling was damaged.

And just as UEFA are attempting to curb Mourinho's excesses, the Chelsea coach is to have his own television show! The 50-minute live show will be broadcast monthly in Portugal and, given that Mourinho is said to be 'willing to talk about anything but politics', there is potential for more controversy. The first show is scheduled for 18 April at 9pm – after the watershed.

Meanwhile, chairman Bruce Buck meets with chief executive Peter

Kenyon to plan Chelsea's defence as William Gaillard accuses the club of turning their problems with UEFA into a vendetta. Gaillard is a central character in the feud. A former media director of the International Air Transport Association, he had to reassure the public about worldwide airline safety in the aftermath of 9/11. Gaillard, 53, quit to become UEFA director of communications a year ago.

Chelsea's lawyers are trying to convince the disciplinary panel to dismiss the case and will cite Article 6 of the European Convention on Human Rights, governing the right to a fair trial. Mourinho reportedly says, 'They have taken sides without listening to our side of things and we have already been found guilty before UEFA passes judgment. We simply passed on what we saw – not in my case because I could not see, but those who work with me saw. And when they tell me what they saw I believe them.' The quotes attributed to Mourinho in the newspaper *La Vanguardia* provide an untimely reminder of his ability to court trouble. Chelsea move swiftly to deny that Mourinho uttered the words.

All in all, the situation has reached a farcical stage, with Chelsea saying that Mourinho did not say something about an event that UEFA say did not happen.

On the eve of the hearing, a five-game ban to include the Champions League final is being touted. But Chelsea stick to their line that Steve Clarke and Les Miles saw Frank Rijkaard in an area forbidden to coaching and playing staff and reported their concerns to Jose Mourinho. They are also claiming that there are many inaccuracies and discrepancies in UEFA's report.

In the event, Mourinho is handed a two-match touchline ban and a 20,000 Swiss francs (£8,900) fine, Clarke and Miles are reprimanded and the club receives a 75,000 Swiss francs penalty (£33,000). Significantly UEFA withdraws its key allegation that the club manufactured a conspiracy that 'created a poisoned and negative ambience'; UEFA privately concede Gaillard overstepped his authority.

Mourinho stays away from the hearing. Peter Limacher, head of

UEFA disciplinary services, says, 'As far as the touchline ban is concerned, a team manager who is suspended from carrying out his function may follow the match, for which he is suspended, from the stands only. He is not allowed in the dressing room, tunnel or technical area before and during the match and he is not allowed to get in contact with his team.'

Claude Makelele is not too worried about the ban. 'Jose's absence will not affect us totally although it will be a blow. Mourinho has a massive presence and having him on the bench helps us enormously. Mourinho is a marvellous boss and can change a game with his instructions. That talent makes him the best boss there is. He has the ability to think on his feet regarding his substitutions and the positional or tactical changes to the shape of the team. We just look to Mourinho on the bench and we instantly know what we are doing and what we need to correct.'

Chelsea are unbeaten in their last nine home Champions League games – their last defeat was against Besiktas in 2003 – but Bayern Munich striker Roy Makaay reckons Chelsea are weak at the back and have taken too much for granted. He says, 'I know Mourinho from my time in Spain when he was Bobby Robson's assistant. Now he is the coach and things are going well for him, but the good results are perhaps going to his head. I don't like it that he takes it for granted that they will knock us out. They say that Chelsea have the best defence in Europe, but they still haven't played against Bayern. Playing the return leg in Munich will give us a slight advantage, but we can't afford to drop our levels of concentration. Maybe this fame that they have will end after these two games.'

Germany's national newspaper, *Bild*, does not mince its words either. 'And you thought Bayern were arrogant? Meet Chelsea's manager-lout' is their headline, while underneath are some of Mourinho's more outrageous quotes.

Meanwhile rumours spread that Mourinho is set to quit Chelsea over the club's failure to fully support him against UEFA. The club are not appealing against UEFA's decision, believing that this would almost certainly lead to a longer ban for their outspoken coach. Roman Abramovich flies in to London to talk with Mourinho, something he always does before a game. But this time the headlines shout, 'Crisis!' Mourinho's agent, Jorge Mendes, joins the talks to provide even more 'evidence' that Mourinho's future is on the line.

Mendes is there to help deliver the message – some of Europe's biggest clubs are understood to have been in contact, with tentative enquiries as to whether Mourinho would be keen to move. However, Mendes is not demanding an improved contract or making threats. He wants reassurances for his client.

Mourinho, though, is not genuinely close to resigning, but he and his employers realise that the matter has to be resolved before it escalates further.

Certainly Chelsea do not want to lose the coach who has taken them to the brink of a first title in 50 years. Mourinho, equally, prefers to remain at Stamford Bridge despite numerous other offers. 'He likes Chelsea, the players, the club and the country,' says a friend. 'It is not important that he has offers from anywhere else. But Jose is not someone to keep his mind in his pocket. Remember the way he left Benfica; he wanted to clarify his situation with the president, a public statement that he would be the coach the next season, but it did not happen. Jose just wants to work in clear waters.'

The cracks in the manager's relationship with the club hierarchy are confirmed by his assistant Baltemar Brito, who also reveals Mourinho will watch the Bayern game in a 'private place' on television and there will be no contact with the bench via mobile phone or any other means of communication.

When asked about the manager's future at the pre-match press conference, Brito does nothing to silence the persistent rumours. He says, 'When Jose comes to a club or starts a new job, he gives 100 per cent and expects 100 per cent back. Jose is not too happy because he feels slightly hard done by around the ban situation.' It is the first public acknowledgement of a problem but Mourinho is keeping his thoughts to himself.

For the first leg against Bayern, UEFA appoint hardline referee Rene Hemmink, 6ft 6in and 17st, who abandoned a game in October between Den Haag and PSV Eindhoven with ten minutes to play after racist chants from fans. Hemmink was in charge of Chelsea's goalless draw with Paris Saint-Germain in November.

Bayern boss Felix Magath is careful not to follow Ottmar Hitzfeld in describing Mourinho as arrogant. 'If I don't know the person, I can't make judgments,' he says, 'but I am clearly aware of Jose Mourinho's great achievements.

'The advantage of having the return leg at home is that Chelsea must do something tomorrow,' he continues. 'They can't just rely on counter-attacks but they will have to bring the game to us and that could help us. I believe that tomorrow we will not lose and that we can score one or two goals. Germany have the winter break so our players now are fresh and in top condition, whereas England has played non-stop until today. I think there were signs of that when we played Arsenal.'

Despite the ban, Mourinho will get his chance to do his stuff at half-time after all. UEFA will be unable to stop him addressing any of his players – and the nation – who are watching television when his advertisement for American Express airs for the first time during ITV's coverage of the match. That'll do nicely, then.

WEDNESDAY, 6 APRIL 2005
CHELSEA 4, BAYERN MUNICH 2

Mourinho is supposed to be the man who isn't there but his presence is everywhere on a night of mystery and intrigue, cloaks and daggers.

He is there in the banners, then in the boos that greet the playing of the UEFA anthem before the tie and in the words of support from John Terry in the programme. Chelsea add to the melodrama by refusing to give any clues as to his whereabouts, except to say he is 'in a quiet place'.

Mysteriously, notes are being passed around among his assistants in the dugout. Are they from Jose? Is he in a health club a mere 50 yards away? Someone says he is in the Chelsea Village Hotel, holed up in a room overlooking the pitch. No one knows for sure, although one paper manages to snap him leaving in a baseball cap and tracksuit top.

Mourinho's ban has created a siege mentality at Stamford Bridge, which is immediately evident when Chelsea fans boo the UEFA anthem before the game and chant Mourinho's name to drown it out. 'Jose,' a giant banner says, 'They May All Hate Us But We All Love You'. Another reads, 'Jose Is Simply the Best'.

Soon Frank Lampard shows there are leaders on the pitch as well as off it. And two left-footed goals demonstrate how he is maturing into arguably the best midfielder in Europe. After substitute Bastian Schweinsteiger capitalises on a rare instance of fallibility from Petr Cech to cancel out Cole's deflected early opener, it looks as if the absence of Mourinho could prove costly. At this point it looks as if the remainder of Chelsea's season hangs in the balance. Enter Lampard ...

His first, which puts Chelsea back in front just seven minutes after Schweinsteiger's equaliser, is simple in construction; Glen Johnson's high ball is knocked down by the head of Drogba, for Lampard to take a step back before steadying himself and directing a low accurate shot past goalkeeper Oliver Kahn.

The next is even better as Makelele clips the ball into the box. Lampard controls it on his chest, then spins 100 degrees to produce a thunderous finish on the half-volley – a special strike.

The Germans are unable to deal with the long-ball tactic, with Drogba making life a misery for the centre-backs Robert Kovac and the Brazilian Lucio. Later Owen Hargreaves is rather unflattering about Chelsea's style, describing them as a 'long-ball' team who resorted to direct tactics because they could not pass their way through the Bayern defence. Taking advantage of costly absences in the Bayern ranks, where Roy Makaay has joined Claudio Pizarro on the sidelines denying Felix Magath's side two players with 40 goals between them this term, it is all looking so good, particularly when Drogba forces the ball home from close range with only ten minutes remaining.

Yet deep in stoppage time comes the final twist on a night that is becoming, in its own way, as dramatic as those unforgettable events against Barcelona. This time, Ricardo Carvalho's tug sends Michael Ballack into sufficient histrionics to alert referee Rene Hemmink. Terry later accuses Ballack of diving to win Bayern's late penalty, which the Germany international successfully converts, as Chelsea become embroiled in yet another Champions League refereeing controversy.

Magath says that Ballack's goal has raised his side's chances of overturning the two-goal deficit in Munich. 'It was good to get the goal before the end – it has given us hope,' he says. 'We will also hopefully have some of our other players back for the return game. We had difficulty coping with the high balls and it was disappointing to concede four goals. This was an exception for us tonight. Normally we cope with such tactics.'

Magath hopes to have Makaay and Pizarro back for the return. "But only three teams have ever overturned a two-goal deficit in the Champions League at this stage and, with Lampard so imperious, Mourinho's men will fancy themselves to score in Munich.

A further note of controversy emerges: did Mourinho use coaches Rui Faria and Silvino Louro as contact points to deliver messages to his assistants Clarke and Brito? There was certainly some very suspicious behaviour by the man in the hat, fitness coach Faria. Faria, rarely on the bench, was wearing a 'beanie' hat and seemed to be leaning back and listening to an earpiece on several occasions before scribbling notes and speaking to Clarke and Brito. Goalkeeping coach Louro, at the centre of punch-up claims in the tunnel after the Barcelona game, appeared three times clutching a piece of paper – and three times it led to a Chelsea substitution. During the second half, UEFA press officer Hans Hultman was seen standing by the home bench keeping watch on the trio and, in the 75th minute, he asked fourth official Pieter Vink to question Faria. Later Brito denies having any contact with Mourinho during the match.

Bayern promise an electrifying second-leg performance at the Olympic Stadium. 'We want to attack so hard that the stadium walls are going to shake,' says Bayern's director of football Uli Hoeness. 'We have to take them down, and that's that. We've got to get two goals – it doesn't matter how. I'm very confident.'

> **Team**
>
> Cech, Johnson (Huth), Carvalho, Terry, Gallas, Cole (Tiago), Lampard, Makelele, Duff, Gudjohnsen, Drogba (Forssell).

One mystery is solved soon after the game. It transpires that Mourinho watched the Bayern match on a huge plasma screen television inside the Chelsea Club & Spa, which is part of the Chelsea Village complex.

And just after 11pm, as the crowds drift away, Mourinho's agent Jorge Mendes slips through the entrance to the Chelsea Village Hotel. A few minutes later Kenyon also rounds the corner, passes the old Shed End, but heads in the opposite direction towards the VIP car park. A new contract has been finalised for Mourinho and they can both go home safe in the knowledge of a job well done.

Of course, Roman Abramovich was always going to give Mourinho exactly what he wanted. But talks were brought forward because Mourinho was so exasperated when he read the comments from chairman Bruce Buck after the UEFA ban was announced, when the Chelsea chairman declared the hearing to be 'full and fair'. Mourinho feels the club has not been backing him and Buck's remark added salt to the wounds.

Chelsea can now justifiably claim there has been a cover-up over what really happened in the Nou Camp during the Champions League first leg on 23 February. The club always insisted referee Anders Frisk spoke to Frank Rijkaard outside his room and remain adamant that such a conversation took place – a claim now supported by UEFA. Chelsea's version of events is now backed up by the venue director's own report to the UEFA disciplinary panel.

Above: In 1997, Jose Mourinho had his first taste of success as assistant to Sir Bobby Robson at Barcelona. The pair are pictured here with star player Ronaldo and the European Cup Winners Cup.

Below: Having already won the Portugese league, cup and the UEFA Cup, Mourinho added the coveted UEFA Champions League trophy to his collection at Porto. Chelsea came so close to winning the same title in 2004-05.

Above: Jose Mourinho is no stranger to the cameras and press. Since leaving Porto for Chelsea, Jose's feelings and comments have been no stranger to the British media.

Below: Jose on his first visit to Stamford Bridge as the manager of Chelsea Football Club.

Mourinho on a family outing to the premiere of the film *The Incredibles*. His wife Tami, daughter, Matilde and son, Jose follow his successes closely.

Above: The team prepare for another big game. Before each game, one of the players gives a motivational team talk. Mutu hit the headlines in 2004 when he was sensationally sacked for using illegal substances.

Below: Damien Duff, Joe Cole and Claude Makelele celebrate.

Jose Mourinho very quickly won the hearts of the Chelsea fans, who feel nothing is impossible with Mourinho at the helm.

Mourinho contemplating tactics as he watches his team play.

Above: Frank Lampard tussles with Ronaldinho for the ball in the Champions League match with Barcelona.

Below: Drogba disagrees with referee Anders Frisk. The referee resigned shortly after the tough fixture between Chelsea and Barcelona.

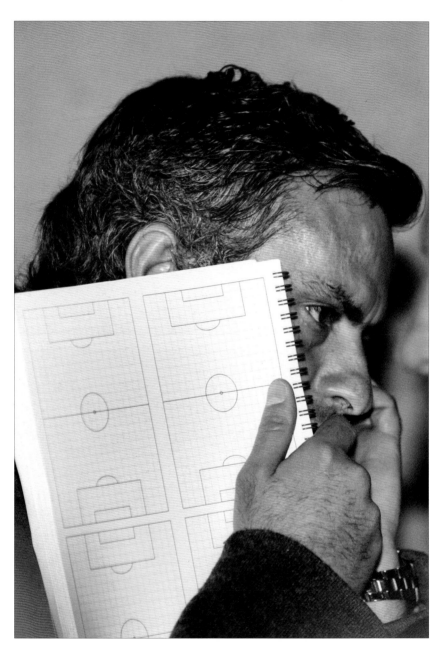

Following allegations made by Jose about Barcelona coach Frank Rijkaard approaching referee Anders Frisk, UEFA gave Mourinho a two match touchline ban. He is pictured here phoning his coaching staff with tactical advice prior to the game against Bayern Munich.

It really is astonishing that UEFA apparently chose to ignore the written testimony of the man at the centre of the dispute. The 25-page report compiled by investigator Edgar Obertuefer for UEFA's Control and Disciplinary Body does not appear to contain a single reference to the referee's version of events.

Chelsea contacted UEFA to ask for Frisk's report and, when it arrived a day later, they discovered that the Swede had bolstered their version. Frisk said that Rijkaard approached him on three separate occasions until he finally lost patience and told him to return to his own dressing room. Although UEFA confirm that Chelsea have 'waived the right to appeal', the club are discussing whether or not they can pursue other avenues to seek redress as they feel Mourinho, who is still furious they did not appeal, has been made the scapegoat.

UEFA are in no mood to wipe the slate clean for Mourinho, but the failure to bring Rijkaard to book is rapidly becoming a farce. Chelsea, though, will be punished following events during the first leg against Bayern. As is mandatory under UEFA law, the club will be fined because they had four players cautioned – Drogba, Carvalho, Gallas and Makelele.

Frank Lampard's last trip to the Olympic Stadium, Munich, was for England's unforgettable 5–1 World Cup triumph in September 2001. He says, 'It can be an imposing ground, especially with their fans and the atmosphere they're going to produce. But we don't believe in giving things up when we have them in our grasp.'

Mourinho admits that his role in the dugout will not be as vital as the preparation of his squad. 'I am not on the bench but the players are on the pitch. And as I have been saying to them, our work – the management team's work – is done during the week. During the 90 minutes my direct actions are not that important. I never say after a first leg, the result is good or bad, because you never know. In the first leg, I never feel the pressure of having to win or not concede. The second game will be more important than the first, like against Manchester United in the Carling Cup semi-final. We played them at home and couldn't beat them, but we didn't panic and we went away and won the second leg. I think the players are well prepared.'

As they arrive in Munich every member of the party is still livid about the long-ball tag. Joe Cole says, 'If anyone really thinks we can't play football they should look at any of our last ten games when we've carved teams open with our passing movement. Of course we can pass the ball. But we played a more direct game against Bayern because we felt they couldn't deal with it. There wasn't a moment when somebody told us to start looking for Didier in the box. It just happened naturally.

'Sometimes you need to fight and sometimes you need to get the ball quickly into the box. What's the point in playing pretty stuff if it's not effective? Why should we play to Bayern's strengths? The way we played last week was very effective because we scored four and should have had more.'

But Magath is plotting an upset. 'We are capable of scoring two goals in 45 minutes and that is what we need against Chelsea,' he says after his side recovers from going a goal down to beat Borussia Moenchengladbach 2–1 in the Bundesliga. 'That will comfort us, even in the Champions League. We can now go into that game with added self-confidence. We go into the game convinced we can knock Chelsea out.'

Chelsea deliver another snub to UEFA by putting fitness coach Rui Faria and fringe striker Mikael Forssell up for the pre-match press conference. The event degenerates into farce as Faria arrogantly fields questions about his infamous woolly hat and launches a personal rant against UEFA's touchline ban on Mourinho. Faria denies he passed on mobile phone messages to Brito and Clarke at Stamford Bridge and adds that he had nothing to hide under his hat!

Faria is dubbed 'Mini Mo' the next day in the press. Unable to keep a smile off his face as he winks at his audience, Faria shows he is a chip off the Mourinho block as he declares himself a 'Special One' in his own way. UEFA representative Wolfgang Eichler, close to tears when he realises what Chelsea are doing (poor chap), says, 'I'll be reporting everything that has gone on to UEFA. Just look at the difference. Bayern put up Magath, Kahn and Hargreaves and Chelsea did this.'

But Bayern are not interested in Mourinho's latest tricks. Hargreaves jokes, 'They were handing notes around like naughty schoolchildren in a class. We saw the TV clips. It's not a big deal and we're not going to be sidetracked by the circus.'

Meanwhile, experienced goalkeeper Oliver Kahn calls on his lightweight team-mates to stand up and be counted. 'It was a big shock to me to concede four goals last week. It was unprecedented in Bayern's Champions League history. That result has come as a real warning to us and we will only have a chance of turning this match around if we don't let Chelsea catch us by surprise again. They are known for their aggressive style and their powerful physical contact. We must respond with aggression and a firm resolve of our own. Otherwise we will lose.'

The incorrigible *Bild Zeitung* chooses the game as the subject for its front-page headline: 'Bay-Bay, Chelsea'. On the football page, there is a cut-out paper aeroplane to be aimed at the Chelsea dugout with messages in English purportedly from Jose Mourinho: 'Substitute Drogba and Lampard!'

TUESDAY, 13 APRIL 2005
BAYERN MUNICH 3, CHELSEA 2

Mourinho arrives on the front seat of the team bus with an air of affected nonchalance: feet up and eyes shut. If his entrance is unusual, his exit is spectacular. As most of the stadium's photographers train their lenses on the VIP seats, Mourinho suddenly appears on the giant screen in the stadium; he's back outside and stepping into a beige Munich municipal taxi for the short ride back to the team hotel. A Chelsea spokesman later announces that Mourinho's 'privacy' had been invaded at the stadium. He fully intended to watch from the VIP area but felt harassed by cameramen and left the ground minutes before kick-off.

Once the whistle goes, Bayern make good their promise to take the role of aggressors and Robert Huth makes an inauspicious start to life as a right-back when he is skinned by Ze Roberto down the wing. The Brazilian cuts the ball back to Michael Ballack in the area and only a flailing leg from Cech keeps the shot out.

Down the opposite wing comes Bastian Schweinsteiger who begins by causing equal trouble for William Gallas, the young German inflicting the old-fashioned 'nutmeg' humiliation on the French full-back on 18 minutes and then going on to beat Lampard before unleashing a cross that curls menacingly across goal.

Yet Bayern have to beware of Chelsea on the counter. In fact, after just a few minutes, Lampard's ball over the top sends Drogba away behind the square backline with the flag staying down, but Oliver Kahn, racing from his goal, just gets his foot there first to clear the danger. Before the half-hour, Chelsea take a daring lead. The goals Lampard keeps scoring, and the games he has dominated, mean that his triumphs are no fluke. But when he strikes his 15th of the season, the ball goes in after a big deflection off a defender, just like Cole's first last week.

Michael Ballack is swiftly up to his first-leg trick of diving but the Spanish referee nips that tactic in the bud. There are two scares for Chelsea before half-time, not least when Ze Roberto offers further evidence that Huth is not a natural full-back by beating him down the flank and cutting back another inviting ball. But Ballack wastes his best chance when Huth misjudges a header and presents the midfielder with a simple chance from close range. The talented midfielder cannot keep his shot under the bar.

Duff is then presented with a glorious chance to kill the tie. Lampard's innocuous free-kick is allowed to trickle through to the Irishman and, holding off Willy Sagnol's challenge, he shoots from close range. Somehow Kahn turns the ball away.

The Bayern goal arrives on 65 minutes and, by then, the home side are in control. Sagnol crosses from the right and Ballack, who has established himself as the match's most influential man, produces a stunning header. Cech is equal to it, but turns the ball against the inside of the post and, as the ball ricochets back along the line, it is turned in by Pizarro. The Chelsea defence is no longer looking invulnerable. Pizarro's tap-in means only one clean sheet in the past 11 games.

Bayern pour forward. Within four minutes Huth deflects a Bixente Lizarazu cross on to Cech's bar. From the corner Ballack once again proves dominant in the air and it requires Eidur Gudjohnsen to volley off the line.

Out of nothing, Chelsea appear to seal the tie with 11 minutes remaining. Cole makes the crucial breakthrough, running unselfishly to keep the ball by the corner flag. As the defence expects him to waste valuable time, instead he crosses from the left for Drogba to power-flick his header past Kahn into the far corner. Drogba, kicked twice by Kovac, who is eventually booked, takes revenge by climbing above the Croat to score.

Bayern manage to rouse themselves from the depths of a display that sees most of their supporters exit before their winning goals go in. The first comes from Jose Paolo Guerrero, who turns in Schweinsteiger's cross from the right at the near post. Then in injury-time Mehmet Scholl scores with the last kick of the game. It is the first time that Mourinho's Chelsea have conceded three goals but they are through. In the semi-finals Mourinho's team will play against either Liverpool or Juventus, who face each other in Turin tomorrow night.

While the game is going on, UEFA officials confront fitness coach Rui Faria during the half-time interval to prove he is not in communication with Mourinho. Faria is ushered into a side room and told to remove his hat after allegations he has been passing on messages from Mourinho to Brito and Steve Clarke during the first leg. Despite protests from Faria, who claims such a request is not in UEFA rules, the Chelsea coach duly removes his hat to prove he has no communication device attached to either ear.

Chelsea have a fitness scare over Terry, who admits that his leg is 'in bits' after the match. Terry has a week to recover before the home game with Arsenal. But the next round of the Champions League is even more important.

Can Mourinho become the first manager in the modern era to win the European Cup with different teams in successive seasons?

Team
Cech, Huth, Carvalho, Terry, Gallas, Makelele, Cole (Morais), Lampard, Gudjohnsen (Geremi), Duff (Tiago), Drogba.

After the match Mourinho goes window-shopping in Maximilianstrasse, Munich's equivalent of Chelsea's Sloane Street, until his team return. When they do, around midnight, he joins his players and staff for a celebration party thrown by Abramovich at Munich's trendy Cafe Roma restaurant, a regular haunt of the rich and famous just 400 yards from their hotel, the five-star deluxe Hotel Kempinski. As he makes his way out through the hotel lobby after the game, Mourinho is applauded on his side's victory.

Later John Terry follows his team-mates through Gatwick airport 20 paces behind them. He returns from Munich with only one leg in complete working order. But he has managed what so few traditional English hard men have achieved in European football before: aggression and dominance without loss of temper.

The tone for the night was quickly set. The clattering of Kahn by Terry and the long balls to Drogba in the first leg had been part of a successful tactical ambush by Mourinho; then Terry and his team-mates did a remarkable job of subduing a Bayern side intent on revenge.

Liverpool Manager Rafa Benitez announces he is 'proud and delighted but not surprised' after his side secure an unexpected aggregate victory over Juventus in Turin. Liverpool have sealed a first-ever all-Premiership semi-final against Chelsea, which also guarantees an English side will be in the final. Benitez says, 'Chelsea have won three times against us already this season. But over the last two games we have got closer and maybe next time we will manage it. We certainly have a lot of confidence when it comes to the Champions League, though it will be difficult. Chelsea are top of the table and, for me, are the favourites. But we have nothing to lose, only something to win.'

Defender Jamie Carragher believes Gerrard will snub a £35m move to Chelsea if Liverpool can knock them out of the Champions League. Carragher says, 'Why would anyone want to walk away from a club who had reached a European Cup final? These are good times at Liverpool at the moment and this result shows the club are going places. We're desperate for him to stay but it's his decision. If we get to the Champions League final, it must have an influence.

'For me, Stevie G is the best in England and he'll be out to prove that against Chelsea. I want to be in the final – we all do – because we all want success. If Stevie has a decision to make at the end of the season, that's up to him. But the club will move on whatever happens, although we're all hoping he'll stay.'

Benitez knows Chelsea are overwhelming favourites to make it through to Istanbul. But his side's own European pedigree must disturb even the single-minded confidence of Mourinho. 'All the pressure is on Chelsea. If you spend £10,000 on a suit, you'll get a better suit than if you spend £1,000. You might think it's the same with football – that, generally, if you spend a lot of money you will win. But this is different. You only need one goal to win and that can come from a corner or a free-kick, or something you haven't even thought about. In Spain, Real Madrid and Barcelona spend all the money, but Valencia still won the title, so you can see football is so different to anything else. Chelsea are one of the best teams in the world and are favourites ... but we can beat anybody on our day. We will go without any fear of Chelsea or the game.

'We're the underdogs because they're one of the best teams in the world. But the way we beat Juventus in the quarter-final was important because it made the players believe we can win games we're not expected to. It is just a case of mixing what is in the heart with what is in the brain. The important thing is that we are not afraid of Chelsea.

'Against Chelsea, I've identified what I believe are weaknesses and we've been working hard on ways to give them problems. But

Mourinho will be doing the same. Away from home in the Premiership we sometimes have three or four weaknesses. At home, I hope one or nil. When you lose by only one goal, you know you're very close. They'll play like they play in the Premier League, I'm sure, but we'll be treating this as a European game. I don't know why exactly it's been that different between Champions League matches and the Premiership. Maybe the players feel it's more special in the Champions League. If you'd said to me six months ago that we'd be playing at Anfield against Chelsea for a place in the Champions League final, I'd have taken it.'

Luis Garcia is out for revenge after the Carling Cup final. 'The final left a bad taste because we should never have lost. Now it is the moment for revenge. It is the best time of the season to play this semi-final because we have key players coming back from injury and we are playing a better game. To play the final of the Champions League is a dream for any player and we are only 180 minutes away from it. I've fixed our defeats against Chelsea in my heart and to beat them now would be magnificent.'

It has taken foreign leadership to make English football a Euro force again. Mourinho claims, 'English football needs to adapt to Europe in certain aspects. English managers are very good. But maybe the mentality of me and Rafa Benitez to play in a more tactical way gives us a little bit of an advantage.'

Mourinho is ready for an ear-bashing from the Scousers who will be within touching distance behind his dugout. After Gerrard's own-goal equaliser in Cardiff, Mourinho was sent down the tunnel for putting his finger to his lips and telling their fans to be quiet. He also had a running verbal battle with Jamie Carragher, who did not like Mourinho shaking hands with the Liverpool players. 'I told him where to go and he said the same, so it's 1–1.'

Mourinho adds, 'My reception is always bad from rival fans and always negative. I think that is normal; it's not just Liverpool fans but every fan. They sit behind me and can almost touch me. I think we are a special club because we give opposition fans the best seats in the stadium. When we go to Liverpool, Newcastle and Manchester

United our fans are stuck up on the moon at the top. But they come here and get the best. That shows we are special. They always try to disturb me a bit but I try to calm them down and be nice to them.'

There are stirrings of unrest when defender William Gallas says that Barcelona are keen to sign him and Mateja Kezman announces he wants to leave because Mourinho will not give him a regular place. Gallas's revelation comes a fortnight after he spoke about wanting to clarify his situation at Stamford Bridge at the end of the season when he made it plain that he was uncomfortable at left-back. Frank Rijkaard regards him as a central defender. 'Yes, Barcelona want to sign me,' Gallas tells the city's newspaper *El Mundo Deportivo*, without stating whether a move there would interest him. Mourinho is expected to try to persuade him to stay to compete for a place in central defence once he signs a new full-back.

Meanwhile Damien Duff has an injured left hamstring and needs a late fitness test. He trains on his own the evening before the game against Liverpool but is seen to grimace repeatedly while doing shuttle runs. Arjen Robben, though, could be fit but he is still being treated for a sore ankle after playing 45 minutes against Fulham.

WEDNESDAY, 27 APRIL 2005
CHELSEA 0, LIVERPOOL 0

At 5pm Damien Duff fails a fitness test on his hamstring. Arjen Robben is in a slightly better condition but his ankle problem means he can only come on for the last half-hour and, lacking these two creative forces, the game heads towards a goalless draw as Liverpool dig in. Chelsea are unaccustomed to being without both Duff and Robben. Excluding two FA Cup ties for which Mourinho rested players, this is the first time they have started without either player since mid-September.

The game is tactical rather than end-to-end. Throughout its 90 minutes, goalkeeper Jerzy Dudek makes no noteworthy saves but Petr Cech has to pull off two to avoid a perilous away goal before the trip to Liverpool. It falls to Joe Cole to provide the bulk of the team's runs from his flank because Eidur Gudjohnsen, on the left, always moves inside to link with the midfield.

Gudjohnsen does, however, release Cole with a pass that springs the offside trap after 14 minutes but, although Didier Drogba's power sees him get the break of the ball from the ensuing cross, he badly screws his finish wide with only the keeper to beat. Within five minutes a better opportunity is manufactured on the left. When Drogba lays play out to William Gallas, he works the ball on to his right foot and flights in a deep delivery. The diminutive Cole outjumps Djimi Traore and heads down but Frank Lampard inexplicably fires over from point-blank range.

Gathering a pass from Xabi Alonso in the 19th minute, John Arne Riise, having put the ball on to his unfavoured right foot, comes across Ricardo Carvalho but can do no more than steer the ball straight at a relieved Petr Cech. Six minutes before half-time the goalkeeper makes one of the best saves of this tournament when, after going one way, he somehow manages to recover and tip away a goal-bound Baros header.

'Welcome Home Stevie G – Another OG Please,' reads a cheeky banner in the Shed, a double-edged reference to the glancing header past his own goalkeeper that gave Chelsea a late equaliser in the Carling Cup final. Gerrard's battle with Lampard for supremacy in the central areas sets England's two strongest midfield men in direct opposition, with the added piquancy of a possible link-up next season.

'There's only one Steven Gerrard,' sing the blue-clad fans in the North Stand as he collects Alonso's short free-kick in the last minute and slices a 30-yard pile driver into Row Z of the Shed – interestingly, his ritual post-match handshake with Mourinho is not accompanied by eye contact. Meanwhile, Alonso is cautioned for a disputed foul on Gudjohnsen and leaves the arena pointing angrily at the Icelandic striker, implying he coaxed the booking from the referee. The booking will keep him out of the second leg.

There is no sign of panic from Mourinho at the end, though. He slaps hands contentedly with Steve Clarke at the final whistle. It turns out Mourinho is one of the few people who can be inspired to a bout of nostalgia by a goalless draw at home. Mourinho's conviction that Chelsea will secure passage to the final is unswerving. 'We need to be strong mentally but I think the pressure is on them. At this moment 99.9 per cent of Liverpool people think they are in the final but they are not. It's an easy thing to come and play for a draw, and they defended well, but it will be different in the second leg. I like this situation very much because it is now like an FA Cup tie with the result being decided over 90 minutes.

'Don't forget that Manchester United drew 0–0 here in the first leg of the Carling Cup semi but we went up to Old Trafford and won the second leg. And in last season's semi-final with Porto, we were held 0–0 at home by Deportivo La Coruna but they lost Mauro Silva through a booking late in the game and we beat them at their ground. Tonight Liverpool have lost Xabi Alonso for next Tuesday's game so there are a lot of similarities.'

Rafa Benitez refuses to abandon the belief that his team will snatch a place in the final. 'They did not have a shot on goal and that was because we controlled the game. If someone had said at the start of the season, we'd play at Anfield for a place in the Champions League final, I'd have thanked them. But tonight I am a little disappointed we have not won.'

On the final whistle Liverpool celebrated as if they had won a trophy, but Eidur Gudjohnsen believes that they will feel the pressure in front of their expectant public. 'We're not going to panic and will go to Anfield full of confidence. It'll be a difficult game but they have to come at us as they're playing at home. That could work in our favour as they're under pressure but we'll go out to win the game as we normally do.'

Team

Cech, Johnson, Carvalho, Terry, Gallas, Tiago (Robben), Makelele, Lampard, Gudjohnsen, Drogba, Cole (Kezman).

It transpires that before the first leg with Liverpool Mourinho asked Arjen Robben to begin the match after Duff failed a late fitness test, but the Dutch international declared himself not fully fit despite being cleared by the club's medical staff. The media interpret this as a conflict between the star and coach, which is strenuously denied. Although frustrated by the player's stance, Mourinho understands Robben's predicament and has resolved to ration his playing time strictly until the end of the season.

Steven Gerrard warns that, when Chelsea visit for the return leg, Anfield will be no place for faint hearts. 'We need 11 gladiators and the subs and the fans have all got to be ready as well. Anfield is the best place for a big European night by a mile and Tuesday night is going to be a great spectacle for everyone. The confidence running through all the players on these occasions is incredible.

'The Carling Cup was a huge disappointment. It was not my day then but hopefully it will be my day next month when I get the chance to lead the boys out in another final. The important thing before the game at Chelsea was to stay in touch and give ourselves a fighting chance in the second leg. It was a good performance; it's a massive achievement to get a clean sheet at Stamford Bridge. But we know we are not home and dry. Chelsea are a brilliant side capable of coming to Anfield and beating us. We will show them a lot of respect – but it's going to be some night.'

The Chelsea players are oozing with confidence after encouraging words from their coach. Ricardo Carvalho insists, 'Chelsea will get into the final – and that is for certain. I am very confident. We will run out at Anfield with our heads held high. We know we're capable of winning. We have what it takes to score goals and win up there. It was important for us not to concede in the first leg. Now we know we have to score in order to win the tie – and we will do all we can to achieve this. The main priority for us now is to reach the final of the Champions League.'

As the war of words grows, Rafa Benitez tries to turn the tables on his Chelsea counterpart by insisting all the expectation lies with Mourinho. 'Chelsea are saying that we are too confident, but I think that only goes to show that they are worried. What they are trying to do is put the pressure on us because they know that in reality it is them who are under all the real pressure.

'When you have the most expensive team in the world then you need to win titles to justify that. Chelsea have spent £200m. They should be expected to win the Champions League after spending that kind of money and that's why they now feel under so much pressure. I know people think that if Chelsea score, we cannot win because of the away goal, but that is something that does not concern me. The only issue is that we win the match. If Chelsea score once, then we have to score twice. If they score twice, then we have to score three times. I don't think about the away-goals rule, I only concentrate on winning the game.'

Before the second leg, Robben is still not fully fit but says he is willing to risk it. Robben, left out at Bolton as the Blues clinched the Premiership title, says he will put his hand up for selection at Anfield even though he does not think his body is up to it yet.

Mourinho is not giving too much away about his plans – apart from admitting his continued doubts over Robben and Duff. Asked whether Liverpool will miss the suspended Alonso, he replies, 'They'll miss him no more than we miss Robben or Duff in other matches and maybe tomorrow again. Alonso is a very good player, of course, but they have Igor Biscan, Steven Gerrard, Dietmar Hamann and Harry Kewell. They have a lot of solutions. For us, it's more difficult as we only have two wingers. If we lose one, we are in trouble. If we lose two, then it's a problem that you cannot solve.'

Mourinho invites the Kop to make as much noise as they can. The new Premiership champions, their manager says, are unafraid to claim their European Cup final place in one of the most imposing football stadiums in the competition's history.

Both Mourinho and Benitez insist that the pressure to triumph in the Premiership's private European battle is weighing more heavily on their opponents and yet neither can deny that defeat will irredeemably scar their season.

Mourinho bemoans the relentless tide of crucial fixtures that pile up week after week in England. Chelsea beat Bolton to clinch the Premiership on Saturday which allowed his team just one hour's celebration – 'no families, no wives, no kids, no dinner, no champagne, nothing to enjoy' – before they had to begin preparations afresh for the Liverpool game. He dismisses the magnitude of the achievement that awaits him – winning two successive European Cups with different teams – but says his team have not been affected by the exhausting pursuit of the Premiership.

'They [Liverpool] have more power in their legs but we have more power in our minds from winning the championship,' Mourinho says. 'It is more difficult to win the Premiership than the Champions League. You have to go all over the country in all conditions, in wind and rain, sleet and hail, on good pitches and bad ones and in the north and the south, and all the time under pressure from United and Arsenal.'

Duff and Robben are both consigned to the bench after failing to fully recover from injuries, while several other players are shattered following their efforts in winning the Championship at Bolton on Saturday. But Mourinho says, 'Motivation can make miracles. Chelsea are tired but ready to go to the final. Liverpool rested six or seven players this Saturday, but with a little more effort we can get to the final. We played our best team at Bolton because winning the title would help us forget our fatigue. We're confident that we can win.

'I said last week that details could make the difference. At Stamford Bridge the game was very balanced but we deserved to win 1–0. Now I think the game will be very balanced and only a detail will determine who goes to the final.'

TUESDAY, 3 MAY 2005

LIVERPOOL 1, CHELSEA 0
(LIVERPOOL WIN 1–0 ON AGGREGATE)

After the stalemate at Stamford Bridge, the last thing anybody expects is an early goal, but Liverpool seize the initiative after four minutes. Steven Gerrard plays a delightful first-time ball over the top to Milan Baros. Petr Cech collides with the striker as he rushes out, but referee Lubos Michel allows play to continue. Luis Garcia hooks the ball towards goal and the linesman rules his effort has crossed the line despite Gallas's desperate last-ditch clearance.

Having given his side the lead, Garcia almost gifts Chelsea an equaliser midway through the first half. He is caught in possession on the edge of his own box by Frank Lampard who feeds a ball through to Joe Cole, but the angle is acute and he lifts his shot over Jerzy Dudek but wide.

It is the same at the start of the second half as it becomes blue attack against red defence. Jamie Carragher is awesome at the back as Liverpool see off wave after wave of Chelsea attacks. A tiring Baros is replaced by Djibril Cisse on the hour.

Two minutes later, Didier Drogba curls a free-kick just over the bar as Dudek waits to make his first save. Liverpool concede a free-kick in a dangerous position on 68 minutes and this time Dudek is called into action. Lampard's free-kick is sweetly struck and heading for the bottom left-hand corner, but the Pole makes a superb save at full stretch to turn the shot round the post.

Ricardo Carvalho escapes a booking for a foul on substitute Harry Kewell which would have forced him to miss the final had Chelsea made it to Istanbul. Mourinho introduces Arjen Robben for the disappointing Joe Cole and Mateja Kezman for Tiago. Robben is instantly in the thick of the action, seeing one effort superbly blocked by Carragher and then firing over.

In a last act of desperation, giant centre-back Robert Huth is sent on up front in place of full-back Geremi. But the next chance falls at the other end as Djimi Traore's cross drops perfectly for Cisse. The Frenchman's header is weak and straight at Cech.

Chelsea then waste a glorious opening of their own. Drogba looks odds-on to bury Robben's centre from the left, but he misses the ball completely and it rebounds off Traore for a corner. Carvalho is then almost caught out at the back on a rare Liverpool raid. He gifts the ball to Cisse but his shot is deflected just wide of the post with Cech scrambling across his goal.

Chelsea have a glorious chance to level deep in injury-time. Terry launches himself to win a header in the box and Dudek flaps at the ball, gifting Gudjohnsen an incredible opening at the far post. But staring at goal, he snatches at his shot and it goes inches wide. The final whistle sounds soon afterwards.

Rafa Benitez claims that he always believed he could outwit Mourinho, 'I said that, with our fans behind us and the players playing so well, we had a great chance of winning – and we have. Yes, they put us under pressure but we controlled it more in the second half. The boys are jumping around; it's very joyous in the dressing room. The whole team was superb.'

Mourinho, who congratulated all the players and Liverpool staff individually on the pitch, backs Liverpool to lift the European Cup. 'They were lucky and the best chance came in the last minute, when, if we had scored, we would have killed Anfield. So maybe it was good not to happen.'

Despite this Champions League semi-final defeat, Mourinho insists that Chelsea will rightfully still be hailed by their fans for their title success. He is frustrated, claiming the 'best team lost' as Benitez's side benefited from a controversial refereeing decision when Luis Garcia's fourth-minute goal was allowed to stand, even though Gallas appeared to clear the ball before it crossed the line.

'My players are still heroes, for sure. They have done what nobody at this club has done in 50 years. They won the Premiership. So for me, they are heroes. They can lose and lose, but if our group is so solid and so strong, for me they will always be my heroes. I think the fans have the same feeling as I do for my players.'

Even in defeat, Mourinho has lost none of his innate self-belief, claiming he still regards himself as the 'Special One'. 'For sure I am. You want to try and succeed in your job like I have done in mine inside three years? You have no chance,' he tells one reporter. 'Of course, the players are upset. Everyone reacts differently but they are all sad. William Gallas is crying but he is not more unhappy than me.'

Mourinho adds, 'What can I say? Just that the best team lost. No doubt, that is for sure. The best team didn't deserve to lose. But football is sometimes cruel and you have to accept the reality. Sometimes it goes for you and sometimes it goes against you. Now I hope Liverpool can win – with all my heart I hope that.'

Meanwhile as tears roll down the battered and cut face of Gudjohnsen. A slashed shot across the face of goal in the sixth minute of injury time was the difference between Chelsea booking their trip to Istanbul and returning to London as unfulfilled champions. Gudjohnsen says, 'It was a tight angle and actually Jamie Carragher cleared it off the line. I controlled the ball, hit it quite well and thought it was going in, but it came off Carragher's thigh. I would have loved to see the net move at that moment, but it seemed that Carragher cloned himself last night. He was just about everywhere.'

Gudjohnsen is more composed than after last year's semi-final defeat, but insists that the pain inside hurts more this time. 'It was even more disappointing than last year because we're a better team and more mature. It's a bitter disappointment, but we've taken a big step forward this season. We've won two trophies. After getting over this result, we'll bounce back with a smile on our faces.'

Mourinho sees grounds for optimism. 'This is an historical group of players for the club and I hope the fans give them the credit they deserve. The group are together and next season we will be together again. We don't change the group; we can have two or three new players and no more than that. Now though, at the end of the season, I want the Chelsea fans to show these players the love they deserve.'

Mourinho gives his players two days off before Saturday's league game against Charlton but confirms that he, for one, is not resting on his laurels. 'I want the players to rest. But I will be at Stamford Bridge tomorrow starting to prepare for next season. It will be coming soon and it will be another chance to get some trophies.'

> **Team**
>
> Cech, Geremi (Huth), Carvalho, Terry, Gallas, Tiago, Makelele, Lampard, Cole (Robben), Drogba (Kezman), Gudjohnsen.

Computer technology later shows Luis Garcia's strike did not cross the line. Sky's hi-tech image reveals Gallas cleared the ball in time and the goal should not have stood. Sky commentator Andy Gray insists the computer programme, developed from Israeli missile technology, proves Slovakian linesman Roman Slysko got it wrong.

But Slysko says, 'I believe my decision was correct. My first feeling, which I remain convinced of, is that it was a goal. I am 100 per cent convinced. I saw it clearly. I was adequately positioned for that situation. It was a very hard situation and under those circumstances you only have a few hundredths of a second to react. There will always be those kind of situations in football matches. There was also an incident just before involving Petr Cech and Milan Baros which could have resulted in a penalty and a red card.' Cech insists his challenge on Baros in the lead-up to the crucial goal did not warrant a spot-kick or sending-off. 'I just occupied the space,' he says. 'Milan hit the ball and then he jumped into me. In my opinion it could not be a penalty.' But Baros, Cech's international team-mate, raps, 'It should have been a penalty. He flew at me. I think he even did not hit the ball. But it is not important now.'

Referee Lobos Michel observes, 'I believe Chelsea would have preferred the goal to count rather than face a penalty with just ten men for the rest of the game. If my assistant referee had not signalled a goal, I would have given a penalty and sent off goalkeeper Petr Cech. Jose Mourinho shook my hand after the game and did not complain about the goal. I appreciated his gesture. I was quite ready to explain everything, but no one asked me about the situation.'

Mourinho is again under attack by UEFA. Lars-Ake Bjorck, the Swedish vice-chairman of UEFA's referees committee, responds to Mourinho's criticisms of the referee in the *Telegraph*, saying, 'It is unbelievable he does not have the decency to learn anything, especially considering that he was recently punished with both a suspension and a fine. This damages football a lot. We can only hope Mourinho's initiatives do not have the same consequences this time.'

But it is a far more hostile comment attributed to the same official in the *Sun*. 'It's unbelievable he hasn't got the brain to learn from his mistake last time. It's incredible, especially when you put in mind he recently was punished hard with both suspension and payment charges. If UEFA get a report we will treat it rapidly. This kind of statement damages football and everything around football.'

Swedish head of referees Bo Karlsson says he hopes Slysko does not suffer the same fate as Anders Frisk. 'I hope with all my heart this linesman will not get the same terrible threats Anders got,' says Karlsson. 'We can only hope Mourinho's words will not bring the same, bad, sad consequences as last time.'

The defeat is still sinking in for John Terry. 'We are absolutely devastated at going out in the semis again – especially as we reckon we were the better side and their goal should never have been given,' he says. 'We feel it should have been us in the final but it wasn't to be. Hopefully, next season we can win the Premiership again and reach the final. We believe it will be our turn next. It's something all the lads wanted desperately – and over the two games we felt we deserved to go through. We've stepped up the ladder this season by winning the Carling Cup and the Premiership, which was a massive achievement. It's still been a great season for us but this defeat will put a bit of a downer on things. It was especially disappointing to go out at this stage for the second year running. Having come this far and beaten teams like Barcelona and Bayern Munich we felt we could go all the way and win it. We've played Liverpool five times this season and they've beaten us only once, so I think overall we are entitled to feel we are the better side.'

William Gallas, who wept on the pitch at full-time, says Chelsea's stars went missing at Anfield. 'We were one match from the final. Why couldn't we get there? You shouldn't be tired with just one match remaining to be played. We should have played with our hearts and minds. That had been our strong point all season. Not this time.'

Eidur Gudjohnsen says he and his team-mates will be back in a positive mood by the time the Premiership trophy is presented. 'We should try to enjoy the moment and still remember that is has been a very successful year and we'll be even more together next time.'

FA Cup

'I CAN SEE WHAT THE FA CUP MEANS NOW AND I THINK IT'S FANTASTIC.'

Jose Mourinho after Chelsea's FA Cup tie against
the League two team, Scunthorpe United.

The late Brian Clough was Brian Laws' manager at Nottingham Forest. Laws, now boss of Chelsea's third-round FA Cup opponents Scunthorpe, considers it a privilege to have served under Cloughie at the City Ground for five years. Laws can see many similarities between his old boss and Jose Mourinho. 'They used to call Cloughie "Old Big 'Ead", but Mourinho should be known as "Young Big 'Ead" because he is only 41!' says Laws. 'And having heard Jose in interviews, he does remind me very much of how Cloughie used to act. But that is not just about being big-headed. It is more of an arrogance or confidence – not only in himself, but also in his players. Cloughie had a great belief in us and he was prepared to upset people with it. He just didn't care. And I think that is where Mourinho has shown his colours. He marched into Stamford Bridge and said straight from the start that he knew his team were going to win things this year – and I find that really refreshing.'

Laws adds that he felt like he had 'won the lottery' after drawing Chelsea. He was doing his Christmas shopping in Sheffield with his wife when the draw was made but managed to watch it in an electrical goods store. 'I was in a television shop at the time, and saw it 40 times on 40 different screens. They must have thought I was an absolute lunatic, because I was screaming and jumping up and down. That's just how much it means to me and this club. We're not going to Chelsea just to lap it up and say, "Thanks very much." We're going to try and cause an upset.'

Chelsea's chief opposition scout Andri Villas warns they must not take Scunthorpe lightly. 'For a Division Two team they have good organisation. The principles are direct football, but direct football with some basics and quality. The guy who impressed was Peter Beagrie, with his experience. In one-to-ones he can still beat defenders.'

Beagrie was watching from the comfort of his settee when he heard the draw, but could have done without the reaction of his nine-year-old son. 'Dad, you're going to get hammered,' said Sam. The last time he played at the Bridge he was marked by Mario Melchiot, and before that Albert Ferrer. 'Maybe they will go easy on us this time, and only play Glen Johnson! If we had been playing Arsenal or Manchester United, they might have put out a team of fringe players, but even Chelsea's youngsters are worth £6m–£7m. The likelihood is that, whatever the line-up, it will be worth about £150m. In those circumstances, all we can ask is that we don't embarrass ourselves. If we can keep the score-line below five, we'll have nothing to be ashamed of.'

Jiri Jarosik experiences English football for the first time after signing three days earlier. He says, 'I hope I will become an important part of the squad and help Chelsea to achieve their goals for the season. There is a great chance for me here, and I will do everything to take it. Jose Mourinho explained the situation in Chelsea to me and said that I will certainly be given my chance.'

Keeper Paul Musselwhite is sure Steve Clarke, Mourinho's assistant coach, will warn his superstars about the perils of facing the League Two side. Former Scotland international Clarke was Chelsea's right-back when they were hammered 4–1 in a League Cup clash at Glanford Park in 1988. Musselwhite played in goal for the Humbersiders that day as a teenager. Seventeen years on he cannot wait to get to grips with Clarke's Chelsea. He says, 'Obviously it's a bit different from 17 years ago because Chelsea are now a team full of superstars. But they still had a very good side back then with Kerry Dixon up front. And they won the old Division Two title that season. I was a kid of 19 playing just my ninth game for Scunny – but we were brilliant that night and battered them. We did the same in the second leg at Stamford Bridge when people down at Chelsea thought it would be easy for them to get a result. Their fans were so sure they would do it that only 5,000 turned up at the Bridge. But in the end we drew 2–2. I don't suppose many of their top players now have even heard of Scunthorpe. But Stevie Clarke will remember that game. So I'm pretty sure he will have revved up his squad and told them not to take us too lightly.'

Clarke admits, 'I've tried not to tell the players about it. I'm too embarrassed. It was a humiliating night for all of us. We'd just been relegated from the old First Division. But it was still considered a big upset. It was 1–1 up there for a long time and then the roof fell in on us, as it often did for Chelsea in those days. I think they scored three goals in five or six minutes. I remember walking off feeling so ashamed. We thought we could turn it around at Stamford Bridge but could manage only a draw. It is a reminder of what can happen in cup competitions. We've done the same preparation for Scunthorpe as we would for Arsenal, Manchester United or Barcelona. We don't treat them any differently.'

SATURDAY, 8 JANUARY 2005
CHELSEA 3, SCUNTHORPE UNITED 1

Jose Mourinho presents Brian Laws with the five-page dossier he has had compiled in preparation for the tie to show that Chelsea are taking nothing for granted. Yet the match proves even tougher than the score-line suggests.

Striker Paul Hayes' smart eighth-minute turn and shot through Cudicini's legs puts the 6,000 travelling fans into ecstasy. Then, after Kezman's volley and a cruel own-goal by Crosby have restored the natural order, substitute Cleveland Taylor is the width of the post away from putting Laws' men back on level terms.

Only a late close-range strike by stand-in skipper Gudjohnsen kills the game off and Laws says it is a day his side can be proud of. 'Chelsea treated us like kings – but we nearly took a ransom. We showed that they're only human beings and not from another planet – even if they can play like they are. Jose came in and gave me the scouting report he'd compiled on us. I was ready to swap him mine, although I'm not sure he needs it too often. The only weakness I'd spotted was that the pies were cold. But after the game he said to me, "If we keep on being that lucky, we'll win the Premiership." That was a nice touch and he made my players feel very special. It's easy for the big clubs to ignore the smaller teams but he couldn't have done more.'

Goalscorer Hayes is also full of praise for Mourinho. 'Scoring that goal was a dream come true – I just assumed I was going to wake up. But the whole day was fantastic, thanks to Jose Mourinho. He was brilliant towards us. He showed us around, let us go into both dressing rooms, and after the game he said "well done" to each of us on the pitch and came into the changing room as well.

'Jose told us that we could go into the home dressing room and talk to anybody we wanted to and get any autographs and shirts. I got Joe Cole's, which is the one I really wanted. He didn't have to do any of that, but he did. I've seen him called arrogant and rude but he couldn't have done more to make our day great.'

Mourinho rests Terry and Gallas, with Smertin given a run-out at centre-half alongside promising young defender Steven Watt. Cech has not conceded a goal in over 500 minutes; it takes his replacement Cudicini just eight. Sparrow picks up some scraps carelessly left by another Chelsea reserve, Nuno Morais, and clips in a cross to Hayes' feet. His turn is sharp enough to leave the hopeless

Smertin on the seat of his pants and the Scunthorpe striker drills a low shot between Cudicini's legs.

Drogba passes up the chance to tackle Sparrow in the build-up – a snapshot that gives you the picture of Chelsea's early approach to the tie. Chelsea don't underestimate Scunthorpe – they just don't estimate them at all.

A slice of normality is brought to proceedings when Gudjohnsen swings over a cross and, after Drogba's token effort to challenge, the ball falls to Kezman, whose precise volley produces the equaliser.

Then Drogba isolates himself against Byrne and races past him in three strides. The Chelsea striker's intended low cross is a touch sloppy but the hapless Crosby cannot break his lumbering stride and merely wrong-foots Musselwhite with his unwitting diversion.

Chelsea preserve their lead by Cudicini's full-stretch save from Taylor's ten-yard header that shakes the post. But Gudjohnsen wraps up the victory with a six-yard finish five minutes from time after shots from Robben and Cole are saved and the rebound falls to him unmarked close to goal. He smashes the ball into the roof of the net and turns to signify the cup fighters have finally been finished off.

Laws observes, 'We were very much on top in the first 20 minutes – there was only one team in it and we were looking the more likely to score. But as the game went on the Chelsea players stepped up a gear. They knew they had to get a result. But overall, the players did the town, the fans and the club proud.'

As Manchester United begin to plot a route to Exeter after surprisingly being held at Old Trafford, Mourinho suggests that such trips should become compulsory. 'When it comes to the cup, the Premiership sides should always play at the stadium of the lower division side if they're drawn against one,' he says. 'If we'd played our game at Scunthorpe, I can imagine we might have lost it. I can understand that maybe it was a great feeling for them to come to Chelsea and play in front of 40,000, especially as their fans made the atmosphere magnificent. I guess it was the same for Exeter when they went to Old Trafford. That would have been a big day out for them. But I think we should all have to play away. It would give the smaller sides a bigger opportunity of winning and give the fans the chance to see Premiership football players which they normally don't.'

Joe Cole, watched by Sven-Goran Eriksson, pleases Mourinho with another fine performance. 'Joe is improving a lot as a tactical player. The talent he has he will always have, but two months ago I told him it was impossible for him to play in my team as a midfield player. Last week he played against Middlesbrough as a midfield player and he was fantastic. Now he can think the game, not as an individual but one of 11 players. He understands the organisation of the game, what the team needs, what he has to do when we do not have the ball. He is improving a lot as a player and is a good boy. He is open and, instead of crying, wants to improve.'

While the FA Cup is a chance for Cole to continue his breakthrough in the side, it provides Kezman with a strike to lift his confidence. Kezman observes, 'There is a feeling we have something really special going on here. Why not win all four competitions! Normally it would be difficult to talk about the Premiership, Champions League, FA Cup and Carling Cup, but the spirit and belief within the club is tremendous. We all want to make history. It is wrong to look too far ahead but we'll just keep going.'

Mourinho admits, 'We needed a lot of luck. Scunthorpe had a great chance to equalise but were unlucky to hit the post. They played not only with commitment but also with a lot of quality and we had to work hard for the win. The atmosphere was fantastic and I hope the experience inspires them to get promoted.'

So concerned was Mourinho that he brought on Robben for the final nine minutes. And it was the Dutchman's turn and shot which Scunthorpe failed to clear that provided the final flourish. Mourinho adds, 'I can see what the FA Cup means now and I think it's fantastic. The good thing was that Scunthorpe came to Chelsea with a dream of winning, not just to look around the stadium and try not to lose too heavily. If we'd had to play at

Scunthorpe, I couldn't have afforded to play the team I did at home. I'd have been pushed to play a better team because I'd be afraid of losing. I have respect for these guys.'

> **Team**
> Cudicini, Johnson, Watt, Smertin, Morais, Geremi (Ferreira), Tiago, Cole, Drogba (Jarosik), Gudjohnsen, Kezman (Robben).

Back at Glanford Park, Laws glances through the Mourinho Report: four pages of computer-generated Technicolor triumph, fronted, of course, by a glossy corporate cover. 'The main thing was that he guessed correctly at our formation and how we would play,' Laws says. 'He knew that sooner or later we would give the ball back to them and the dossier is all about our weaknesses. We are at our most vulnerable when we are on the attack. The attention span of players farther down the league is not very long. Instead of concentrating on individuals, Chelsea concentrated on our shape and how we would attack and defend.'

The fourth round draw pairs Chelsea with Birmingham, and the club's owner David Sullivan admits, 'I'm gutted. We couldn't have had a worse draw. Chelsea are the best team in Britain and probably the best team in the world at the moment.'

John Terry helps brother Paul try to spring an FA Cup shock on Charlton. John fixes it for Yeovil to train at the Blues' training ground ahead of the League Two leaders' fourth-round visit to The Valley. Yeovil manager Gary Johnson says, 'It is thanks to our Terry connection. Paul spoke to his brother and I believe John had a word with Jose Mourinho. I am very grateful to PT and JT and of course Chelsea and Mr Mourinho. It will be an ideal place to prepare for our big game.'

Mario Melchiot reached two FA Cup finals in his five years at the Bridge, winning one and losing the other. Melchiot left Chelsea at the end of last season, initially with the intention of playing abroad. He changed his mind after falling for the charms of Brum boss

Steve Bruce! The season has not panned out as expected and Birmingham hover only slightly above the relegation zone. Melchiot says, 'I made my decision before the season finished. I needed something new and fresh. I was at Chelsea for five years. Everyone knew I wanted to go to another country and try there. But I've never played for any coach who wanted me as much as Steve Bruce wanted me. Things are not going like we expected but I have no regrets. I also have no negative thoughts about Chelsea. The club has been waiting for a long time and I want them to win the title. I think Mourinho has got everyone's head straight. He has enough quality to take the team to a different level and I think he's done that already. He is a man who psychologically is strong. He knows what he wants and he knows how to get it and he's going to get all his players to believe in it as well.'

Melchiot vows to give old pal Claude Makelele a good kicking. 'When I saw we were playing Chelsea, I smiled because I thought it was funny,' he says. 'We want to go further and it would be easier to play a team not doing as well as they are. But you can't do a lot about it. This is a nice game and a nice moment to play. When the draw was made my friends started calling me, but this week I've spoken to Claude. He was joking with me. He told me if the chance arose to give me a kick, then he would. I told him, "Don't worry, if I get the chance, I'm going to do the same!"'

Birmingham boss Steve Bruce is the latest to be spellbound by Mourinho. 'He is a breath of fresh air,' says Bruce. 'We've all been watching him. I don't know whether it's his personality or whether he's a maverick but he's very good and his team reflect it. I had a chat with him earlier in the season and he's very interesting. He's only been here six months and we are all intrigued.'

Bruce, in charge of Huddersfield five years ago, reveals he almost lured John Terry to a club that was then going places. Bruce says, 'When I was at Huddersfield I had agreed a fee of £700,000 with Chelsea for him. And I was led to believe he'd join us. I don't know what it was that I saw in him. Potential, I suppose. And who knows what might have happened if I had signed him? I could have made him a star in Huddersfield!' Terry's move to Yorkshire fell through because the Huddersfield board could not raise enough cash.

Now Bruce believes Terry is one of the main reasons for Chelsea's success. 'John and Frank Lampard are the heartbeat of this Chelsea team,' he says. 'He has been a bit unlucky in some respects inasmuch as he has strong competition for a regular England spot. But for my money he's right up there. And he is unbuyable now. You don't come across the likes of him very often. He's brave – as tough as they come – and a leader. Mind you, you can run through this Chelsea side and there aren't too many weaknesses in it anywhere.'

Mourinho approaches the FA Cup with the same attitude he had towards the early rounds of the Carling Cup. 'There, we played every round with a stronger team, and when we reached the semi-final we used our best XI. In the third round of the FA Cup, against Scunthorpe, we rested a few players, now against Birmingham we'll field a stronger side. Fortunately, all our players are up to it, and I don't think three or maybe four changes will make us weaker.'

SUNDAY, 30 JANUARY 2005
CHELSEA 2, BIRMINGHAM CITY 0

John Terry's goal ten minutes from time spares Chelsea a nervous finish with the team effectively down to ten men and only a goal ahead. Mourinho has already put on Lampard, Drogba and Robben as substitutes when Huth, scorer of the opener, is injured. The centre-half eventually goes off straight after Terry's strike. 'In the first half I think we played very, very, very well and we should have been two or three or four goals up,' says Mourinho. 'In the second half we didn't. It was our fault and they improved a bit. The most important thing is to be in the next round.'

In just the sixth minute Terry's cleverly executed block on Taylor gives Huth the space to head home from a corner. Terry heads the second from a Lampard cross ten minutes from time – his seventh of the season. Terry is honest in his assessment of the opener, which he admits was no 'accidental collision'. He says, 'It's not something we work on in training. Robert and I just said one will win it and the other will do the block. I was pleased with my goal. It was good to get on the scoresheet. The lads were a little bit relieved after we went 2–0 up. Birmingham started quite well. Emile Heskey was winning a lot of headers, which was disappointing defensively. But overall I think we deserved the win.'

After Huth's goal Bridge carves out another opening for Duff four minutes before the break, but this time his effort is deflected for a corner. When the ball comes across Huth again finds space but crashes his shot into the ground and against the crossbar.

Chelsea swap one rampaging winger for another during the interval with Mourinho deciding it is Robben's turn to terrorise the City defence instead of Duff.

But it is City who almost got on level terms in the 52nd minute when a cross from Gray falls to Darren Anderton at the far post. The former England midfielder's volley is good enough to bring the best out of Cudicini, who tips the ball over the crossbar.

Terry makes a slip with a back-header that falls short of his keeper, but the chance is wasted, and the Chelsea skipper then strikes to finish off the visibly wilting opposition.

Most of the post-match talk centres not on the game itself but on allegations that Chelsea have made an illegal approach to Ashley Cole. Mourinho makes light of the suggestions. 'I was in Milan with Adriano,' he jokes. 'On Thursday I flew to Milan, so I couldn't be with Ashley Cole.' In case anyone is in any doubt, he quickly makes it clear his words are in jest. 'Steven Gerrard, Adriano, Ashley Cole – and next week it will be another one. I have a perfect and wonderful squad and I don't need any more players this season. Next season I will need one or two. It is names after names with us, because it is Chelsea. Everybody wants to come and everybody wants to connect players with us. But I have no time to meet players. I am concentrating on my job with the club, and that is to get some silverware.'

> **Team**
>
> Cudicini, Johnson, Huth, Terry, Bridge, Cole, Smertin, Jarosik, Duff (Robben), Gudjohnsen (Drogba), Kezman (Lampard).

With all the off-field controversy the FA Cup draw seems to go ahead virtually unnoticed. Chelsea are drawn away to Newcastle, who they beat en route to the Carling Cup final. But Newcastle boss Graeme Souness is confident of stopping Chelsea's charge. 'We were unlucky not to beat them in the League Cup earlier this season and we cannot wait for this one,' he says.

Newcastle's spy in the camp is Celestine Babayaro, who spent eight years at Chelsea and outlasted three managers: Gullit, Vialli and Ranieri. Nothing prepared him for the impact of Abramovich. 'What has happened at Chelsea under Abramovich is like nothing else that has happened before,' says the Nigeria international who, after almost a decade in west London, delivers his words with an accent more King's Road than Kaduna, his family home in Nigeria. 'He came out of nowhere. Nobody expected someone like him to take over Chelsea. The amount of money he has invested is unbelievable. So many players came and went; the dressing room always had different faces in it. Everything changed so quickly.' Babayaro made 197 appearances for Chelsea following a £2.25m move from Anderlecht in 1997. Significantly, though, only five of those were made during this historic campaign.

Having left Nigeria aged just 15, Babayaro was still only 19 when he moved to Chelsea. He grew up at the club and became a familiar face in a river of new arrivals. But, having survived the cull under Ranieri, the first manager given unlimited access to Abramovich's chequebook, he was not so fortunate under Mourinho. 'There was no hesitation when I found out Newcastle were interested in me,' says Babayaro. 'I'd been at Chelsea for eight years, but I had five months left on my contract. I could've stayed, the manager told me that. I'd thought about signing a new contract, but I wasn't playing regularly. I was the longest serving player at the club. I'd seen players and managers come and go. I'd played under four different managers and that is not an easy thing to do.

'Until Roman Abramovich took over Chelsea there was nothing to choose between them and Newcastle. We were at the same standard. Both looked like they might be able to win the title, but never managed it. Then it all changed because of Abramovich. It is not the same Chelsea I joined, but they are doing so well and I'm pleased for them. I'm happy here, though. It was the right decision. Things have not gone as well as we'd like on the pitch, but we can change that.

'Do I think they can do the quadruple? No, because I hope we knock them out of the cup. It would give me a lot of satisfaction. Beating Chelsea is the sort of result which could make a season. Chelsea are nine points clear in the league and still in every cup competition, so you have to say the quadruple is possible. It's our job to knock them out of the cup, though I'd be happy if they win the rest. Chelsea are flying at the moment but no team is unbeatable and anything can happen in football.'

Babayaro won an FA Cup winner's medal and the European Super Cup with Chelsea, and he believes the transformation from also-rans to runaway leaders is largely down to one man. 'Mourinho's great strengths are confidence and organisation. He knows exactly what he is doing. He came into Chelsea and changed everything. Some people say he's arrogant but I just think he has confidence in everything he does. He's instilled that into the boys and they really believe in themselves, which is a big change for Chelsea. Last season we went into games thinking it was going to be hard and we might get a draw, but this year they expect to get three points from every game. No one even thinks about the possibility of losing. Mourinho's approach to the game is so professional – the most thorough manager I've worked with. We used to watch videos before every game, but Mourinho made us watch the same video three times. A couple of days before the game he puts down notes on each player's peg of who you're playing against so that everyone knows their job. There's this incredible feeling of togetherness and belief that they're going to succeed.'

But against Newcastle Mourinho has Robben, Parker and Drogba injured and Terry suspended. Lampard and Bridge have flu, while Cech, Makelele and Duff are rested with the Champions League blockbuster against Barcelona to follow in midweek. Mourinho says, 'We will go to Newcastle to play against a strong team with my second team.' He adds, 'If the match had been on Saturday, as I believe it should have been, I would have played my strongest side. I don't have supermen here, and it would be asking too much of them to play on Sunday, then travel to Barcelona and arrive in the early hours the next morning. Newcastle played on Thursday, and in those circumstances I can understand that they didn't want to play us on the Saturday. I would be the same. But my point is that there are two days allocated for Uefa Cup ties, and Newcastle could have played Heerenveen on Wednesday. If they had played on Wednesday and Saturday instead of Thursday and Sunday, we'd have played our full team in the FA Cup. The FA should have done something. They should defend the interests of all clubs representing England in Europe.

'Nobody can say I don't respect the cups in England, because when others were playing reserve teams in the Carling Cup I was fielding our best team. Ourselves and Manchester United played our strongest sides in the semi-finals, which was the biggest compliment we could pay the tournament. But this time I cannot do it.'

SUNDAY, 20 FEBRUARY 2005
NEWCASTLE UNITED 1, CHELSEA 0

Chelsea's quadruple dream collapses after Mourinho's double gamble backfires spectacularly. Mourinho, who already has Terry suspended, chooses to rest six more key players ahead of the

Champions League trip to Barcelona, a decision he is forced to rethink after seeing Patrick Kluivert head the home side into a fourth-minute lead.

Duff, Gudjohnsen and Lampard all come off the bench at the break, but 'Plan B' is ripped up within two minutes when Bridge is stretchered off with a suspected broken ankle. Chelsea end the game in disarray, with Duff a virtual passenger for a long spell, and even Gallas limping after a collision with his own keeper. With Cudicini sent off in injury-time, Chelsea actually finish with nine men on the field – two of whom are injured. Little wonder Mourinho starts shaking the hands of Souness and his coaching entourage a minute before the end of the five minutes of added time!

It is Chelsea's first defeat in 16 games and only their second in 30. The Magpies' eagerness to clear the snow off the pitch may have much to do with Terry's ban and the absence of Robben and Drogba, although the Chelsea captain is aware a postponement would rule him out of the Carling Cup final.

The Toon Army are in good voice from the off as they sense an opportunity and they are on their feet with just four minutes gone when their side surges into the lead.

Cole is on the attack but falls, and Kieron Dyer and Nicky Butt combine in the middle of the park to find Laurent Robert on the left. He whips in a cross and Kluivert gets in front of marker Gallas to power an unstoppable header past Cudicini and into the top corner.

Kezman is desperately unfortunate to see his lob clear Shay Given but not the crossbar on 24 minutes, and the Newcastle keeper has to make a solid save from Jarosik nine minutes later.

Mourinho's reaction is as decisive as it is swift, replacing Cole, Geremi and Tiago with Gudjohnsen, Duff and Lampard at the break. But he is left to wish he had not been so bold when Alan Shearer tackles Bridge from behind just two minutes after the restart.

The England defender is in agony and, after extensive treatment on the pitch, he is stretchered off with his left ankle in a protective brace, leaving his side down to ten men as he heads for hospital.

Souness makes his own moves as the game enters its final quarter, replacing Shearer and Dyer with Shola Ameobi and James Milner. Kezman and Gudjohnsen both try their luck from distance to keep Given on his toes.

Full-back Stephen Carr has a chance to wrap things up 16 minutes from time after being played in by Milner, but Duff and Cudicini do enough to deny him only for the keeper to injure his own winger. Cudicini, though, has to suffer even more with his dismissal, ending his dream of a Carling Cup final farewell. 'A selfish person would have let Ameobi score a goal,' Mourinho says. 'Instead Carlo thinks of the team and he bets. He bets, he gives away a free-kick and he gets sent off, but Newcastle do not score. I think it showed the professional that he is.

'You can put a big headline: "Mourinho Guilty Of The Defeat",' the Chelsea manager admits. 'Putting three on at half-time is a risk. But I don't regret it. My life is a risk. I have done it before and would do it again. I am the manager and I make decisions. I am responsible for the defeats; my team are responsible for the wins. I thought the subs would be the best thing for my team. We had ten men for most of the second half and we were better than them. Imagine if we had eleven.'

Bridge is now out long term and Duff (hamstring) and Gallas (groin) are doubts for the trip to the Nou Camp. Mourinho refuses to moan about his injury list in the most crucial week of his reign. 'I don't cry about injuries,' he says. 'When we get on the plane I will think about the Barcelona team. It is time for that now. We can do nothing about the injuries. The medical department will do their best. Sometimes you're proud of your team when they win and sometimes you're proud of your team even when they lose, and I was proud of them today.

'I think the mentality was fantastic – the way the team reacted after losing the goal and playing with ten players during the second 45 and then nine and a half men when Duff was injured. Sometimes defeat makes you think your group is a great one and you are not afraid of the future. I know four trophies is possible. I did it in Porto.

But the domestic competitions are more difficult to win here in England. The result is not fair for us. But I have to be fair and say at Stamford Bridge they did better than us in the first half and we won 4–0, so that was not fair. This is football. We played really well for the team I put on the pitch.'

Shearer describes the win as 'huge'. Asked if the home side were under pressure in the second half, he says, 'I don't think so. If you look at the chances we created and the chances they created, I don't think they really troubled Shay. On the Bridge injury, I don't think we touched each other.'

Souness reiterates the importance of grinding out results without the stylish quality football some fans demand. 'The last two games against Chelsea, luck was not with us. This time is was. They controlled possession after our goal. We are not used to holding on to leads and winning 1–0. That is the first time we have done it since I have been here. Football has never been more cat-and-mouse, never been more cagey. We got a 1–0 and we are delighted. We are in the next round of the cup. Chelsea were criticised at the start of the season. But they kept winning, their confidence grew and they started to score goals.'

As Tyneside celebrates a famous win amid the blizzards that blanket the North East, suddenly Mourinho faces his toughest challenge. They must put behind them their third defeat of the campaign, and find the mental and physical resolve to take on Ronaldinho and friends in the Nou Camp and then a fired-up Steven Gerrard and Fernando Morientes in the Carling Cup final, with the first stirrings of doubt and the sense that the good fortune that has been with them all campaign has turned its back on them at the time of greatest need.

Lampard issues a defiant rallying call, insisting greatness is still within their grasp. 'When you've been winning, it really hurts to drop out of one competition, but there's other things for us to concentrate on. We've got a massive week ahead of us with a lot hinging on it and we need to make sure we're on our game. We can still go on to have a great season. We've got great spirit and belief in ourselves here and will always keep fighting to try and win games. There's disappointment at the minute and the defiance will probably come tomorrow. We'll get together and realise that we're on the verge of some great achievements this year. There's a long way to go on a lot of fronts but we have to make sure we carry through the journey and finish it well.'

Mourinho says, 'Today is not a good moment but there is no time for dramas, especially as we're in a fantastic position to win what we really want to win: the Premiership trophy. I have only good words for my players.'

Team

Cudicini, Johnson, Gallas, Ricardo Carvalho, Bridge, Jarosik, Smertin, Tiago (Gudjohnsen), Geremi (Lampard), Kezman, Cole (Duff).

The Carling Cup

'I LIKE JOSE. HE HAS A GREAT SENSE OF HUMOUR AND A DEVILISH WIT ABOUT HIM. HE SEES HIMSELF AS THE YOUNG GUNSLINGER COME INTO TOWN TO CHALLENGE THE SHERIFF WHO'S BEEN AROUND FOR A WHILE. HE WAS FULL OF IT, CALLING ME BOSS AND BIG MAN. IT WOULD HELP IF HIS GREETINGS WERE ACCOMPANIED BY A DECENT GLASS OF WINE. WHAT HE GAVE ME WAS LIKE PAINT-STRIPPER AND I NOTICE THAT HE DIDN'T HAVE ANY ... NOR DID ROMAN ABRAMOVICH.'

Sir Alex Ferguson after the Carling Cup semi-final at Stamford Bridge
against Manchester United, 12 January 2005

The Carling Cup campaign begins when Chelsea are drawn against fellow Londoners West Ham at Stamford Bridge. A trio of former West Ham players – Frank Lampard, Joe Cole and Glen Johnson, all once idolised at Upton Park – are expecting to run a gauntlet of hate. Assistant manager Steve Clarke says the three players are bracing themselves for a rough ride. 'Having spoken to the lads, they are not expecting a very nice reception from the West Ham fans.'

Lampard has played against West Ham since his move in 2001 but it will be the first opportunity for Cole and Johnson to renew old acquaintances. 'They all want to play against their old club – that is normal,' Clarke adds. 'But it won't affect team selection. All three might play, but it could be two or even one.'

Chelsea will field a strong team because Jose Mourinho is aiming to make the League Cup his first piece of silverware in English football. During his final two seasons with Porto, Mourinho won five of the six available trophies and he is intent on ingraining the same winning mentality at his new club. 'The only difference between Porto and Chelsea is that at Porto we won everything but not at Chelsea,' states Mourinho. 'When you win things together, it makes you stronger. We had two and a half years at Porto of winning and winning and winning and winning ...'

Last season Chelsea lost in the quarter-finals of the Carling Cup to Aston Villa and Clarke says Mourinho has already spelled out what he wants this time around. 'He has told the group that he expects us to win this game and then to go all the way in the League Cup. That is a shift from previous managers.'

WEDNESDAY, 27 OCTOBER 2004

CHELSEA 1, WEST HAM UNITED 0

Last week's Champions League match against CSKA Moscow was played out in near silence at times but there's a much more vibrant atmosphere to this cup tie – that is, until a minority in the crowd loses its self-control and the mood sours. Mourinho makes several changes but still fields a competitive side. In come Carlo Cudicini, Celestine Babayaro, Geremi and Tiago, with Scott Parker starting his second successive match.

The game sees Mateja Kezman's first competitive goal for Chelsea, something which has taken an inordinately long time to arrive. Indeed, after appearing to squander a couple of nailed-on chances in the first half, the Serbian has been receiving stick from a section of the Chelsea fans in the 41,774 crowd. In the 56th minute, however, he gets the reward he deserves for sheer perseverance. Joe Cole plays him in and the striker's shot just evades the groping fingertips of goalkeeper Jimmy Walker to shave the inside of the upright and go in. After the game the Serbian's relief is palpable. 'This was an important goal for me,' says Kezman. 'I feel very free now and I am sure I will score more. Although I missed chances I never gave up. I thought from the first moment of this match that I would score and, in fact, I could have scored a hat-trick.'

The game degenerates in the last 15 minutes after Kezman, who has just been awarded a penalty, is struck above the eye by a coin thrown from among the 6,000 West Ham fans massed behind the goal. With blood pouring from a wound in his forehead, the former PSV Eindhoven striker receives treatment for the cut. Former Hammers favourite, Frank Lampard, is then pelted with more coins before missing the spot-kick.

One of Chelsea's substitutes, Eidur Gudjohnsen, deflects a header against the crossbar and West Ham just fail to force a draw in the dying seconds when Anton Ferdinand, sent forward in a last desperate attempt to salvage something, heads against the bar from Rufus Brevett's cross.

In further outbreaks of crowd trouble, at least two plastic water bottles are thrown onto the pitch as West Ham fans target their former hero Joe Cole. During the evening a Stamford Bridge steward is crushed and has to be taken to hospital after riot police clash with fans who have been pelting the pitch with coins and bottles. Violence flares again after the final whistle when West Ham fans in the Matthew Harding Stand's lower tier fight with police, while Chelsea fans in the top tier appear to throw rubbish from above. It takes 15 minutes for order to be restored inside the ground. Rival fans then clash outside Fulham Broadway tube station as the crowd heads home. Police make 11 arrests for public order offences, carrying offensive weapons and possessing drugs.

It's just a pity that the focus of media attention is falling on a second successive night of football violence in London. These unsavoury scenes come only 24 hours after Liverpool fans threw coins and seats at police during their 3–0 win at Millwall.

After the game West Ham manager Alan Pardew says, 'What happened is a shame. There had been some good English banter between the two sides. There is a big rivalry behind these two clubs and both sets of fans were in good voice.' A police spokesman adds, 'The majority of fans behaved well.'

Pardew meanwhile is comparatively happy with his team's

performance. 'It's difficult to get the ball off Chelsea, but when we did our performance level was good.'

'West Ham played well,' admits Steve Clarke, 'but we could have scored more goals and won more convincingly.'

Team

Cudicini, Ferreira, Carvalho, Gallas, Babayaro, Geremi, Parker (Lampard), Tiago, Kezman, Robben (Gudjohnsen), Cole (Duff).

Chelsea's next Carling Cup opponents are Newcastle United. Having spent two seasons as assistant manager with Newcastle, Steve Clarke knows all about the pressures of working in that football-mad city. He says, 'Newcastle have a good squad of players and great support, but they need to win a trophy. They've invested a lot of money in the squad and need something to show for it. They desperately want to be successful and will be smarting from Sunday's defeat by Fulham as they don't like getting beaten on their own ground – 4–1 is a very heavy defeat and they'll come out wanting to make up for it.'

Meanwhile, Mourinho's side have moved to the top of the Premiership for the first time following Saturday's 1–0 win over Everton. Clarke says, 'We've never really thought about being top of the league, second, third or fourth. We just want to win as many games as we can. It's the Carling Cup, so we'll have a totally different psyche. There's pressure every time these boys pull on a Chelsea shirt, because they're expected to perform. I'm sure they can all handle it.

'We'll make one or two changes, but it won't necessarily weaken the team as we've lots of top international players. It's the time of year when we need to rest one or two because we've got a difficult schedule and a lot of games. It doesn't get easier between now and Christmas.'

WEDNESDAY, 10 NOVEMBER 2004

NEWCASTLE UNITED 0, CHELSEA 2 (AET)

Until extra-time Mourinho cuts a frustrated figure in the dug-out. Laurent Robert is the main architect of Newcastle's territorial domination and has three long-range efforts well saved by Carlo Cudicini. Plan A – with Joe Cole up front, Damien Duff down the left and Tiago in midfield – isn't working, so Mourinho switches to Plan B, unleashing Frank Lampard and Arjen Robben on Newcastle with 20 minutes to go. The game is transformed.

Robben immediately looks the greatest threat on the pitch, and so it proves when he jinks down the left wing and dinks a ball to Eidur Gudjohnsen, who has only been on the pitch for three minutes but still manages to power home a drive low past Shay Given in the 100th minute of an absorbing game. It marks the end of the home side's challenge. Twelve minutes later it really is all over after a superb individual effort from wonderboy Robben. He picks up the ball 45 yards out and dribbles at the heart of Newcastle's defence before flashing his shot across goal and into the far corner.

In the post-match press conference, Mourinho admits, 'We were ready for penalties. But I told them Newcastle would be more tired than us in extra-time and we would get the space. The answer was magnificent again. All of my players gave a fantastic performance. Carlo and Glen Johnson gave a fantastic answer. John Terry and William Gallas were great behind this team.'

Newcastle manager Graeme Souness contributes his personal viewpoint. 'It was a very close call. We had better chances than them and this is hard on us. We leave with nothing after lots of hard work. We defended really well and shaded it in normal time. But Chelsea are a really class side. The first goal was important and they got it. Chelsea will be right up there at the end of the season.'

After watching his skipper guide the club into the Carling Cup quarter-finals, Mourinho insists that John Terry is worth every penny of his lucrative new contract. The England international has just signed a new five-year deal, worth £80,000 a week, and Mourinho is convinced it is money well spent. 'He's ready for everything; he's a top player. To be fair, in this country, maybe you have the best central defenders in the world – John Terry, Sol Campbell, Rio Ferdinand, Ledley King and Jonathan Woodgate. But John Terry is the one for me, partly because he's a Chelsea boy – he grew up here, he was born in Chelsea and he feels Chelsea like nobody else – besides he's a big influence in the dressing room and he deserves every coin.'

This is Chelsea's tenth win in 11 games and their seventh victory in a row, a sequence which has seen the Blues concede just four goals in 18 games with only one defeat. The Blues make the short trip to near neighbours Fulham in the next round.

> **Team**
> Cudicini, Johnson, Terry, Gallas, Bridge, Ferreira, Tiago, Parker (Gudjohnsen), Duff (Robben), Kezman, Cole (Lampard).

With Fulham next up in the quarter-finals, Chelsea are taking the Carling Cup seriously because they want to lift *all four* trophies this season. Arjen Robben says, 'We are still in four competitions and our aim is to win them all. You can't go into a competition with any other attitude. It will be very hard to win all four but we'll try.'

'We are now in a time of rotation,' Mourinho says as the Fulham game looms into view. Chelsea could showcase the strength in depth that makes them increasingly likely to win the title. Chelsea's second string is truly first-class: Scott Parker (England international), Wayne Bridge (the second best English left-back), Alexei Smertin (captain of Russia), Mateja Kezman (prolific for PSV Eindhoven), Joe Cole (England awaits his imminent development) and Carlo Cudicini (last season's first-choice goalkeeper).

'You can have the top stars; you can have the best stadium; you can have the best facilities and the most beautiful project in terms of marketing, but if you don't win, all the work these people are doing is forgotten. You have to win and especially, as I have, you have to win a trophy for the first time,' Mourinho says.

After scoring four goals in each of their last three away Premiership games, only Arsenal have a better goalscoring record than Chelsea. But Arsenal have not won the League Cup since 1993 and Manchester United's only triumph in the competition came a year earlier. It would underline the opulence of Chelsea's resources if they were to succeed in the Carling Cup while maintaining a push for the Premiership, the Champions League and FA Cup glory.

TUESDAY, 30 NOVEMBER 2004

FULHAM 1, CHELSEA 2

In the first half Fulham's four-player midfield gives them a man over and it is only after a half-time change of formation that Chelsea start to open up their hosts. Chelsea look to be on their way when Damien Duff's 54th-minute shot from the edge of the box takes a horrible deflection off Ian Pearce's outstretched leg and hops past the wrong-footed Edwin van der Sar. This deflection is a cruel blow for a Fulham team bidding to reach the semi-finals for the first time.

Yet Fulham are determined to make a fight of it and gain their reward in the 74th minute when Ghana-born striker Elvis Hammond, who has only been on the pitch a matter of seconds, whips an inviting low cross past John Terry for Brian McBride to force his way beyond Ricardo Carvalho and shoot home.

Unfortunately for manager Chris Coleman, his team do not have the finesse to break down the meanest defence in the business, with front man Andy Cole guilty of failing to hit the target on at least three occasions.

In the end, substitute Frank Lampard strikes the winner with just two minutes to go, after van der Sar fumbles in his 20-yard shot. The marathon man of England's midfield has replaced Duff 12 minutes earlier and simply refuses to let this tie drag on when everyone else is steeling themselves for extra-time.

Lampard nearly didn't play because he is in mourning for his grandfather, Bill Harris, who died the previous weekend. Before the game, Mourinho offers to leave him out. 'I spoke with Frank before the game and asked him how he was feeling. He said he wanted to be here to help his team. He is a great guy and a great professional. His attitude is fantastic. I asked him about this game and next week's tie against Porto because the funeral is next Monday. He will travel separately to us next week. We will go in the morning and he will go later, but he still wants to join us there.'

After the game Lampard comments, 'That goal was for my granddad. Now we want to go on and win this tournament and get a cup in the bag by the end of February.

'We don't consider ourselves to be "The Invincibles". That's the term used for Arsenal last season but we want to get to that level. We're not there yet because we haven't won anything. But all the players want to go on and win the Carling Cup.'

Fulham manager Coleman says he got the reaction he wanted from his team after their weekend disaster against Blackburn. 'We've matched the country's best team and it's a huge disappointment to lose like that.'

Coleman believes Chelsea may not win all the trophies they are after. 'There is certainly enough quality in the squad but I think it will be hard for them to win all four. I think they will win two – the Premiership and possibly the Champions League. They are in the semi-finals of the Carling Cup and they could win this as well. But I think that the games build up towards the end of the season and it is a big ask.'

Team

Cudicini, Johnson, Carvalho, Terry, Bridge, Smertin, Makelele, Parker, Duff (Lampard), Robben (Cole), Drogba (Gudjohnsen).

While the Carling Cup remains at the bottom of Mourinho's list of priorities, he believes that winning his first trophy as Chelsea boss will enable his side to cross the last remaining mental hurdle.

'I have told the players that this is a competition which finishes in February. It doesn't go on until May or June. If we can reach the final, it would be great for all of us, and especially for the club as they haven't been involved in big occasions for a few years. If you can get through to the final, you go. If we can win, we win.'

Following alleged missile-throwing by fans during their Carling Cup tie at Stamford Bridge, Chelsea and West Ham are both charged by the FA. On 15 December, the FA announces on their website, 'Chelsea FC and West Ham United FC have been charged for the behaviour of their supporters during their Carling Cup match at Stamford Bridge. The two clubs have been charged with a breach of FA Rule E22(a) for their alleged failure to ensure that spectators, and/or persons purporting to be its supporters or followers, conducted themselves in an orderly fashion and refrained from threatening and/or violent and/or provocative behaviour.'

The Carling Cup semi-final draw pits Chelsea against Manchester United. Manchester United thus get a chance to spoil Chelsea's perfect season and repair their own at the same time. United have been second best to Chelsea since the very first league game of the season, when Mourinho's fledgling side ground out a 1–0 victory over them at Stamford Bridge. Twenty-one matches later, Chelsea are brimming with confidence, having cast an inconsistent United 11 points adrift in the title race. Not only have they left United third in the table, dropped champions Arsenal to second and qualified for the FA Cup fourth round, but Chelsea have also been resolute in Europe and are the first club into the Champions League knock-out stages after qualifying with two matches to spare and without conceding a goal in the first four games.

Fergie abandons his policy of playing his second string in the Carling Cup and recalls his star names. 'It will be a stronger team at Chelsea, without being my strongest team. I know I said I'd stick with the side that beat Arsenal in the previous round, but injuries and circumstances have changed all that. The team will be a mixture of first-teamers and youngsters. I can't risk all our players because we play Liverpool on Saturday. We've got a fantastic record in semi-finals since I came to this club: I've never lost a domestic semi and, when you get this close to a final, you want to go all the way.'

With Chelsea and United not due to meet again in the league until 16 April, Fergie knows this is one of his last chances to land a psychological blow on the team everyone is chasing. 'Chelsea have had a great season, you can't deny that. They've had great momentum. They are 11 points clear of us and seven clear of Arsenal. That tells you the story. But, historically, what the next few months tell you is that they will have a blip. However, they have a lot of players and a strong squad, so it's going to be interesting.'

WEDNESDAY, 12 JANUARY 2005

CHELSEA 0, MANCHESTER UNITED 0

A goalless draw at the Bridge ensures it will be advantage United when the teams square up again at Old Trafford for the second leg. The way the visiting fans celebrate at the end of the game suggests they think they will make it through.

Fergie has said the Blues cannot win all four competitions – and he may be right. But United are fortunate. Twice they clear off the line in the second half and, after the game, Mourinho is furious at the performance of referee Neale Barry after the break.

Mourinho claims United got all the decisions from then on because Fergie 'got at him'; he cites a shocking high tackle by Quinton Fortune on Drogba just before a mass brawl that went unpunished.

For his part, Fergie reckons United are hard done by in the first half when Barry turns down a tenth-minute penalty appeal. Louis Saha, back in the United team after a 14-game absence because of a knee injury, is sandwiched as Tiago and Paulo Ferreira challenge him in the area. Then, within two minutes, Cristiano Ronaldo goes sprawling as he checks away from a sliding tackle by Terry. Ronaldo's reputation as a diver has gone before him. Lampard flicks a header wide and

Gudjohnsen converts Duff's cross only to be given offside. Wayne Rooney then brings out the best in Carlo Cudicini, who flies to his left to save the young Liverpudlian's firm header.

After the interval Chelsea replace Gudjohnsen with Drogba and Mourinho's side up their game. Joe Cole volleys Tim Howard's poor clearance wide and on 48 minutes Frank Lampard shows great skill to break into the box and beat Howard with a close-range shot but Gabriel Heinze gets back to clear his shot off the line.

Heinze is then booked for a foul on Drogba and from the free-kick Lampard squares to the striker whose deflected shot is saved by Howard. The game may be scoreless but it is far from dull and Lampard goes close as he volleys Drogba's headed flick just past the post from 25 yards. Chelsea deserve better than a draw but you cannot fault the way United get stuck in to keep them at bay.

Sub Jiri Jarosik pops up in the box with a crisp angled far-post snapshot but Phil Neville denies him on the post. Mourinho then finds himself wrestling in the middle of a late melee after Drogba and Ronaldo clash when the ball goes out of play close to the dugouts. Drogba has Fortune by the throat while Ronaldo is swinging his arms wildly.

Drogba and Ronaldo are booked but that may not be the end of the matter once the FA have studied the video. And they will be wanting a word with Mourinho after he accuses Ferguson of influencing referee Barry at half-time.

In his cool, calculated style Mourinho fumes, 'There was one referee in the first half and a different one after the break and I suggest he didn't walk alone to the dressing room at half-time. He should go to his dressing room with two linesmen and the fourth official but somebody else was with him and, if the FA ask me about that, I'll tell them.

'Maybe one day when I am 60, when I've been in the same league for 20 years and I know everyone and they respect me, I will also have the power to speak and people will tremble a bit. The second half was fault after fault and diving and more diving. There were dozens and dozens of free-kicks; the ball went into the Manchester United end a number of times and he awarded only two minutes of stoppage time. I'm not questioning the integrity of the referee. I'm sure he is a nice man. It was a question of a big personality influencing another person without as much prestige in English football. I told the fourth official what I felt at the end. It was very important for me to understand a few things of what I saw, what I heard and what I felt at half-time.'

Fergie does not deny his chat with Barry but insists, 'Well, I certainly didn't influence him in the first half!' The United boss says his team should have had a penalty when Saha went down. 'I've seen it on TV and it certainly looks a foul. But we were at Chelsea and it was always going to be difficult to get a penalty.'

Mourinho retorts, 'Manchester United should be forbidden from speaking about referees for at least a year after what happened against Tottenham [Pedro Mendes's last-minute, 40-yard shot which crossed the line, a fact never acknowledged by match officials at Old Trafford] last week. That was the most ridiculous thing I've seen for a long time.'

John Terry maintains that Chelsea will still win through. 'I thought it was a good performance from the lads. It was just a shame we didn't manage to break them down and get a one- or two-goal cushion for the second leg. We said before the game that if it didn't work out for us in the first leg, we would go up there and get a result and that's exactly what we have to do now. We're not going to throw it away now. We're treating the Carling Cup seriously because it's the first final of the season and we want to be there.'

Team

Cudicini, Ferreira, Gallas, Terry, Bridge, Tiago (Kezman), Makelele, Lampard, Cole (Jarosik), Duff, Gudjohnsen (Drogba).

Mourinho initially escapes punishment from the FA for his comments but referees' chief Keith Hackett wants him to apologise.

'What Jose Mourinho has said is rubbish. The truth is that at half-time Alex Ferguson shouted to the referee, "There are two teams out there." Neale is one of our most experienced referees and was not influenced by that. The facts show that in the second half there were 19 free-kicks – ten of them went to Chelsea and nine to United. I'm hoping that Mourinho might reconsider his comments. Managers do not go into the referee's dressing room at half-time and neither did so on Wednesday. Referees are impartial and Neale Barry is one of the best. On this occasion, it is the comments of a manager who didn't get the result he wanted.'

Statistics do, however, show that Barry punishes Chelsea players more often than other clubs. And he is lenient when reffing Manchester United games. Since 1998, he has given Chelsea 17 bookings in seven games. By contrast, he has shown 10 yellow cards to United in 13 matches.

Mourinho renews his war with Ferguson by branding Manchester United 'cheats'. The Chelsea boss is now in deep trouble with the FA after taking his outburst a step too far. Mourinho says, 'Sir Alex was really clever, if you can say that, at half-time by putting some pressure on the ref. In the second half, it was whistle and whistle, fault and fault, and cheat and cheat.'

Mourinho makes his remarks on Chelsea's own TV channel and his use of the word 'cheat' is likely to enrage both Ferguson and the FA. Arsene Wenger was fined £15,000 earlier in the season for branding Van Nistelrooy a 'cheat' and the FA will be under pressure to haul Mourinho to Soho Square.

On the other hand, Ferguson may see Mourinho's rant as a sign that his mind games are beginning to rattle the Portuguese. Having considered Mourinho's comments, Ferguson comes to the conclusion that the main reason behind them is to try and exert influence over Graham Poll who is taking charge of the encounter between Chelsea and Tottenham at White Hart Lane.

The Scot is annoyed enough to recall Porto's diving antics during last season's Champions League clash with United, then to set his sights on John Terry's claim that Barry refused to listen to him during the game. 'I think Mourinho has opened a can of worms for himself. We remember what happened in Porto. Look back a couple of weeks to the penalty decision that went their way against Liverpool and how Rafael Benitez handled that. But I don't think his comments have anything to do with what happened on Wednesday. It was more about trying to influence the referee for tomorrow's game against Tottenham.'

In a fresh charm offensive Mourinho insists he will go mob-handed to Soho Square to fight any disrepute charge and maintains he has no feud with the United boss. Indeed, he reveals he will be taking a bottle of splendid Portuguese wine to share with Ferguson after the return leg at Old Trafford in a fortnight because the United manager complained bitterly about the vintage they had drunk in Mourinho's office after the first leg! Mourinho says, 'I will be happy to go to the FA with the five, six or seven people who were with me in the tunnel. I won't accept any fine; if they fine me, I will have to pay, but I won't accept it because I did nothing wrong. Since the first day I arrived in England, I've done nothing wrong with referees.

'I know I could be punished for pointing out that someone else has done something wrong. So if the FA do it, I think it will be unfair. I don't think they should punish Sir Alex for what he did; I think they should just tell referees not to allow it whether they are the top manager in the country, a guy has who just arrived or a lower-division manager. I always say what I think and feel and I am not worried by the consequences. If Sir Alex can do that in the Stamford Bridge tunnel – and the tunnel at Chelsea is only ten metres long – I can only imagine what he can do in the Old Trafford tunnel, which is 30 metres. If the FA want me to go there and say what happened in those ten metres, I will go.'

Mourinho's 'cheat' comments were not, it seems, directed at referee Barry but at what Mourinho perceived to be the tendency of United's players to fall down at the first touch. He admits that the use of the word 'cheat' may have been wrong in the circumstances, yet he still hints that United's players were diving. 'Maybe the word is not the correct one and it is not in relation to the referee. It was in relation to players trying to get faults after faults. Maybe "cheat" is not the correct word. For me, "cheat" means when a player gets one touch and they dive.'

The last time Mourinho visited Old Trafford he ended up tearing joyfully down the touchline after his Porto side knocked Manchester United out of the Champions League with a late goal. This time he hopes to be celebrating more than just his 42nd birthday, which falls on the day of the game.

Ferguson has not beaten Mourinho in four attempts and Chelsea have lost only three of their 12 visits to Old Trafford in the Premiership. But Chelsea are aiming to win their first cup tie at Old Trafford in seven attempts. Ferguson has never lost a domestic semi-final in his 18 years at the club.

The word from the United camp is that victory is essential to halt Chelsea's title drive; Ferguson is not quite as convinced about the effect defeat would have on Mourinho and his team. 'It would take a lot of damage to allow us to claw back 11 points. That is a big lead at this time of year.'

For an entire week, Sir Alex is full of praise for Mourinho and Chelsea, but the compliments stop when it is put to him that the London club could one day be bigger than Manchester United. 'That's the most stupid question I've heard this year. You should be apologising for even asking it.'

The second leg will be watched by 68,000 compared with the 41,492 who saw the first leg. In two years, Old Trafford's capacity will rise to 75,000. The club museum and the trophy cabinet complete Fergie's argument. Yet overtaking United and Real Madrid as football's greatest income-generators is precisely what Chelsea are aiming for.

WEDNESDAY, 26 JANUARY 2005

MANCHESTER UNITED 1, CHELSEA 2
(CHELSEA WIN 2–1 ON AGGREGATE)

When Mourinho shakes the hands of the Manchester United players in the tunnel before kick-off, they look confused, sheepish and puzzled. Only Ronaldo smiles and grasps his countryman's hand of friendship.

Ferguson's players have set a club record with a sequence of eight consecutive clean sheets but Mourinho has pinpointed a weakness and is as relentless as ever in preying upon it. Didier Drogba persistently pulls out wide, delivering one pass for the opener and providing another from which Arjen Robben should extend the lead.

United find themselves trailing to Frank Lampard's strike just before the half hour. The in-form midfielder gives United an early warning with a typical surge into the box but his effort from Duff's pull-back is scuffed wide. The next chance comes from Lampard again and it gives the visitors the lead. Lampard delivers a straight pass forward from inside his own half to Robben, who in turn feeds Drogba in the United penalty box. He holds the ball up, then picks out Lampard, who bursts past Roy Keane before controlling the ball with his first touch and dispatching the shot with his second past Tim Howard into the far corner.

United enjoy plenty of possession but, with Claude Makelele patrolling the midfield, they cannot break down the Blues back line. They have legitimate claims for a penalty not long before half-time as Bridge sticks out a foot to bring Quinton Fortune down from behind. The left-back has no need to make such a challenge with the ball heading out of the box. Fortunately for Chelsea, referee Rob Styles may be unsighted by Lampard and he waves play on.

Some heroics from Howard save the Red Devils from conceding a killer second not long before Giggs magically brings United back into it. The American keeper may now be a confirmed second choice behind Roy Carroll but his recent form has been excellent, barring his late blunder to allow Duff's free-kick to find the target.

Twice he keeps United in the hunt, scrambling away a goal-bound Lampard effort, before earning top marks for a feet-first stop which denies Robben. Giggs then produces another semi-final beauty to add to his solo effort against Arsenal in the 1999 FA Cup. Gary

Neville clips a curling ball into the box from the right touchline. With Terry back-pedalling and Cech advancing, Giggs slips between them and chips a first-time volley over the goalkeeper and into the unguarded net.

Chelsea respond by rising above the frenzied atmosphere and clinically looking for a second. They get it, although they benefit from Howard's misjudgement as Duff swings a dead-ball in from the right that eludes everyone to find the net.

United rally and it needs a goal-line clearance from Bridge to deny Mikael Silvestre as well as a brilliant Petr Cech save to thwart Ronaldo before Mourinho is able to celebrate yet another famous night at Old Trafford.

Later Giggs points out that Chelsea found themselves on the rack during the game. 'When we upped the tempo of our play in the second half, I didn't think Chelsea could live with us. We all recognise Chelsea are a quality side but I have not seen them rattled like that before. Once we scored it looked like there would only be one winner. We definitely felt we did enough to get something out of the game but I suppose if you make mistakes in a semi-final against a team as good as they are, you will get punished.'

Mourinho says, 'This was perfect. I'll never forget it. We have given everyone a message that we are really strong. The boys were magnificent and we're ready to win the Premiership now. If you can finish your day with such an important victory, it is the perfect day. The plan was just to win the game and be in the final but we knew, with the opponent and the atmosphere, that a semi-final is always difficult and we were ready for anything.'

Ferguson, who has now failed to beat Mourinho in five attempts, is displeased about the defending for Duff's winning goal. He says, 'In 18 years you expect to lose a semi-final some time. But I didn't want it to happen tonight. We're not happy about the free-kick from 50 yards out – you can't expect to win losing goals like that. We played exceptionally well in the second half. It was a great game; you couldn't divide the teams today. They are a threat on the counter-attack but we coped with that well and I thought we had the far bigger momentum in the second half.'

Asked about whether giving Fergie a £240 bottle of Portuguese vintage red was a fair swap for claiming his proud 18-year-old unbeaten semi-final record, Mourinho graciously insists, 'I would love to lose my records at his age, for his records are absolutely magnificent. I would be very pleased if I kept winning and winning and winning and then I lose one semi-final in 20 years.'

Team

Cech, Ferreira, Gallas, Terry, Bridge, Makelele, Lampard, Tiago, Duff (Jarosik), Drogba (Gudjohnsen), Robben (Cole).

A date at Cardiff is the first tangible reward for all the investment and hard work that has been put in at Stamford Bridge. Mourinho says, 'This final is a great gift for Roman Abramovich who has given so much to this club. From the beginning I thought we could achieve good things.'

Mourinho seems genuinely pleased that Liverpool and Rafael Benitez will provide the opposition in Cardiff. 'It's fantastic for Rafa because he had a difficult week and now he's in the final. It's not easy for managers to adapt to a new country. Liverpool is Liverpool, and Liverpool is history, so it's a fantastic final for the clubs, for the pros like we are and for the supporters.'

Attendances at Old Trafford in the last two rounds of the Carling Cup, against Arsenal and then Chelsea, have been the highest, apart from finals, in the competition's 45-year history. This year's final will have a higher profile than last season's, which was between Bolton and Middlesbrough, and will be contested by something close to full-strength sides, allowing for the exertions a few days earlier of Champions League games against Barcelona and Bayer Leverkusen respectively. Chelsea have beaten Liverpool twice already this season – by a single Joe Cole goal each time.

Mourinho believes the opposition will be all the stronger by the end of February when the final is played. 'When we went to Liverpool they had no Morientes, and Baros was injured. In one month's time, maybe they have both and will have a lot of power. And of course there is Steven [note the first-name terms!] and a good defensive organisation.'

Steve Bennett is appointed to referee the Carling Cup final, the first domestic cup final for the 44-year-old from Kent who has been on the FIFA list since 2001.

Mourinho is then charged with improper conduct by the FA for his 'cheat, cheat, cheat' comments after the semi-final first leg with Manchester United. Mourinho denies the FA charge of improper conduct and requests a personal hearing to defend himself.

In a major break with tradition, Mourinho wants to treat the final like any other away match, so there will be no designer suits. Mourinho doesn't want his players distracted; he orders his players and staff to make sure the build-up is low-key. When Chelsea last reached a final, their 2–0 defeat by Arsenal in the FA Cup three years ago, they won style points for their Giorgio Armani blue pinstriped suits. But this time the players will be in the normal Hugo Boss club suits the squad wear to away matches. Mourinho, no doubt, will wear the grey trench coat his wife bought him when the winter weather kicked in, because he believes it brings him luck.

The biggest week in Mourinho's first season begins in the worst possible way, FA Cup defeat at Newcastle, before the team head off to Barcelona for the Champions League with a series of injuries and lose 2–1. Wayne Bridge is left behind with a suspected broken ankle and Carlo Cudicini is ruled out of the final after being sent off against Newcastle.

Chelsea lodge an appeal with the FA on their goalkeeper's behalf. Cudicini has to wait 48 hours to know whether or not he will be cleared to play in the final with Liverpool. The Italian was dismissed after bringing down Ameobi just outside the Chelsea penalty area. Match official Mark Halsey deems Cudicini to have 'denied an obvious goalscoring opportunity', although TV replays indicate

Ameobi was heading away from goal when he was sent clattering to the ground. Mourinho promised Cudicini he would play in the Millennium Stadium showpiece. But Chelsea withdraw their appeal since they stand little chance of overturning the red card without the cooperation of the ref.

Benitez claims Liverpool's 3–1 Champions League victory over Bayer Leverkusen has boosted Anfield. 'The victory gives us confidence for the Carling Cup final. To score three times in a Champions League game is very good and should improve my team's morale. And do not forget that we have Steven Gerrard and Fernando Morientes back.'

Last summer Steven Gerrard's dad Paul, a straight-talking Scouser, warned his son that he was about to become the most hated ex-Liverpool player in the club's history and that his family would become outcasts in their beloved home city if he joined Chelsea. After hearing his words Gerrard stood in the Anfield trophy room and announced he had no intention of joining Chelsea and that his future lay at Liverpool. The club had managed to hold on to its favourite son for one more season at least. Gerrard's decision to stay at Anfield meant he turned down an extra £15m from Chelsea in increased wages.

Liverpool deny it, but Chelsea insiders now insist a deal will eventually be agreed to sign Gerrard. Apparently he made up his mind to join Chelsea while on England duty in Portugal during Euro 2004 and even texted Mourinho and Peter Kenyon to announce his decision. He was 'less than a week' away from completing the move.

Liverpool chief executive Rick Parry is believed to have held at least two private meetings with Paul Gerrard at the exclusive Royal Birkdale Golf Club to convince him that Steven's future lay at Anfield. John Williams, of Leicester University's Football Research Centre, who is also a Liverpool season ticket holder and closely monitors events at Anfield, says, 'The board mobilised his [Gerrard's] family to work on him. It was emphasised that this was more than about football and money; this was about family and loyalty and the fact that Liverpool is where Steven belongs. The family, particularly Gerrard's father, implored him to stay.'

Former Liverpool player Howard Gayle, who is still closely connected to the club and, like Gerrard, was born in the city, adds, 'There was a feeling that, when Gerrard was in Portugal during Euro 2004, his head was turned by some people telling him that he needed to move on. Gerrard's dad soon put him right and had serious words with him. He just told his son, "Look in the mirror, you are a hero around here, can you really turn your back on the club now?"'

This time the mood is different. There is a sense of inevitability about his move and locals are prepared for Gerrard to leave for west London. Gerrard's deal with his father Paul was that he would give the new regime of Benitez one more season and that, if he was still dissatisfied with Liverpool's progress, he could leave. Williams adds, 'Steven is already in the departure lounge and if he was to go this summer it wouldn't be a big surprise to Liverpool fans. Many fans feel he's done his bit and that he should be free to go; it will hurt, but they are ready for it.'

Gerrard leads his side into the final believing that a major upset is on the cards after Chelsea were knocked out of the FA Cup at Newcastle and then stumbled to a disappointing Champions League reverse in Barcelona, with a sending-off in each game. Liverpool hope to make it a treble of misery. Gerrard argues, 'I really think the pressure is on Chelsea now. Everyone is expecting them to go to Cardiff and win the final and that could work against them. We are going there with the intention of upsetting the odds.'

For more years than he cares to remember, Gerrard has dreamt of lifting a trophy as skipper of the club he has supported since he was a boy. 'If anyone wants to know how much lifting a cup for Liverpool as captain means to me, they should just watch my face if I do that on Sunday.'

Benitez's side have been beaten twice by Chelsea but Gerrard is adamant the London side were lucky to come away with two 1–0 victories. Liverpool dominated for long periods in the New Year's Day fixture at Anfield before Cole stole the points with a late winner, just as he had done at Stamford Bridge earlier in the season.

Gerrard says, 'Chelsea are a very good team full of world-class players so it will be a tough game, but we're confident we can win. They were a bit lucky against us at Anfield. It's a big couple of months for Liverpool. We're fighting for fourth place in the league and are still involved in two cup competitions. We are confident we can get to the last eight of the Champions League but our main aim is to upset Chelsea on Sunday. That's our best chance of winning a trophy.'

Mourinho will not receive a win bonus if he leads the club to a first trophy in five years. Although Mourinho's contract includes scope for generous bonus payments on top of his basic £2.25m-a-year salary, they do not cover the Carling Cup, providing a revealing insight into the club's attitude towards the competition. Mourinho will receive huge bonuses if Chelsea win the Premiership, FA Cup or Champions League, but the Carling Cup is not deemed important enough to merit additional remuneration.

But Mourinho is desperate to collect his first trophy in English football and will select a full-strength side.

John Terry is still haunted by the memory of his last visit to the Millennium Stadium when he was ruled out of the 2002 FA Cup final by a mystery ear infection. 'I woke up on the morning of the match and literally fell out of bed. The balance in my eardrum had gone. Apparently it was vertigo. I'd never suffered it before and have never suffered it since. So it wasn't a good day to go down with it! I did come on as a second-half sub but we lost 2–0 and the medal I got that day doesn't mean a lot.

'I got a winners' medal against Aston Villa in 2000 – but I didn't get off the bench at all that day. Now this is a chance for me to go to Cardiff, enjoy the pre-match atmosphere and hopefully pick up a trophy.

'Everyone at the club knows how important it is to get our first cup. Put one in the cabinet and get the confidence to go on. Then, hopefully, we can add a couple more. This is a perfect chance for us to shut up all those people who are saying that this is finally

Chelsea's blip. There is always an element of jealousy in football and people want to knock you down when you're at the top. It's up to us to deal with that criticism. Losing two games is a new experience for us this season but this final is the perfect opportunity to bounce back.'

Terry also has a point to prove to Fernando Morientes after he scored the goals for Monaco that knocked Chelsea out of last season's Champions League semi-final. 'We really thought we were going all the way, so it would be nice to get our revenge.

'Morientes is a tremendous player, good in the air, strong and holds the ball up well for players like Stevie Gerrard to come through from the midfield. We've got to keep those players quiet because we've put a lot of effort into this cup and it will mean nothing if we lose the final.'

Defiant Mourinho, who ordered a media black-out after the Barcelona game, holds a press conference ahead of the final in which he taunts Sir Alex Ferguson and Arsene Wenger, insisting both would want to swap places with him. An indignant Mourinho denies that the Blues are experiencing the blip that Manchester United and Arsenal have been waiting for and insists that, of the three sides, Chelsea are the most likely to go through to the Champions League quarter-finals. 'They can't speak to us about blips because they're not in a better position than us. Do they want to change positions with us? We are top of the league by nine points and in the Carling Cup final; we didn't lose at home in the Champions League to Milan and didn't lose 3–1 in Munich. If you think two defeats makes me doubt our work or what we can do in the future, I tell you: no chance. The only thing they can say they are in a better position than us in is the FA Cup.'

Asked about the importance of his first piece of silverware, he says, 'I'm not the point. I prefer to analyse it as Chelsea's first trophy of a new regime. People speak a lot, and rightly so, about all the money this club has invested in buying players, but the reality is that we are talking about a process – the process of building a team and a football club – and Chelsea are nowhere near a finished product. We are at the beginning of the process. If you can win trophies during our stage in that development, it is fantastic, because normally you have to wait until it is finished. To get a trophy now would be fantastic, and I'm sure Liverpool feel the same. They have not spent the same sort of money, of course, but they have the same ambitions as us. My friend Rafa Benitez hasn't come to England just to visit; he's here to make Liverpool a winning team again. Maybe he has more time to do it, but they also want to win a trophy.

'We're on top at the moment, but not because of the club's financial power. We are in contention for a lot of trophies because of my hard work, coaching sessions and the team ethic I have instilled here. My philosophy is that you don't win a game during 90 minutes. A winning team is made day by day, training session by training session, minute by minute. Winning the Carling Cup will be a testament to that. A team has to play in the image of their coach. They have to be able to do things with their eyes closed. That isn't about money or having people working together for years. It is about me making them work hard and putting on good training sessions. Then the success will come.'

SUNDAY, 27 FEBRUARY 2005

LIVERPOOL 2, CHELSEA 3

Mourinho shows another side of his character before kick-off when Carlo Cudicini leads the team out despite being unable to play. However, first-choice goalkeeper Petr Cech finds himself picking the ball out of the back of his net with just 45 seconds gone as Fernando Morientes arcs over a searching deep cross. John-Arne Riise is unmarked at the far post and produces a thunderous first-time volley to leave Cech rooted to the spot. Steven Gerrard responds by setting a captain's example by winning his first full-blooded, 50-50 tackle with Lampard.

Sami Hyypia comes close to being sent off just after the break.

Already booked for bringing down Joe Cole, referee Steve Bennett looks set to issue another yellow card before realising what this would entail. Hyypia instead escapes and Mourinho starts to lose his temper when he berates both Luis Garcia and Jamie Carragher from the touchline as the match grows in intensity.

The Chelsea boss changes the pattern of the game with his introduction of Eidur Gudjohnsen at half-time, replacing Jiri Jarosik. Gudjohnsen re-energises his team as Chelsea lay siege to the Liverpool goal, even if Jerzy Dudek conjures up a fantastic double save first from Gudjohnsen and then from William Gallas. Benitez brings on Milan Baros and, just moments later, Gerrard comes agonisingly close to putting his side 2–0 up only to divert Antonio Nunez's cross inches wide from close range.

After Didi Hamann brings down Frank Lampard in full flight, the Blues duly equalise from the free-kick. Gerrard jumps highest, challenged only by his own players, to meet Ferreira's mis-flighted delivery but succeeds in diverting the ball past Dudek. At this point Mourinho cannot contain his celebrations and is dismissed from the touchline. Dudek is then injured in a clash with Damien Duff, and, with his side's three substitutes already on, there is a nervous wait for Benitez before he carries on.

Just a minute into the second period of extra-time, Hyypia fails to cut out substitute Glen Johnson's long throw and Drogba bundles the ball over the goal-line from close range. Then Dudek fails to hold Gudjohnsen's fierce cross and Kezman succeeds in prodding the ball just over the line before the keeper can react in time. Liverpool rally immediately, with Nunez just beating Cech to a header as he flicks the ball into the net, but after this there is no more scoring and Chelsea run out 3–2 winners.

Mourinho is guaranteed a hero's reception from the Chelsea fans when he finally reappears after the final whistle. In his first season, Mourinho has just brought the club their first trophy in five years and only the tenth major success in their entire history.

But he has endured a controversial afternoon. He was shocked that it was a policeman who intervened to send him off after he appeared to gesture to Liverpool fans following Chelsea's 79th-minute equaliser. After Gerrard's own-goal, Mourinho turned to the crowd with his finger to his lips and then was ordered from the dug-out by fourth official Phil Crossley, in conjunction with the head of the national group of referees, Jim Ashworth. 'For me it is unusual to be sent off by the police and not by a fourth official. The policeman told the fourth official Mr Mourinho has to go off, so this is a special situation for me. But again if I made a mistake, if I do something I cannot do in English football, I have to adapt.'

A league official confirms Mourinho was asked to leave the technical area to preserve public order.

Earlier Mourinho had been warned for berating Liverpool players, notably when he pointed an accusing finger at Jamie Carragher, and he was then censured seemingly for inciting Reds fans by putting a finger to his lips after Chelsea's late equaliser.

He later tells a news conference the gesture was not to Liverpool fans but to his critics in the media. 'It was a gesture to be cool, to put your pens back in your pockets,' he says.

In the end, it was Didier Drogba who persuaded Mourinho to go back out on to the pitch to celebrate with his players. 'I had to do this for my team-mates,' says Drogba. 'I told him that we win together, we lose together and we celebrate together. It was me who went back for him but it could have been any of us. That is the spirit of this team.'

Drogba 'had to score' as he later explains, 'I knew I had let my team-mates down in Barcelona by being sent off and I had to make up for that. I know I will not be there for the second match but I am confident the team will win through without me. If I had played one or two more matches before Barcelona, then I am sure I would have been quicker and would not have been sent off. This trophy is very important for us though. We have not been down in many matches this season and won. This will give us great confidence now to go on in both the Champions League and the Premiership.'

Mourinho says Chelsea, who dominated possession

throughout, deserved victory. 'We were the best team. They fought a lot. They defended a lot and well and they were very well organised. They did their best. But when we scored with ten minutes to go, at that moment we had a big advantage from the psychological point of view.

'The attitude of my players was magnificent and we deserved to win, no doubt about it.'

Benitez says his side deserved to win after holding on to the lead for 79 minutes. 'If you have clear chances at 1–0, if you get a second goal, you finish the game. We made mistakes and in the end we conceded a goal. I said to the players we must be proud, we have had a good game; they controlled the game but we were organised as a team and had opportunities. It is difficult to play against Chelsea, but we scored two goals and worked hard. I think that after the game we need to analyse things.'

Gerrard's face is a mask of suppressed rage when his name rings around the Chelsea areas of this magnificent stadium: after his own goal, the idea of his defection to the west London club is mingled deliciously with implied gratitude for his contribution to the cause. The clear implication of the chants was that this was his first significant contribution to his 'new club'!

Later Benitez is adamant his captain must not shoulder any blame and praises his side's defiant performance. 'I spoke to Gerrard afterwards, just as I spoke to the rest of the players, and I said that they should be proud. It's a pity for the team and the fans. It's not a problem for any one player. At the end, to score in your own goal is bad luck, that is all.'

Gerrard is distraught at the end of the match and tries to avoid Mourinho, only to be pursued by the Chelsea boss for a handshake. The significance of that is not lost on fans, but Mourinho says, 'I didn't see Gerrard move away from me; he was feeling very down because he had scored the own goal and I was trying to console him. I went to every member of the Liverpool staff and I didn't see that as a negative thing. I didn't single Gerrard out, I just felt for him.'

During the game Roman Abramovich could be seen willing the ball to cross the line, fidgeting and then jumping for joy as the goals went in. This is the beginning: the first trophy for the owner and the new manager, but it won't be the last.

> **Team**
>
> Cech, Carvalho, Gallas (Kezman), Ferreira, Terry, Cole (Johnson), Duff, Jarosik (Gudjohnsen), Lampard, Makelele, Drogba.

In an interview with Portuguese television, Mourinho continues to insist that he was banished to the stands by the police. 'I wasn't sent off by the fourth official but by the authorities. This country is different and has its good and bad stuff. It was all because of a gesture to shut up the British Press. For them this is First World and Portugal is Third World. I won't shut up because Chelsea needed a Third World manager to win a trophy, something that didn't happen in the last five years.'

Captured on Sky TV, Mourinho can be seen telling Jamie Carragher to 'f*** off' *five times*. But another rap for Mourinho looks unlikely as the FA await the formal reports. Sifting through the information has taken longer than expected because of the conflicting stories. South Wales Police say that it had nothing to do with Mourinho's removal after Chelsea's equalising goal, an assertion backed by the Football League. 'The decision to ask Jose Mourinho to leave the technical area came from the match officials and was initiated by the fourth official, Phil Crossley,' a spokesman says. 'The match referee, Steve Bennett, was aware of what was happening on the touchline and was content that it was being dealt with correctly.'

Chelsea's director of communications, Simon Greenberg, says Mourinho has apologised if there was any misunderstanding among Liverpool fans over his gesture. 'The manager apologised, which is something people have not made a lot of. He was measured and said that, if he had made a mistake, he apologised for that. He is a guy who knows his own mind and also a guy who does listen. He knows why he did it and we don't have a view on whether that was wrong or not.'

Abramovich, according to John Terry, was 'over the moon' as he joined the players in the dressing room. 'He was having pictures taken with the lads and the trophy,' Terry says. 'He had a couple of glasses of champagne as well, so it is great.'

Inevitably Abramovich's riches have brought envy and resentment. Terry says, 'We don't get irritated by people having a go at us. It is frustrating at times, because we have done really well this season, but it is up to us to stop people from talking. There is only one way to do that, which is on the pitch. We have shut a few people up. It is a great win for us and hopefully that will stop people talking for a little bit. There is definitely no crisis here. When you are at the top, people want to shoot you down. That is where we are at the minute and we have to deal with that.'

Terry calls it 'a massive cup' and adds, 'This trophy means the world to us. The players, the management, the club, the fans – everybody involved with the club. It is a great achievement and a great starting point for us. We are professionals, we are grown up and we deal with that. We can build from this and, if we keep on showing great fight like that until the end of the season, hopefully it will be a great year for us. This is the start of our trophies.'

What counts above all else is that Chelsea had to recover from their lowest ebb to capture the Carling Cup, as Cech points out. 'Our black week is now over. After our failures in the FA Cup at Newcastle and the Champions League at Barcelona, we were under big pressure but we showed we had the inner strength and will to win. We were in our worst position of the season but we came back and defeated Liverpool. We were like a good working machine.'

As he toasts his first winner's medal, Frank Lampard offers further insight into Mourinho's mentality. 'The manager can handle the pressure. He reacts to it in a positive way. He likes a fight, he likes a battle and he stands up to it. This was our message: we won't give in and we will continue that in the league and against Barcelona because we want to win them all. If we had lost, the pressure would really have been on. It would have been a case of going from the quadruple to almost nothing. But we have thrived upon the fact that there has been so much pressure and criticism from outside.'

Mourinho receives news that he has escaped a fine or touchline ban from the FA after his behaviour in Cardiff but he is reprimanded and asked to behave more responsibly in future. 'Jose Mourinho has been reminded of his responsibility to abide by FA rules governing the conduct of managers,' the governing body says. 'He will not face any formal disciplinary action and the FA now considers the matter closed.'

And finally, Wayne Bridge gets to lift the Carling Cup – from his hospital bed. Led by skipper John Terry, players visit the broken-ankle victim and take the trophy along with them. Bridge, who broke his ankle at St James's Park during the FA Cup defeat, will still receive a winner's medal after playing in four of Chelsea's six ties on the road to Cardiff.

The Results

After a thrilling season, Jose Mourinho certainly did take his Chelsea team all the way. The team were crowned champions of both the Premiership and the Carling Cup and their sights are firmly set on more successes next season. Their desire and expectations are so noticeably apparent that they can't fail to excite in the seasons to come. For now though, here is how they became champions in 2004/05 ...

CHELSEA RESULTS LIST

DATE	OPPOSITION		F – A	COMPETITION
15/08/04	Manchester United	H	1 – 0	Premiership
21/08/04	Birmingham City	A	1 – 0	Premiership
24/08/04	Crystal Palace	A	2 – 0	Premiership
28/08/04	Southampton	H	2 – 1	Premiership
11/09/04	Aston Villa	A	0 – 0	Premiership
14/09/04	Paris Saint-Germain	A	3 – 0	Champions League

DATE	OPPOSITION		F – A	COMPETITION
19/09/04	Tottenham Hotspur	H	0 – 0	Premiership
25/09/04	Middlesbrough	A	1 – 0	Premiership
29/09/04	Porto	H	3 – 1	Champions League
03/10/04	Liverpool	H	1 – 0	Premiership
16/10/04	Manchester City	A	0 – 1	Premiership
20/10/04	CSKA Moscow	H	2 – 0	Champions League
23/10/04	Blackburn Rovers	H	4 – 0	Premiership
27/10/04	West Ham	H	1 – 0	Carling Cup
30/10/04	West Bromwich Albion	A	4 – 1	Premiership
02/11/04	CSKA Moscow	A	1 – 0	Champions League
06/11/04	Everton	H	1 – 0	Premiership
10/11/04	Newcastle	A	2 – 0	Carling Cup
13/11/04	Fulham	A	4 – 1	Premiership
20/11/04	Bolton Wanderers	H	2 – 2	Premiership
24/11/04	Paris Saint – Germain	H	0 – 0	Champions League
27/11/04	Charlton Athletic	A	4 – 0	Premiership
30/11/04	Fulham	A	2 – 1	Carling Cup
04/12/04	Newcastle United	H	4 – 0	Premiership
07/12/04	Porto	A	1 – 2	Champions League
12/12/04	Arsenal	A	2 – 2	Premiership
18/12/04	Norwich City	H	4 – 0	Premiership
26/12/04	Aston Villa	H	1 – 0	Premiership
28/12/04	Portsmouth	A	2 – 0	Premiership
01/01/05	Liverpool	A	1 – 0	Premiership
04/01/05	Middlesbrough	H	2 – 0	Premiership
08/01/05	Scunthorpe	H	3 – 1	F.A. Cup
12/01/05	Manchester United	H	0 – 0	Carling Cup
15/01/05	Tottenham Hotspur	A	2 – 0	Premiership
22/01/05	Portsmouth	H	3 – 0	Premiership

DATE	OPPOSITION		F – A	COMPETITION
26/01/05	Manchester United	A	2 – 1	Carling Cup
30/01/05	Birmingham	H	2 – 0	F.A. Cup
02/02/05	Blackburn Rovers	A	1 – 0	Premiership
06/02/05	Manchester City	H	0 – 0	Premiership
12/02/05	Everton	A	1 – 0	Premiership
20/02/05	Newcastle United	A	0 – 1	F.A.Cup
23/02/05	Barcelona	A	1 – 2	Champions League
27/02/05	Liverpool	–	3 – 2 (aet)	Carling Cup Final
05/03/05	Norwich City	A	3 – 1	Premiership
08/03/05	Barcelona	H	4 – 2	Champions League
15/03/05	West Bromwich Albion	H	1 – 0	Premiership
19/03/05	Crystal Palace	H	4 – 1	Premiership
02/04/05	Southampton	A	3 – 1	Premiership
06/04/05	Bayern Munich	H	4 – 2	Champions League
09/04/05	Birmingham City	H	1 – 1	Premiership
12/04/05	Bayern Munich	A	2 – 3	Champions League
20/04/05	Arsenal	H	0 – 0	Premiership
23/04/05	Fulham	H	3 – 1	Premiership
27/04/05	Liverpool	H	0 – 0	Champions League
30/04/05	Bolton Wanderers	A	0 – 2	Premiership
03/05/05	Liverpool	A	1 – 0	Champions League
07/05/05	Charlton Athletic	H	1 – 0	Premiership
10/05/05	Manchester United	A	3 –1	Premiership
15/05/05	Newcastle United	A	1 – 1	Premiership

All The Way... To More Records And Trophies

'I THINK I'M A GOOD PERSON. SOMETIMES THE IMAGE I GIVE IN FOOTBALL IS NOT THE REAL IMAGE. ONE THING IS JOSE MOURINHO THE MAN, ANOTHER IS JOSE MOURINHO THE MANAGER.'

Jose Mourinho

Jose Mourinho could have walked away from Stamford Bridge after his incredible first season in charge. He admits as much himself. 'It would be very easy for me – win the Premiership and say goodbye and go to another club and try to bring success to that club,' he says. 'But I don't want that. I'm very happy with my decision to stay.' Mourinho says a text message sent to him by skipper John Terry on behalf of the entire squad reinforced his decision to stay. 'What it said will stay with me for ever.'

Mourinho formulates his plans for the new season. 'The most important thing is to keep what we have, in other words to retain the Premiership title, and we have a squad powerful enough to do that. But we also have to change one or two players. In every group, in every squad, there are always one or two players not very happy with their personal situations. Of course they are happy with the success, because they belong to the success, but some of them are not very happy because they are not my first choice. So those are my key tasks – to keep what we have, bring in a left-back, a midfielder and an attacker, and improve in every department of the squad. And our group will be even better next season. It's simple.'

Frank Lampard collects his Footballer of the Year award from the Football Writers' Association at the Royal Lancaster Hotel, London, and, in a moving acceptance speech, dedicates the honour to Lucy, a ten-year-old girl who died from a brain tumour. He befriended Lucy during his charity work for the Teenage Cancer Trust.

He collects his award and then says, 'This award is massive, an achievement I hold very highly. I watched JT pick up the PFA Award and was genuinely delighted for him. This award is voted for by journalists, who can be your biggest critic and get on your nerves sometimes, but they all know football and I am very respectful of their thoughts, and very proud they have decided to give me this award this year.

'I'd like to say a big thank you to Ken Bates and Suzannah. I am very privileged that they have decided to fly over especially for tonight. I know Ken has the money, but he still had to make the effort! Ken took a chance on me and paid what people thought was a lot of money at the time. He had belief in me, as did Claudio Ranieri, and without that move, without him putting his money on the table and doing that... I had another offer to go to Leeds, and no disrespect to Leeds, but things might have gone slightly differently. Claudio was the man, the manager, who made the decision. I met him when I first went to Chelsea and he showed great belief in me, he improved my game no end in the three years I played under him.

'For this year I have to thank Roman Abramovich. I know what you're thinking: thanks very much for that five-year deal I signed last year and I'll be back knocking on the door in a couple of years! You have to understand this man and it's not easy when you see it from the outside. What the man does is he comes in the changing room, win or lose, and shows the emotion that every fan shows and he really means it – and to the players that means so much. We respond to that. I would like to thank him for moving Chelsea on from the fantastic club it was to a club that really is one of the best in Europe and is hopefully going to be a force for future years.

'Jose Mourinho? I cannot say enough about the man as a manager. He has ultimate confidence in himself and the amazing thing is that he manages to transmit that confidence to the players around him. He has given me real belief. I hope to work for him for many years and to be very successful.

'I would also like to say a big thank you to the England manager. It is a bit embarrassing when he is sitting two seats away from you to give him big praise.

'The main thank yous are to my family, who have lived everything with me. First to my granddad, Poppa Bill as we used to call him. He died earlier this year. He was a fantastic man and someone I looked up to. I really would have liked him to have seen me here tonight. He would have been really proud. Also my Nanny Hilda, my dad's mum. She used to be at West Ham giving out wine gums to everyone who sat around her – now she does it at Chelsea. Unfortunately she still keeps calling the manager Joseph Mourinho. She will never learn.

'This is a personal award, but the main one I won this season was the Premiership – and I could not have done that without the players around me. Everyone has seen how strong we are this year and I would like to say thanks to all of them – and also a massive thank you to all the Chelsea fans. They took me to their hearts very, very quickly and I have nothing but appreciation for them. They give me the confidence to be the player I am today. They are a piece of my heart now and I really mean that.

'A lot of the reason I am here is because of my strength, my determination and character. I would just like to talk about a girl called Lucy. I went to her funeral today – she was ten years old. She came to the game against Charlton where we lifted the Premiership trophy. She had a tumour on the brain – really she should have died the week before that game. But she was so desperate to come and see that game, to watch us play. The character and strength she showed made me put everything in perspective. I would like to dedicate this whole award to her, her family, especially her mother, and I would like to say thanks to everyone tonight. Thank you.'

Lampard knows keeping the title will fully test Chelsea's resolve the following season but he remains confident. 'This was a fantastic club when I signed but in the position we're in now, we can really dominate for some time to come. We know there will be new faces coming in but everyone has total confidence in the manager not to rock the boat. He will improve where he sees fit but he won't want to upset what we've built here. It's not just the team here but the spirit and the togetherness and I am sure he will take all these things into account when he looks to strengthen the squad.'

Mourinho is just as complimentary about Lampard. 'Chelsea are very lucky to have two English players who lead by example,' he says. 'I see no reason why Frank cannot use those leadership qualities for international work. If you are looking for a player to score goals, to give everything he has as a player and lead a team, he has the ability. England have other players who fit those criteria but, in my opinion, Frank is one of the best. There is more to come from him – a lot more. Mr Eriksson is fully aware of what he can do. The next World Cup could be exciting for Frank.'

Mourinho writes a report for Abramovich each week outlining the reasons behind his team selection, tactics and substitutions. In a BBC1 interview with Gary Lineker, entitled *Jose Mourinho – The Special One*, he details his relationship with the billionaire Russian.

'He wanted the best for the club,' Mourinho says. 'So did I. He wanted to know the club life. I have to tell him because he's the owner. He has to know everything and from that point I told him he will know why every decision was made. Why I did not play this one and I played the other one. Why do you want Paulo to be your right-back? Why do you want Ricardo Carvalho to be your central defender? I have to explain. More than explain, I have to give a written report where they can understand and I can commit myself with that responsibility.'

Mourinho and the owner communicate on an emotional level. 'I don't understand the language but I understand emotion,' says Mourinho. 'So when he needs to explain something in Russian I get the emotion before Eugene Tenenbaum or other friends translate.' Mourinho is adamant that Abramovich will be at Stamford Bridge for the foreseeable future. 'He is so much in love with the club. He's not a person to sell the club in a few years [and] go away. He's completely committed and that's good. The club is growing day by day and he's not the sort of person to stop. He told me when I took over that he wants to create the conditions to make Chelsea the best club in the country and the best in the world. He eats football and he likes to be surrounded by football people because he loves the game so much. It's fantastic to speak to him, to explain things to him and share with him my ideas and thoughts. I think it's good for me to have somebody next to me who I can share things with.'

He also reveals that his 'special one', super confident image is not the real him. 'Sometimes I feel I need to be like that to play a little bit with emotions,' he says. 'I can be speaking with you but I know that my players are watching, and players from other teams are also watching. Yes, it's a bit of an act. I think you have to act a little bit and to show sometimes a different face. I am not bad at it. I'm not the "special one". I was under pressure when I arrived as a European champion and I thought I wasn't respected.'

Some of his bold public statements have been made to galvanise his players. 'I put myself in the firing line straight away by saying things that some people understand and some don't,' he says. 'Like, for example: "I'm special, I want to win in the first season, I don't care about the power of Manchester United and Arsenal, and I don't care that no one in English football was champion in his first season." I might have put myself in the spotlight but, at the same time, I woke up my people. And I put them also under a little bit of pressure. I said, "All of you are top players, but nobody won a Premiership or a Champions League, and you are not successful players until you win." So I made them think. I hurt them a bit, but I created a big ambition in the team. It was risky, but it worked.

'The first step is to make the big guys understand and accept and be on my side. Once they accept this rule, it's easy to manage the group. I couldn't be luckier than when I got Terry and Lampard and, immediately behind them, Makelele. They are the perfect example of big players with a notion of the needs of the club.'

One of his motivations for signing more top players is to guard against complacency, which he talks about at length during the closed season. 'I could say I don't need another midfielder, I have enough,' Mourinho says. 'But if you don't need it from the football point of view, you need it from the mental point of view. A player cannot think that because I was good, I have my place, and because I have my place, I don't need to have the same commitment. For a manager it is difficult, especially after success. You can think you don't need new players and you don't push. You can't be emotional, you have to think of the most important thing and you have to think about the club. I hope the hunger will be there – that's what we're aiming for. When you decide to bring in two or three new players, it is to bridge a new reality. Nobody knows who is going to play. Drogba had a good season, so did Gudjohnsen, but if I bring in a striker, who will be first choice? Nobody knows.'

Hernan Crespo marries his Italian girlfriend Alessia and claims, 'Staying at Milan is the best wedding present I could ever have.' Yet with Chelsea seeking the return of at least half of his £16m fee, negotiations with the Serie A side have stalled over his price. Barcelona and Inter Milan are also both interested in signing the 29-year-old. Crespo keeps all his options open by diplomatically claiming he wants to win the Champions League final for both his current clubs. 'Maybe I can take revenge for Chelsea. They lost to Liverpool in the semi-finals. It is a good personal motivation for me.'

Chelsea round off their title-winning season with a trip to Korea and a lacklustre 1–0 victory over local champions Suwon Bluewings. Cole scores in the 16th minute and despite all the tireless running of the hosts they cannot find a response. Mourinho travels with a squad of only 17 players and, with no recognised striker, he names Cole, Duff and Jarosik in his forward line.

Johnson is deployed in an unfamiliar position in the centre of defence alongside Huth while Cudicini and Pidgeley are both named among the substitutes. Cole gets between two defenders to run on to Tiago's looping header and fires left-footed past goalkeeper Woon Jae Lee from just inside the area.

Back at home on board Chelsea's victory parade open-top bus, Mourinho makes it clear his first priority is to keep his title-winning squad together. 'I just need to keep my champions, no more than that,' he says. Lampard savours the occasion. 'The celebrations have been unbelievable. It gives you a taste of it and you just want more,' he says. Clutching the Premiership trophy, he adds, 'I want a few more of these.' Terry echoes the sentiment. 'I never expected to see so many people – they are everywhere. The fans have been amazing all season and this just gives you a taste for success. You want to do it again and again.'

Cole says, 'We want to do this for as long as we can. There is no reason why we can't do it again next year. We've got the players and the management.' And Gudjohnsen adds, 'These are the people we do it for. They have been waiting a long time.'

In west London, blue is the colour as the streets around Stamford Bridge are packed. They turn the pavement into a sea of waving flags and many fans wait patiently all morning for the Premiership winners' bus. In 1955 when Chelsea last won the title, wooden rattles and rosettes were the football accessories of choice, but these days it's shrill air horns, whistles and replica shirts. One canny street trader is also doing a mean trade in £5 balloons, shaped just like the Premiership trophy, while every T-shirt printer inside the M25 seems to be cashing in with makeshift stalls along the route.

Metropolitan Police estimate the crowd size at 200,000, with fans travelling from all over the country to take their place on the three-mile route. One family even make a special journey from Bremen in Germany.

Mourinho has never been a great fan of celebrations but he allows his players to bask in the crowd's glow, while standing quietly at the back of the bus with Abramovich. However, he raises a smile as the bus passes a King's Road restaurant called La Reserve, whose staff have allowed Carling to drape a giant flag of the Portuguese manager's face from their second-floor window.

No lover of ostentatious celebration, the Chelsea manager shyly takes the microphone to join in a chorus of 'One Man Went To Mow', to the delight of supporters. Cudicini and Drogba record the scene on video cameras while Cole leads the crowd in a rendition of 'Have You Ever Seen Chelsea Win The League?'

While Chelsea celebrate the realisation of their dreams, Hernan Crespo, on loan at AC Milan, sees his disintegrate in the Champions League final. The trophy and his nomination as man of the match look to be in the bag at half-time as he scores twice and Milan lead 3-0. But Liverpool produce an incredible second-half comeback to snatch the Champions League trophy on penalties. 'It's impossible to explain what has happened to us,' says Crespo.

Chelsea are fined £300,000 and hit with a suspended three-point deduction by the Premier League after being found guilty of making an illegal approach to Ashley Cole. The points penalty will only be imposed if Chelsea commit a similar offence during the 2005-2006 season. Cole is fined £100,000 for his compliance, despite the Premier League declaring that he has been 'manipulated to a large extent by his agent', and Mourinho is ordered to pay £200,000 as punishment for his role in the saga. The independent commission concludes that Cole did meet at a London hotel with Chelsea officials, including manager Mourinho, to discuss a potential transfer to Stamford Bridge.

Mourinho admits he is unhappy with the way the club dealt with the Cole affair. 'It was a moment of frustration, impotence and injustice. I felt a lack of enchantment and was thinking that Chelsea were not defending me in the way I thought was ideal. But I am where I want to be and where I believe I will be for the next five years. I sincerely believe that. I'm proud of my story in football but understand that I have more ambitions. It's unthinkable that someone would say they don't want to go to England because it rains a lot and they want to eat sardines in Setubal on Monday. Or that they don't want to go to Germany because they don't speak the language, or they want to be in Portugal to drink coffee every morning. A football professional has to go to the top of his capacity and not think about sentiment.

'If I had stayed in Portugal, I would've broken every record – most victories in the championship and Portuguese Cup – but what would I think at the end of my career? I would be the best in Portugal, but would I be the best in England or Italy? I would be happier to go to England, not succeed, get fired and come back to Portugal than win ten Portuguese Championships. One day I would like to go to Italy and also take charge of the Portuguese national squad.'

Chelsea are hit with claims from Spurs that they illegally approached Tottenham's sporting director Frank Arnesen. Spurs suspend Arnesen and consider what action to take. A Chelsea statement reads: 'Chelsea Ltd made an official approach to Tottenham Hotspur for permission to speak to Frank Arnesen two weeks ago. Chelsea Ltd has been in direct discussions with Tottenham for the last two weeks on this subject.'

Mourinho has his appeal against a fine for improper conduct dismissed. Mourinho was charged and then fined £5,000 for comments he made after the Carling Cup semi-final first leg against Manchester United at Stamford Bridge. The club opt not to contest the £300,000 fine and suspended three-point deduction from the Cole affair, as it is in 'the interests of the game' to move on. However, they fully support Mourinho's appeal against his £200,000 fine. Chelsea are also keen to stress the decision not to appeal is an entirely separate issue from the controversy over their move to employ Arnesen.

After some lengthy negotiations, Tottenham accept a 'significant' cash settlement that paves the way for Arnesen to join the Premiership champions, while Spurs withdraw the threat to lodge a complaint of an illegal approach. Tottenham's stance is prompted by the publication of photographs showing Arnesen relaxing on Abramovich's yacht. Chelsea claim the meeting was purely social. Although 'confidential', the deal is £5m down with a further £3m should Arnesen see out his Chelsea contract.

Chelsea's first major on-field summer capture is Spain left-back Asier del Horno in an £8m deal. The 24-year-old agrees a three-year contract. Mourinho says, 'Asier is an outstanding international player who will add quality to the squad in a position we needed to strengthen. I'm sure he will be a key player as Chelsea continue with the goal to achieve greater success both in England and in the Champions League.' Del Horno promises to prove he is a better player than Ashley Cole. 'I don't believe I was second choice for Chelsea or that they got me because they couldn't get the Arsenal player,' he says. 'Mourinho is a very intelligent coach and he knows what he's doing and who he's signing. I hope I can repay the confidence he has placed in me. Cole is an excellent defender with more international experience than me, but that doesn't worry me. On the pitch is where you demonstrate who is the best player and I know I am not an inferior player to Cole.'

Kakha Kaladze's proposed move is finally off as the Georgia international agrees a new long-term contract with Milan. Milan's director in charge of transfers, Ariedo Braida, does not say how negotiations between Chelsea and Milan are progressing with regard to Crespo. But Mourinho now considers making Crespo part of his plans. Juan Sebastian Veron signs a two-year deal with Inter Milan, making his move permanent. Meanwhile Chelsea clinch the signature of rising Swiss star Jonas Elmer from Grasshoppers Zurich. The 17-year-old left-sided player joins the Blues on a three-year deal. He is a highly rated Switzerland under-17 international and was spotted by Chelsea scout Gwyn Williams. Another young talent signed for the future is French midfielder Lassana Diarra from Le Havre. 'Mourinho told me he wanted me to be the next Claude Makelele,' Diarra says.

With Milan apparently not able to come up with the cash to buy Crespo, Chelsea pull the plug on his loan deal and call him back to Stamford Bridge. 'The return of Crespo is a big plus for us,' says Mourinho. 'We gave Milan the chance to buy him and we arrived at the conclusion they were not ready to buy. Why should I leave a player like him on loan at Milan? I think also Crespo convinced himself to come back. He has been a successful player everywhere he has been, the only place people still have a question mark is in England. He is a proud player, he wants to come and prove himself and score goals. And I think he will do it. We haven't spent any money. He already knows what England is like and he is a different sort of striker to the ones we already have.'

And Chelsea's summer spending spree continues when they finally agree to pay Manchester City £21m for Shaun Wright-Phillips. A dramatic weekend, which starts with City boss Stuart Pearce insisting the 23-year-old wants to stay at Eastlands, ends with Wright-Phillips agreeing personal terms, then passing a medical before heading across the Atlantic on Chelsea's pre-season tour of the United States. The Manchester City squad heads out to Thailand for the FA Premier League Asia Trophy shell-shocked by the loss of their talisman.

As recently as the Friday night, when Wright-Phillips signed autographs after his final outing in a City shirt at Tranmere, Man City officials were convinced he wanted to stay and they rejected a £20m bid from Chelsea. That bullishness evaporated within 90 minutes on a sunny afternoon at Macclesfield, when Wright-Phillips pulled out of the Moss Rose friendly with a stomach bug before telephoning chairman John Wardle to inform him of his desire to speak to Chelsea. Wardle recognised the inevitability of the situation. Although Wright-Phillips was initially refused permission to speak with Chelsea, it was only to allow City chief executive Alistair Mackintosh to broker the best possible deal. Mackintosh prises an extra £1m out of Abramovich's wallet, with the entire fee paid up front.

Mourinho says the 23-year-old will give him a back-up for wingers

Robben and Duff, while Cole will also compete for a first-team place to give strength in depth on the flanks. Mourinho admits a lack of cover cost Chelsea dear in their Champions League semi-final defeat and expects to rotate his team more often next season. Mourinho says, 'Shaun is one of the best young players in England. He is young and has the space for development. He has the qualities you look for in a modern footballer. He's quick, intelligent, creative, can break by himself and shape the balance of the team. With Shaun, Joe Cole, Arjen Robben and Damien Duff we have a fantastic group of wingers to compete to give us the best whenever picked.

Olympique Lyon president Jean-Michel Aulas announces Chelsea will have to pay €45 million (£31m) for their final summer target – Michael Essien. Aulas, who previously said the player was not for sale, signals a U-turn in comments to French sports daily L'Équipe. 'Chelsea had accepted the price Liverpool asked for Steven Gerrard [£31m]. I told them Mike would leave only at that price.'

Chelsea score their second win in as many pre-season fixtures with a 1–0 victory over Benfica in Lisbon, following up a 5–1 defeat of League Two Wycombe. An own goal from Ricardo Rocha settles this clash of the champions of England and Portugal at the Stadium of Light. Rocha is under pressure from Carlton Cole when he diverts Robben's cross into his own net two minutes before half-time.

Mourinho is determined to build a legacy beyond the club's first title in half a century. 'I never tell Mr Abramovich I want this player or that player,' he says. 'We just have conversations. I never told him I wanted Shaun Wright-Phillips; it just came up in a conversation we had after the Champions League semi-final. One of the reasons we didn't make it was because Duff and Robben were injured. What can you do about that? You can have another winger. If we want another winger, we then ask where are the best in the world, who are the best in the country? And we arrive at Shaun.'

At the start of pre-season, Mourinho talked to his players about the challenges facing them as champions and his own expectations for the campaign ahead. The squad he has now is better equipped to cope with the vagaries of form and injury than it was this time last year, and the manager has a more intimate knowledge of the Premiership. The idea that his squad of millionaires may not always be as motivated as their manager to build on their initial success is not something he entertains. 'I don't have meetings with them every day but I did have one in the beginning of the season trying to analyse that kind of situation,' he says. 'Everybody knows that the distance between us and Man United and Liverpool and Arsenal is not what we created last year. It's not 37 points or 25 points or 15 points, it's much closer than that. This season, it will be even closer.'

Terry needed an injection every day to help win the title and to mask how much pain he was enduring. Terry was immediately sent for surgery on his long-running toe injury as soon as Chelsea wrapped up the championship. He now admits the problem is not completely solved. 'Bits of bone were growing on either side between two toes. Every time I put my boot on, they were rubbing against each other, bone on bone, making it very painful. I had surgery in the summer when both bits of bone were shaved away. I've still got a bit of pain, but I think that's just down to the surgery. It's good to be back, fully fit, fully trained and ready to go. I've had the problem for five or six years and it got to the stage where only a quarter of the way through the season I was having injections every day just to train. It was a numbing injection, and then going into games I had an extra one as well. So, once we'd won the title at the end of the season, I just got it done as soon as possible.'

Terry has his sights set on retaining the crown – and matching Arsenal's 2004 'Invincibles'. He says, 'Everybody says the hardest thing of all is winning the title in back-to-back seasons and we know that United are the only side who've done that since the Premiership started. The challenge for us is to make sure we can do it as well. It's the job for all of us to make sure we come back next season and try even harder to ensure we do improve. That's the task for everybody. The bar has been raised by what we have done this year and we need to clear it. Our aim next season has to be to go through the season without losing in the league at all. We've only lost once so far, at Manchester City. It was a game we should never have lost and it hurt. But Arsenal showed last season that it can be done. They did it, so why can't we? None of us see any reason why we shouldn't be able to do that.'

Terry knows the glory is just beginning under Mourinho. 'People accuse us of spending millions to buy the Premiership,' he says. 'But it took something else to make it happen and that was the manager. Last year we spent a lot of money and brought in a lot of big players but there was one thing missing. We've got him now, and that's the gaffer. I would die for the man both on and off the pitch. He's been the big thing for a lot of the players, not just myself – the real difference between last season and this one. He's a great guy and a great character. Every team meeting he is tactically spot-on. He knows what players want and what we need.

'When you've got someone you respect that much you all want to do everything for him and he still surprises us in training. There are things he asks us to do without explaining them, and you wonder why and what it's all about. But then we go through the meeting before the match when we look at the opposition, and when he points to their strengths or weaknesses we understand why he had made us do that drill the day before. He finds weaknesses in other teams nobody else has seen. It's new for me to have this amount of faith in a manager. I completely trust him.'

Chelsea start their pre-season tour to the US with a 1–0 win over AC Milan. It's a significant psychological blow as Milan will undoubtedly be one of the Blues' main rivals for the Champions League again in the coming season. The goal comes in the 13th minute after some neat passing between Geremi and Gudjohnsen. The ball finds its way to Makelele, and his incisive pass picks out Robben, who places a low shot just inside the post. Mourinho changes nine players at half-time, only leaving Lampard and Makelele of the original starting line-up, but Chelsea's strength in depth means Milan are still unable to wrest control.

Next up are local champions DC United. As he did against Milan, Mourinho changes his entire team, with Wayne Bridge returning. Bridge, who has been linked with a move to Spurs, plays 45 minutes – his first action since breaking his ankle at Newcastle in February. DC go ahead after half an hour, but Duff equalises with a smart angled volley five minutes later and Crespo scores the winner after the break to make the final score 2–1.

It is not a great performance, and one of the most notable aspects of the match is the display from DC's exciting 16-year-old Freddy Adu. Mourinho is clued up on the teenager. 'I spoke to him before the game,' says Adu. 'He congratulated me for the goal I scored last week. I would love to end up playing [for Chelsea]. When I'm 18 I'll start exercising my options so hopefully I get a call from a big club in Europe.'

The tour ends with a rematch against Milan. The Italians bring back some of their big hitters and it makes for a much tighter match. Drogba opens the scoring when he is put away by Tiago and bustles past Alessandro Costacurta to fire into the corner. It's a good striker's goal, but the equaliser from Rui Costa is even more impressive. The Portuguese midfielder brings down a corner on the edge of the area and somehow finds the space to clip a curler into the corner of the Chelsea goal. The match finishes 1–1, and Chelsea can be pleased with an unbeaten tour.

Chelsea's resources are the envy of football yet Mourinho explains it's not as easy as everyone thinks spending Abramovich's money mountain. 'Buying players for Chelsea is the hardest job in the Premier League because of our quality,' he says. 'It's very difficult to buy players for Chelsea because of the level of players we want. Shaun was the most important player in Manchester City, so he is difficult to get. Del Horno plays for the Spanish national team and is the biggest face in Athletic Bilbao, while Essien is a crucial player for Lyon. Because of Chelsea's squad level, we want big players from good teams and they don't want to sell. They make it difficult, they ask for sometimes crazy prices, so it's very difficult. If

I'm in a medium team and you give me £20m, I can buy six players. I think it's easier. You think it's easy to buy a goalkeeper for Chelsea? Where is the goalkeeper better than Petr Cech or Carlo Cudicini? How can I improve that position? I can't. Where can I get a better central defender than what I have? I can't. Where can I find a midfielder to improve our group?'

The arrival of Arnesen to oversee player development indicates the seriousness of Chelsea's intention to source promising youngsters, as Arsenal and Manchester United have done. It will also save the club money as they attempt to become profitable. 'For the big teams it's more difficult to choose players because you might buy a player that doesn't improve you,' Mourinho says. 'You don't want to spend money on flops. Instead, you invest a small pot of money in a player of good potential, a player you want to be your future solution. Instead of buying a new Makelele in three years' time for crazy money we bought Diarra, who we believe can be the new Maka. We have three years to work with him to make him the one.'

Demarcation between first-choice and second-choice players will become less clear as the squad has greater strength in depth. 'Against AC Milan we played with two teams and you couldn't say which team was the better one,' he says. 'We have one of the best squads in Europe. I don't know which is the second team. I put a question to my staff because I wanted a laugh. The question was, "If we play tomorrow against Wigan in the first game of the Premiership, what is your first XI?" In four hats there were four different answers and all of them different to mine.'

Mourinho is sure Steven Gerrard's decision to stay at Liverpool will hurt the player more than it will hurt Chelsea. 'Gerrard is a great player and we want an English core very much,' says Mourinho. 'We normally play a midfield triangle and you can imagine that Gerrard and Lampard, with Makelele just behind them as protection, could be a very strong team. But I think it is Gerrard's loss more than Chelsea's. Why? Because Chelsea have good solutions – a good team with the conditions to improve and a club which will be one of the best in the world in a short period of time. So when he decides not to join this club, I think it will be a loss for him, for his career. He can say "I was European champion at Liverpool" and I have to say that is correct. But I can say to him in the next ten years we will compare trophies at Chelsea and trophies at Liverpool. And he will lose.'

Mourinho's rise has earned him a multi-million pound three-year deal with adidas. At the launch of their partnership in New York, his new sponsors look thrilled with their investment. Why adidas? 'Because they are at the top of their trade,' he says, 'and so am I.' Mourinho has become one of the sportswear giant's global coaching ambassadors and joins a roster including David Beckham and Zinedine Zidane. Adidas also agreed a £90m eight-year deal to become Chelsea's kit suppliers from 2006. Mourinho has been cashing in on his success, with a high-profile campaign for American Express and features in billboards in his home country to promote a Portuguese bank. He has been inundated with offers, and he is already the best-rewarded manager in the world.

Mourinho prepares for the start of only his second season in English football maintaining, 'I have already done enough to be regarded as one of those top managers. I took a Portuguese club to win the European Cup. That is enough to be regarded like that. I won the Premiership with Chelsea after 50 years – and I was voted by the fans manager of the century. When you win the European Cup for the first time at 55, it's the perfect end for your career. If you win it at 40, when you have another 20 years to go, you have to win it again. I think we have to win trophies every season. That's what I think and what I feel, in spite of being in a top football country where it shouldn't be a frustration to lose to big teams. It shouldn't be a drama. But we have to look at our club and make it a motivation for us to turn it into a habit for Chelsea to win. And we must do it again. We have four competitions plus the Community Shield. We have to win trophies. That's the point of what we do.'

As the new season approaches, Mourinho's thoughts turn to his counterparts in the Premiership. Mourinho and Arsene Wenger are 'professional' in their dealings with each other. 'Every time we play against Manchester United, Sir Alex Ferguson and Carlos Queiroz wait for us,' he says. 'They invite us into their room. During the game we're not friends but after the game it's the same story. The bottle of wine is there, the television is there, the food is there. We sit, we speak and we laugh. If next week we have some words, a fight in the press, we are intelligent enough to understand that it's football, but the next time we see each other we respect each other again. This relationship is very good, a relationship I have for example with Steve Bruce, Harry Redknapp and Chris Coleman. With Arsenal we have a professional relationship. Nobody treats us badly. It's correct. But one thing is to be correct and another thing is to be correct and have a relationship.'

Mourinho promises to avoid unnecessary squabbles over the coming campaign, but there is a clear message of intent for Wenger. 'You have to ask Arsene Wenger if he would like to be in my position. My philosophy this season is to think about us and forget about the others. We will go our way and not look at other people and not be worried about what they say. But when I feel it is hurting too much or when I feel it hurts my players I will jump in. As I said once, the dogs bark but the caravan goes by. The caravan goes on through the barking dogs and carries on. I will carry on.'

Mourinho is keen to leap to the defence of Peter Kenyon after the chief executive predicts that the champions will come from 'a small group of one' – in other words Chelsea. 'He said what was in his soul and his heart,' says Mourinho. 'That's normal. All summer I've been reading things from Manchester United players, from Ryan Giggs and Gary Neville, saying that next season they will kill Chelsea and be champions again. It's normal; there is nothing wrong with it. What Peter said was taken out of context. But even if it wasn't, his meaning should stay the same. What he said shouldn't disturb anyone. For three years everyone has called me arrogant. Now they say the same thing about Peter. I don't call what he said arrogance. He says what he has in his soul. He says what he wants – this is normal.'

Mourinho insists the Community Shield result is not all-important, but agrees there is plenty at stake. 'In relation to the championship, the Community Shield means nothing. But when it is Chelsea against Arsenal, nobody likes to lose. When we play Arsenal, it is not a friendly, it's more than that.'

Wenger declares that Chelsea pays double the normal market value for players such as Wright-Phillips and he refuses to be lured into wasting his remaining transfer kitty. Wright-Phillips, the 23-year-old adopted son of former Arsenal legend Ian Wright, had been tipped as a potential Highbury signing before Chelsea swooped. 'It is not Chelsea's fault or my fault, it is just like it is,' says Wenger. 'But everyone knows that they have plenty of money and, when they come in, they will buy for £20m what costs £10m. Do you really think Wright-Phillips would have cost £21m had Chelsea not come in for him? Frankly, we have to be honest. What would be his price?'

Dual Chelsea Player of the Year Lampard feels he has been at Stamford Bridge 'for an eternity' after being named in the club's greatest XI of all time. Lampard is the star of the show at the Blues' centenary celebrations. 'It's a nice feeling,' he tells Chelsea TV. 'This four years or so seems like an eternity, I find it hard to remember the West Ham days and I don't mean that as a lie or a joke. I just feel very Chelsea now. Chelsea has become part of my life. To be named in that team, and player of the year again, is a fantastic feeling.'

Chelsea fans will beg to differ, but Mikhail Gorbachev calls on Russian oligarchs to return their 'plundered' wealth to their homeland. 'I do not want to undermine the motherland of soccer and I don't have a problem with a Russian buying shares in Britain but it is clear we should close the book on the period of plundering,' he says. 'Some think $1 trillion has been hidden away by Russian businessmen. If they don't return that, our courts are likely to decide they acquired it illegally. Then they couldn't use that money anywhere. One day it will be used for the benefit of Russia.' Gorbachev was giving his backing to a plan by President Vladimir Putin to offer Russia's oligarchs an amnesty in return for the 'repatriation' of their wealth. He accepts the plan is 'risky' but says the businessmen should be reassured that they will not be heavily taxed in Russia.

Abramovich, however, remains in favour at the Kremlin. Although the opinion of Gorbachev carries more weight abroad than at home – where he is regarded as a figure of yesteryear – the thinking behind it will likely strike a chord after Russian oil tycoon Mikhail Khodorkovsky is jailed for nine years for tax fraud and embezzlement.

Peter Kenyon reveals that Abramovich is obsessed with winning the Champions League. 'I think the Champions League is very important to him,' says Kenyon. 'We shouldn't underestimate the impact of winning the Premier League but winning the Champions League is enormous. Only two English clubs have won the Champions League and even during their dominance of English football in the 90s Manchester United only won the Champions League once, and that tells you how difficult it is. So it's the Holy Grail to Roman but it's within our grasp. And we will do it within Jose Mourinho's tenure, for sure. That's what will set us apart from other clubs. We have a manager who has done it, who knows what it takes to do it. We have a squad that is young and better this season than last season. It's far from its peak and I've got no doubts we will do it.

'Jose is not satisfied with where he finished last season; he wants to do more. Our aspirations are to be the most successful club in Europe. Now I think he has the resources, the facilities and the team that is capable of doing that. We shouldn't underestimate our achievements in the competition over the past two seasons. We have been in the semi-final two years in succession.'

But that has not prevented Europe's elite clubs from blocking Chelsea's attempts to join the powerful G14 group. Kenyon claims they are fearful of his club's presence and Chelsea should take that as a compliment. 'They're the clubs who have dominated Europe for the past 25 years and they see us a real threat and that is a compliment. Yes, not being part of the group causes us grief, but overall it tells us we are on the right track with what we are doing.'

As Mourinho completes his final preparations for the Community Shield against Arsenal, he reveals he takes time out to make each player feel special. 'I think I do it by analysing them as individuals,' he says.' The old theory that you must treat every player the same – the type of communication must be the same for everybody, the rules must be the same for everybody – I think this is old-fashioned leadership in football. For example, I can say to one player after a match, "You are the best player on the pitch." To another player I cannot say that because they react in different ways. I can say to a player, "If you don't perform tomorrow, you don't play again with me." I cannot say this to another player. So I have to analyse people individually and to have different feedback and different communication and a different relationship with all of them because all of them are different.

'I have in my team about 12 different nationalities. Players of 20 [years of age], players of 34, different cultures, different philosophies in football, in life also. I must be intelligent in the way I lead them, and I think leadership is crucial in modern football. In my job I have to be a leader and the strong one and I have to fight for our success and I have to lead a group to try to achieve success.

'When you depend on other people you gamble a little bit. Take substitutions. One thing is the tactical change and when you do it, everything is prepared. I play with four defenders, I prepare the team during the week to play with three, so if I want to change from four to three the team is ready. The organisation is automatic and the players can, just with a click, change because they are prepared. That is the part that you can work on and you have no doubts that it's going to work. The other thing is the human side. You change a player and put another one on. It falls to you to make a change and to make it work. But then the player you put on doesn't perform the way you expect. This is a little bit of luck. Yes, I believe in luck. I believe that the good ones have a better chance to have luck, of course. But I think that luck is important.

'I have in my hands the best example. When I was European champion, we scored at Old Trafford in the last minute. Last season I had a good chance, an open goal in Liverpool in the last minute also. If we score we are in the final. But we didn't. You have the star in that moment or you don't have the star. In every game I think luck is also there.'

Chelsea's growing dominance over Arsenal continues with a 2–1 victory in the Community Shield. Arsenal enjoy a deal of possession but fail to find a cutting edge against the Blues' impenetrable defence. The same cannot be said at the other end, and a brilliant Drogba double is enough to seal victory despite Arsenal pulling a goal back through young midfielder Cesc Fabregas.

Wenger says Chelsea use long-ball tactics and time-wasting to beat Arsenal and also insists that he is not worried about Chelsea's strength in depth. 'Chelsea were dangerous with the long balls,' says Wenger. 'They were very direct and we tried more to play our usual game. I'm not here to judge Chelsea's game; they play their game and we play ours. I just feel that Drogba gave us a hard time on the long balls, but that's not a criticism.'

Terry is satisfied with the preparations for the forthcoming Premiership season. 'It was important for both teams to get off to a good start – and thankfully it's us who have,' says the Chelsea captain. The teams are set to meet in the league at Stamford Bridge on 21 August and Terry adds, 'It's been a long time since we beat Arsenal so psychologically it's given us a massive boost. I think we gelled pre-season in America. The season starts next week so we've got another week's training – but we look sharp and I'm pleased how it went today. Look at Arsenal and Manchester United; they have dominated for four or five years. We want to do that – it's a tough task but we are up for the challenge.'

Drogba's goals come early in each half. The first is with the match just eight minutes old. The Ivory Coast striker is quicker to read the flight of a pass from new boy Asier del Horno than Arsenal defender Philippe Senderos. Drogba deftly brings the ball down on his chest and uses his strength to hold off Senderos and then clips the ball past Jens Lehmann in the Arsenal goal.

Drogba demonstrates the raw power he possesses in dispatching the second goal. A Gudjohnsen flick sends him free and a powerful run takes him past Senderos once more. The combined attentions of Lehmann and Lauren cannot dispossess him and he keeps his composure to fire the ball into the back of the net.

Arsenal quickly pull a goal back when a rare lapse in composure in the Chelsea backline allows Fabregas to fire in from close range, but from there the Blues defence close ranks and secure the victory. Makelele is at his best, smothering every attempted Arsenal attack, while Shaun Wright-Phillips comes on for the last 20 minutes but has a quiet game.

The plaudits go to two-goal hero Drogba, who strikes the first blow in the battle with Crespo to be Chelsea's first-choice striker. 'We wanted to start the season well against a big team with good players, so it's good to win,' says Drogba. 'I'm very happy to score again. I've had one month's holiday and I'm fresh now.' New signing Wright-Phillips, who replaced Robben midway through the second half, says, 'It's my first game and I have come out of it with a medal – it's fabulous! The lads made it easy for me; someone was always there to help me every time I got the ball. I'm just trying to wake up at the moment. It's great to celebrate our first trophy and hopefully we can go on to win more.'

Mourinho responds to suggestions that Chelsea rely too heavily on the long ball by declaring that he will do whatever it takes for his team to win. 'The style of Chelsea football is a winning style,' he says. 'That means playing on your opponents' weaknesses. Sometimes the winning style is to play direct football, sometimes to play possession football; sometimes it is to build long, sometimes to build short; sometimes to press up, sometimes to invest in set-plays because the opponent is not good on defensive set-plays. It is the style of somebody who works hard every day to have the team ready to adapt to circumstances.'

Mourinho also aims a gentle barb back at Wenger, who says he is not too concerned about losing the Shield having won it on four previous occasions to little avail. 'It was the first time I had heard a manager say, "I don't care about the result because I won it before four times." How many times have they won the Premiership? Three? So they don't need to win it any more. If Sir Alex says the same, I would be very happy, but he wouldn't. He wants to win again. We have to try to win every time.'

But on the eve of the new season, can the pressure to keep improving, keep producing and keep winning become too much? While he was learning his profession and coaching Vitoria de Setubal under-18s as a young man, Mourinho was also working with disabled children in his home town. He would happily be doing the same work if his career had not taken off in the manner it did, but the experience taught him a sense of perspective when winning the Premiership threatens to become all-consuming. 'I did it for three years and at the same time I was coaching Vitoria de Setubal under-18s,' says Mourinho. 'I worked from 8am to 2pm and then had a training session at 4pm. I was happy. I think it taught me to think that we, and especially the players, are privileged people and sometimes you create a nightmare for nothing. I realised a lot about these kids and when I think of players and how they can make a war or be unhappy because they are not playing or not selected, it is ridiculous. It helped me the same way it helps people who travel to Africa and sees kids who are dying in every corner. I don't feel pressure because I have seen people with real problems.'